ANALYSIS OF BUSINESS MODELS AND FINANCIAL FEASIBILITY OF FRINGE BANKING INSTITUTIONS

by **Daniel M. Leibsohn**
Community Development Finance
San Francisco, California

2005

Community Economic Development Press

SCHOOL OF COMMUNITY ECONOMIC DEVELOPMENT
SOUTHERN NEW HAMPSHIRE UNIVERSITY

WORKING PAPERS IN COMMUNITY ECONOMIC DEVELOPMENT

Author: Daniel M. Leibsohn

Series Editors: Yoel Camayd-Freixas & Michael Swack

First Published, March 2005

Published by: COMMUNITY ECONOMIC DEVELOPMENT PRESS
Applied Research Center
School of Community Economic Development
Southern New Hampshire University
2500 North River Road
Manchester, NH 03106

Tel: 603-668-2211 • email: arc@snhu.edu

ISBN: 0-9743372-2-6

Table of Contents

Summary of Findings

Context and Background

It is expensive to be poor. Low-income households often pay more for many goods and services those with higher incomes. Financial services cost more and a full range of financial services are often unavailable for low-income people.

Lower-income households tend to pay a very high percentage of their available income for interest and fees to obtain these services. These higher payments significantly affect their ability to move out of poverty and attain higher living standards.

The purpose of this report is to describe the findings of analysis in Community Development Finance (CDF). Community Development Finance began exploring financial services issues in 1998-99. It is considering new ways, approaches and paradigms for community development financing efforts to be implemented alongside the primary existing financial means.

A Dual Financial Economy. The estimates of the number of people not served by conventional institutions, or the "nonbanked" or "unbanked" population, range from 10% to as high as 15% of the U.S. population. And the percent in low-income neighborhoods, where most of the nonbanked are clustered, must be significantly higher.

For the most part, the full range of financial services and investment institutions does not reach low-income neighborhoods. A "dual financial economy" now exists. *There is an entire set of financial institutions and practices in low-income neighborhoods that replaces the institutions that the rest of the society uses. It is not just check cashing companies or payday lenders that create issues. low-income households tend to use the entire range of services, not just an occasional or isolated service. It is this entire range of institutions that constitutes a dual financial economy.*

The lack of conventional, lower cost financial services and the existence of harmful financial institutions and programs in low-income neighborhoods work against economic development efforts. Wealth building programs, for example, are less effective when payday lenders charge high fees or predatory mortgage lenders take large amounts of equity out of homes that the owners have worked a lifetime to build. The savings provided by affordable housing developments or affordable child care can be reduced when the interest and fees on financial services are so high that they can cancel out part or all of the housing and child care savings.

Most of the activity and research in the Community Development Finance field currently focuses on programmatic and policy options. However, there is also a need for work that is aimed at understanding the business models and financial feasibility underlying the industry, which is absolutely necessary to develop new approaches to improve conditions. Therefore, CDF has adopted this approach.

Obtaining information on the businesses in this field is extremely difficult. The information sources used in this report include a wide range of sources: focus groups, site visits, organizations, individuals, reports and other written sources, articles from the trade press and other sources, professionals in the business, public regulatory agencies, some operating statements from businesses, trade associations/conferences, etc.

This report contains the description of the industry and its separate businesses, the range of business models (fringe banking institutions, commercial banks, credit unions, community development credit unions, nonprofit organizations and other institutions) involved and the financial feasibility of this business and its impact.

The Fringe Banking Industry. The report describes the overall industry— numbers of unbanked, reasons for their use of these services, characteristics of the industry and the types of businesses, numbers and sizes of the types of businesses that provide financial services, growth of the industry, reasons for the present conditions, etc. The range of financial service institutions for low-income households includes: check cashing outlets, payday lenders, pawn brokers, rent-to-own stores, consumer finance companies, credit card lenders, Refund Anticipation Loan lenders, remittance companies, mortgage lending companies and automobile title lenders.

Four services—rent-to-own stores, consumer finance companies, money transfer operators and income tax refund anticipation loans—and the products they offer, are examined. Two services—check cashing outlets and payday lenders—are described in greater detail later in this section.

The impacts on low-income households, including an example of effects on a hypothetical family, are discussed to show the effects of these services. Finally, there is a description of focus groups commissioned by CDF and the practice of targeting.

2

The term "unbanked" or "nonbanked" usually refers to households and individuals who do not have checking or savings accounts at conventional financial institutions—commercial banks, savings and loans, credit unions, brokerages and the like. They tend to be poorer households who do not have adequate income to be profitable for conventional financial institutions. They tend to live in neighborhoods that do not have branches of conventional institutions or, if there are bank branches, they do not serve an adequate number of local people. Nevertheless, households in these neighborhoods still have substantial incomes even if many are low-income. Moreover, all of these households are not poor; they may have other reasons for not having banking relationships even though these households may be attractive to banks.

There is a wide range of reasons stated by people for not using conventional financial institutions, including lack of need to write many checks, not liking to deal with banks and/or banks' making customers feel unwelcome, the lack of income to put into a bank, high bank fees, minimum balance requirements, poor locations, etc.

As a result, the fringe banking industry has filled this gap and become quite large by any measure. A 2001 report estimated the sizes of some of the different components from previous years in the following way:

	Volume of Transactions	Gross Revenue	Fee Total
Check cashing:	180 million	$60 billion	$1.5 billion
Payday lending	55 to 69 million	$10-$13.8 billion	$1.6 to 2.2 billion
Pawnbrokers	42 million	$3.3 billion	NA
Rent-to-own	3 million	$4.7 billion	$2.35 billion
Totals	280 million	$78 billion	$5.45 billion

Fringe banking, in contrast to its name, is a major and profitable industry in the United States, although its activities and inner workings often remain hidden. And their scale is undoubtedly much larger now than the above figures indicate.

The industry is also growing very rapidly, for many reasons, including the restructuring of the financial services industry (mergers and consolidations), improved marketing by fringe institutions, expansion of types of financial services offered, the influx of immigrants unused to banking institutions, changes in the banks' policies and business models, governmental attempts to stop money laundering, lowered real incomes of working households over the last two decades, economic conditions, etc. The changing relationships between fringe banks and mainstream financial institutions—for example, Wall Street activities such as securitization, secondary financings, bond issuances and supporting "Initial Public Offerings" or IPOs; fringe banking institutions' enhanced access to capital markets; and banks' financing and/or purchasing of subprime lenders—also played a significant role in the growth of these institutions.

Many of these services that the fringe banking institutions provide are essential for low-income households. Without them, these households might have to pay even more or find other even less efficient methods to address their needs. Nevertheless, there is extensive financial impact on low-income families as demonstrated by the case study of a hypothetical family and the impact of these services on that family.

Some of the businesses appear to heavily depend on households which cannot appropriately deal with the costs of the financial services. Some waste precious funds or are driven into deeper financial problems. A significant level of profit of a number of these businesses is built on use of the payday loan services by these households. This segment of the targeted population faces an explosive and extremely difficult problem.

Economic and Social Elements of Financial Services Delivery in Low-income Neighborhoods: Business Models. Many different types of financial institutions operate in low-income neighborhoods, including both conventional and fringe banking operations. Each type of institution, as well as each individual institution, generally has a different way of operating in low-income neighborhoods in relating to risk, operating costs, staffing, fees and rates, financial products, transaction volumes, capitalization and profitability. A large bank will view these issues in a different way than a small one will. Likewise, a national chain of check cashing stores listed on the New York Stock Exchange will likely consider the situation differently than a local owner of three stores does. Locations will also create differences; rural areas will create different approaches than urban areas. Likewise, the types of clients—income levels, immigrants, age, employment levels and types of employment, etc—will dictate differences such as variations in financial services products.

Nevertheless, certain generalities about the different approaches—or business models—can be observed. This section views some of these generalities, while attempting to account for some of the variations of the following institutions at the same time: commercial institutions (banks and savings institutions), credit unions, Community Development Credit Unions, fringe banking institutions, nonprofit efforts and newer entrants into the field such as large, national chains of retailers, in addition to long time participants such as smaller local convenience stores and grocers.

In the report, the generic business model issues were reviewed and the key elements highlighted. Some of the key issues that emerged included operating cost differences, volume goals and transactions versus relationship business philosophies, the types of financial products and fee structures, profitability profiles, the risk profiles of each, the approaches to reaching scale and the access to capital that allows the achievement of scale.

Commercial banks, for example, tend to use a very different approach—relationship-based with a focus on obtaining loans and deposits to generate earnings—than check cashers, which are transaction-oriented and rely more on volume to aggregate large amounts of relatively small fees. In addition, the range of banks' financial products is much different and often greater and more complex and the staffing is often more skilled, better trained and earn higher salaries. There is a reliance on cross selling opportunities for the different products (which may be one reason for banks' opposition to privacy legislation), which are often less likely in many low-income communities. The bricks and mortar for the branch offices—they are typically well appointed and have amenities— are more costly, which can make achievement of profitability more difficult in low-income neighborhoods; the hours are shorter compared to check cashers and payday lenders; there is a much greater dependence on the use of technology, and there are higher, central administrative overhead costs. These issues also indicate some of the complexities involved in the field of financial services for low-income households

The analysis indicates that they are clearly different institutions that, basically, have different businesses. There is more overlap at present as the more traditional financial institutions are beginning to look at how to better reach low-income and immigrant populations and to modify their business models. Nevertheless, further changes are needed to offer improved financial services to low-income households at lower costs.

The different financial approaches have their own individual requirements and complexities. But there are some key, general issues including:

- It is difficult to provide financial services effectively in low-income neighborhoods.
- Banks and fringe banking institutions are often seen as competitors, but they are really different institutions operating different businesses.
- Stronger legal guidelines can be placed on fringe bankers and some improvements in financial services could result.
- Although it is not really their business or expertise, conventional institutions can be encouraged to offer fringe banking financial services. However, these services will need to be combined with programs and ap-

5

proaches that enhance profitability: mainstreaming as many customers as possible; efficient operations; use of a lower cost model; modification of the overall business models; etc.

- With some of these changes, banks can provide many of the needed financial services. They have been involved in a few situations, generally due to Community Reinvestment Act pressures. A few are involved because of the potential for new markets but they have not achieved adequate scale that would solve the financial services issues in many neighborhoods. It is important to move beyond demonstrations and "exception" activities.

- Subsidy may be necessary for some efforts targeted at very low-income and homeless people and, in some cases, for low-income households as well.

- New financial vehicles, institutions and mechanisms also are needed. These approaches need capital support to work.

Financial Feasibility for Check Cashing and Payday Lending Businesses. Fringe banking is a major and profitable industry in the United States. There are many characteristics that influence the operating costs, revenues and profits of a fringe banking institution, including the demographic profile of the surrounding neighborhood, income levels and sources of income of the nearby households, competition in the immediate vicinity, density of the surrounding neighborhood, etc. Some products can generate almost all profit from their revenues, once fixed costs are covered. This can occur because these operations have a set of fixed costs—rent, insurance, salaries and benefits, marketing, utilities, etc. Therefore, if a store is open a certain number of set hours and it can add certain products with relatively small cost increases, most of the revenue from the new services will create mostly profit.

The volume becomes a critical matter and it depends on many of the issues discussed above—location, demographics, product mix, competition, etc. The stores that have the greater volumes usually can generate more profit. Of course, as the volume grows, some other costs will grow—perhaps an added staff position, more accounting, higher interest on borrowed bank funds, etc.—but these costs typically tend to be relatively small compared to the added revenues.

The report discusses the financial feasibility of a sample store. There is a breakdown and discussion of stabilized annual revenues by source and a stabilized operating budget. There is a separate startup budget for capital costs and working capital needs. Most of the line items have annotations describing the issues for each of them. There are also ranges shown for some of the operating costs that depend on the store size and volume of transactions. The financial information also includes operations that do not include payday loans and operations that include payday loans.

The budgets are intended to show not only the potential for different costs in different locations but also the possible range for a smaller and a larger store. There is a discussion of cash flows and profits at the end of the section.

The numbers presented are more representative of a larger check cashing operation, presumably in a larger city with higher densities. The numbers are also conservative. An experienced owner-operator could likely operate a business with lower costs than those presented here. On the other hand, the payday loan operating costs are understated and the resulting pre-tax income figures are overstated. Finally, the projections do not include any debt service for repayment of start up costs; if a loan or investment had been obtained, the debt service costs would have been included and the resulting net income before taxes would have been substantially lower for several years until the investment capital had been repaid.

The summary of these projected, *stabilized* revenues, costs and pre-tax income figures—including and excluding payday lending—are as follows:

WITHOUT PAYDAY LOANS

	Small Store	Larger Store— no PD Loans Lower Fee Schedule	Higher Fee Schedule
Revenues	$190,000	$281,050	$439,050
Operations	$135,000	$193,200–$294,900	$193,200–$294,900
Pre-tax Income	$55,000	$ 87,850	$245,850–$144,150

WITH PAYDAY LOANS

	Larger Store— PD Loans Lower Fee Schedule	Higher Fee Schedule
Revenues	$385,075	$621,869
Operations	$193,200–$294,900	$193,200–$294,900
Pre-tax Income	$191,875–$ 90,175	$428,669–$326,969

The larger store may have higher possible pre-tax income if the costs can be controlled and the lower end of the operating cost range ($193,200) can be achieved.

The start up costs also needs to be considered, as the figures above represent a stabilized operating budget for a business that has completed its start up phase and has entered a different phase. The early time period may include the startup capital expenses (equipment, remodeling, computers, staff training, marketing, signage, legal assistance, etc) plus the operating losses that would need to be covered. In addition, an estimate of initial working capital for check cashing (but not payday loans) was also included. The analysis concluded with the following start up capital needs:

Startup capital expenses:	$ 110,500– 189,000
Operating losses—year 1	$ 30,000– 100,000
Operating losses—year 2	$ 10,000– 30,000
Working capital	$ 50,000– 150,000
Total	$ 200,500– 469,000

Again, it is important to emphasize that these projections were conservative, especially those for operations and start up capital. They were made using assumptions of start up by relatively inexperienced operators.

Nevertheless, it is clear that there is considerable income potential from a well-managed fringe banking operation. It also indicates that there may be room in the operations of these stores to lower the fees charged to consumers and still make a reasonable profit.

In addition, other measures were analyzed: aggregate data from New York and reports such as the Dove Consulting report prepared for the U.S. Treasury in 2000 which indicated pre-tax returns averaging 20% to over 35%. Due to this profit potential, there are not only smaller businesses, but increasingly, large ones that now exist in the industry. Mostly, they are listed on various stock exchanges. Some operating activities of the larger companies in the field such as ACE Check Cashing and Rent-A-Center were described. Also described was the access to the capital markets—Wall Street, IPOs, banks, etc.—used to finance the activities of large corporations that many other businesses do not have.

The wide range of activities performed by a very wide range of corporations —large grocery and convenience store chains, major banks and other financial services companies, companies manufacturing expensive and sophisticated machines and equipment supporting the industry, investment banks and secondary markets, stock exchanges, credit card companies, consumer lending corporations, etc., in addition to the large corporations that have emerged directly from the industry itself—makes it clear that financial services for low-income people is an extensive and profitable business, with excellent profit growth potential in the future for both small and large scale efforts.

Conclusion. Most low-income people in the United States do not have access to the full range of financial services that most middle and upper income households have. As a result of this inadequate access, these households tend to pay a very high percentage of their available income for interest and fees to obtain these services. These higher payments significantly affect their ability to move out of poverty and attain higher living standards. They also partly counter the efforts of many community development efforts designed to lower costs for low-income households—such as affordable housing and child care or the creation of wealth building opportunities, such as IDAs and small business lending and support.

There is an entire set of financial institutions and practices in low-income neighborhoods that replaces the institutions that the rest of the society uses. It is this entire range of institutions that constitutes a dual financial economy and it is the problem created by this range of institutions, which must be addressed. This range includes check cashing outlets, payday lenders, pawn brokers, rent-to-own stores, consumer lending companies, subprime credit card companies, mortgage lending companies, automobile lenders, Refund Anticipation Loan lenders and remittance companies. Together, they constitute a financial system that can create great barriers for low-income households in their attempts to improve their living standards.

This financial system needs to be altered. It needs to become more affordable for low-income households, although without eliminating profit potential from the industry. It needs to become more efficient. And it needs to offer a more complete range of services so that low-income households can more easily move out of poverty.

There are several ways to help create better options for low-income households.

- Introducing stronger statutory and regulatory efforts for fringe banking institutions.
- Creating political and operational pressures for existing fringe banking financial institutions to change some of their activities.
- Encouraging presently uninvolved, existing institutions—such as many commercial banks and credit unions—to become involved in providing affordable financial services to low-income people.
- Encouraging expansion and new approaches by institutions, such as community development credit unions and some banks, which are already involved.
- Creating new alternative institutions, partnerships and financial products.

Please see the Appendix for a business plan executive summary as one example.

Although the fringe banking industry often has an unsavory reputation, these businesses provide important services to low-income households that no other institutions are willing to provide in any systematic way. Progress has been made in creating more reasonable practices. In some places, the market has created competition and lowered prices. In other situations, political pressure and statutory changes have created important changes.

While some progress has been made, the present conditions are nevertheless inadequate in achieving an appropriate set of financial services conditions in low-income neighborhoods. There is still a very long way to go in many areas before a set of fully appropriate financial services is available throughout the country.

While there are risks in this field, and excellent management is required to be successful, it is clear that this business can be quite profitable. These businesses also do not seem to represent the risk levels that appear from viewing the surface level of the businesses. There is risk, but it does not seem to justify the high level of prices for the services. While there needs to be an appropriate level of profit available to attract and keep businesses in the industry, the risk level does not seem to justify the prices that are being charged. At the same time, it is important to allow adequate profit incentives to maintain the industry and not regulate or overly legislate this field.

While the present profit levels can be quite high, the future levels may be greater, due to several forces. Technological changes may increase the profit potential further. Moreover, as the scale of these efforts continues to increase, the profit potential will probably increase and draw more entrants into the field. Also, it is increasingly clear that large corporations are finding methods to provide or support the delivery of financial services to low-income households—either directly or indirectly.

At the same time, the increasing entrance by large corporations and the consolidation of the industry through large chains are probably creating, or will soon create—barriers to entry for new institutions, capital and branding barriers, for example. While there is still time to begin new efforts, the window of opportunity may be lessening over the long term.

These trends can be positive—if methods can be developed to offer a wide array of financial services, including those not readily available to low-income households at present, in a more efficient manner and at reasonable costs. However, if some of the abusive practices are maintained and even intensified, then deleterious conditions for low-income households will continue.

The appropriate financial services needed by low-income households include the following:

- check cashing,
- money transfers,
- money orders
- bill payments,
- ATM access and credit/debit cards,
- all types of loans and accounts,
- insurance, investments,
- federal income tax preparation,
- IDAs,
- EITC,
- financial literacy training,
- credit repair,
- credit counseling, etc.

The key issues surrounding these businesses are finding ways of making it less costly for those who can afford it the least; finding better methods of delivering the services; and offering a more complete range of financial services. Moreover, the structure of the products that are based on the targeting of households with the greatest lack of capacity to use these services needs to be addressed. The methods and technologies are developing that would encourage this result and still generate adequate profits for participating businesses. *The considerable income potential from a well-managed fringe banking operation tends to indicate that there may be room in the operations of these businesses to lower the costs charged to consumers and still earn a reasonable profit.*

Many different efforts to bring change to financial services for low-income households have been evolving throughout the country and it is likely that many more individual, *ad hoc* projects will be initiated. Presently for example, government officials and regulators have been encouraging banks and credit unions to find ways to offer more assistance to low-income households.

However, a more systemic approach is needed. A more coordinated effort is required and a high level of resources will need to be allocated. The level of assistance required is extensive, due to the large numbers of people across the country who may need assistance and the difficulty of creating a business model that has financial feasibility.

Therefore, future efforts need much more support through a coordinated, systematic method of assisting new programs. These methods include availability of technical assistance and training; availability of development capacity to create these efforts de novo in areas without any existing capacity to create a new effort; availability of a financing vehicle to help new financial services programs begin, including startup funds and investment and lending support; and availability of subsidy.

With this level of effort, major changes in the financial services systems supporting low-income neighborhoods can be made that will assist low-income people in moving out of poverty and participating more fully in the economic future of the country.

ORGANIZATION

This report contains the description of the fringe banking institution industry and its separate businesses, its financial feasibility and its impact.

Chapter I. Context/Background.

Chapter II. The Industry. The market; types of financial services, institutions; impacts; needs.

Chapter III. Review of the economics of financial services delivery in low-income neighborhoods by banks, fringe banking institutions, credit unions, community development credit unions, nonprofit organizations and other institutions. The impacts and implications of different business models and approaches are also described.

Chapter IV. Financial feasibility model for check cashing/payday loan businesses. The experience in New York State. The involvement of corporations and Wall Street in the industry.

A Business Plan, including general strategies/approaches for the field and an implementation approach for CDF or another organization to begin addressing these issues, was separately prepared.

Context and Background

Chapter I

It is expensive to be poor. The costs and availability of financial services for low-income people clearly demonstrate one element of this unfortunate truth.

Low-income people do not have access to the full range of financial services that most middle and upper income households have access to in the United States. The costs of the services that are available to them are higher. These households tend to pay a high percentage of their income for interest and fees to obtain these services. These higher payments significantly affect their ability to move out of poverty.

There is a range of institutions that provides a broad offering of financial services to low-income households. They include check cashing outlets, payday lenders, pawn brokers, rent-to-own stores, consumer lending companies, mortgage lending companies and automobile lenders. Together, they constitute a financial system that can create great barriers for low-income households in their attempts to improve their living standards.

This financial system needs to be altered. It needs to become more affordable for low-income households, although without eliminating profit potential from the industry. It needs to find ways to become more efficient, such as through the adoption of new technologies. And it needs to offer a more complete range of services so that low-income households can more easily move out of poverty.

There are several ways to help create better options for these households.

Statutory and regulatory efforts for the fringe banking institutions.

Creating other pressures for existing financial institutions to change some of their activities.

Encouraging presently uninvolved, existing institutions—such as commercial banks and credit unions—to become more involved in providing affordable financial services.

Encouraging new approaches by institutions, such as community development credit unions, that are already involved.

Creating new alternative institutions, partnerships and financial products.

This step was taken with a separate business plan).

All are needed. All will be discussed in this report in varying levels, as it is the purpose of this report to describe the findings of analysis in the area over the past few years. All of the work has been framed from the perspective of developing and understanding a range of business models, their financial feasibility and possible new, financially feasible models or alternatives as a basis for developing new alternative approaches.

THE COMMUNITY DEVELOPMENT CONTEXT

Most of the focus of community development finance efforts attempting to increase access to capital in low-income neighborhoods over the last fifteen to twenty years has taken place in two main areas:

1) To encourage conventional lenders affected by the Community Reinvestment Act (CRA) to become more involved in housing, business and community development lending in low-income communities.

2) To create and build alternative lending institutions, called Community Development Financial Institutions (CDFI's), such as community development banks, community development loan funds, community development credit unions, micro-enterprise funds, venture capital funds, and the like, that could fill gaps which the conventional institutions could not, and probably should not, try to undertake.

These efforts have been quite successful. Conventional lenders, working under the requirements of the CRA, have had impressive impacts in areas such as low-income home mortgage lending, low-income multi-family housing construction and permanent lending, SBA lending, and so forth. The CDFI's have blossomed all over the country and are increasingly building large and well capitalized organizations capable of successfully leading the lending field into new areas of need to serve low-income neighborhoods.

In addition to these two areas, a third has emerged more recently—building assets and wealth for individual households through a variety of savings mechanisms such as Individual Development Accounts (IDAs)—that is also having significant success. It is still in its early stages of development compared to the other two approaches, but it has gained significant support within the spectrum of community development efforts and has begun to have an impact in some areas.

UNMET FINANCIAL SERVICES NEEDS

Even with this impressive record, however, there are still major segments of the financial lives of low-income people that have not been changed or affected by these new activities. Instead, low-income people are still forced to exist in the most difficult and costly of financial environments. There are various estimates of the number of people not served by conventional institutions, or the "non-banked" or "unbanked" population as they are called. The estimates range from 10% to as high as 15% of the U.S. population. And, if this is the percent for the country as a whole, then the percent in low-income neighborhoods, where most of the nonbanked are clustered, must be significantly higher.

The existing community development approaches do not address these needs very well as yet. The CRA approach, while achieving some spectacular successes, has nevertheless not fully succeeded in this particular area of financial services on any scale and may not be able to make large inroads in the near future. There are similar issues concerning CDFI's. While there are some large CDFI's, these institutions, in general, tend to be smaller, and are not yet able to reach most of the affected population. There are some CDFIs with a mission of providing these financial services, such as credit unions and community banks. However, there is a relatively small number of these CDFIs and they do not cover the entire country. Moreover, many of them do not have the capacity or desire to offer these missing services. Many other types of CDFIs tend to lend to other non-profit or intermediary organizations or developers; the direct lending and improved financial services needed by many individuals and families in low-income neighborhoods is not the mission of many of the alternative lenders. (The exception is small business lending where many CDFIs as well as conventional lenders have been active). The CDFI Fund, a program of the U. S. Treasury, has been helpful in recent years in supporting the increased size and scope of many CDFI's, but there is a long growth curve ahead of these institutions before there will be a major impact on the financial lives of large numbers of low-income people.

These approaches represent important steps and ones that should be continued to the fullest extent possible. Nevertheless, there are still very large numbers of people who live without a wide array of financial services that impact their lives or live under the influence of financial institutions that negatively impact their lives.

In addition, the core issues addressed by these different institutions are partly similar and also partly different as well. The primary issue addressed by CDFIs and CRA lending is access to capital for larger institutions and projects, such as affordable housing, small business needs and community facilities such as child care centers. In financial services, there is also a need for access to credit or access to better credit. For example, many low-income neighborhoods may have to function without the services of a commercial bank or a savings and loan. That, in turn, means that they do not have access to capital needed to obtain reasonably priced loans for purchase or repair of their homes, purchase of a car or household items such as washer/dryers, refrigerators, furniture, televisions or computers. They may not have access to reasonably priced small business loans to start new businesses.

However, the primary issue for many lower income households is only partly access to capital. Undoubtedly, there is still a crucial need for short and medium term credit for short term needs now met by payday lenders, rent-to-own stores, car lenders, and the like. There is also a pressing need for access to non-credit financial services such as check cashing, money wiring, savings vehicles and bill paying without paying a large fee, which other people generally do not have to endure.

Instead, the unbanked use the services of a range of financial institutions that has grown to serve their particular needs—but only at a very high cost. They must pay very high interest rates and fees that create an additional—and very heavy—burden. These costs are so great that they can create true hurdles in their efforts to move out of poverty, as the hypothetical example later in this report demonstrates.

And there is another possible impact. *In effect, the community development work that has been occurring may now be negated to some degree by the framework of financial services that exists.* For example, the savings generated by quality child care or affordable housing may be eaten up by the fees charged by the financial services industry. The small business loan that helped start a new business for a low-income family may be endangered by the high costs of the financial services it is forced to use. The building wealth programs may be jeopardized by the high interest and fees used by the financial services industry available to the targeted low-income household.

For the most part, the range of financial services and investment institutions that serves the larger community does not reach low-income neighborhoods. For example, although there are occasional branches, banks and savings institutions tended to move out of low-income neighborhoods many years ago and generally have not relocated there since. Other financial services, such as insurance, may also be difficult to find.

On the other hand, when some of the mainstream financial services products and companies are available, they may sometimes be detrimental to the financial health of households. These types of institutions include investment banks, credit rating agencies, stock markets, mortgage companies, and the like.

For example, rating agencies may mistakenly base ratings for affordable housing developments on the need for excessive cash flow and set very high debt service coverage ratio requirements. When this debt service ratio cannot be met, the development receives a lower rating. The lower rating results in a higher interest rate, which, in turn, requires rents that can be too high for many low-income families to afford. Another example is the mortgage companies that charge predatory rates for small loans that unnecessarily result in the loss of homes for some low-income people.

There can be a vast gulf in the quality and cost of services, programs and institutions that serve low-income people and those that serve the larger society.

EXAMPLES OF FINANCIAL IMPACT

Although there are no detailed reports describing the impact of the existing financial services on low-income households, there are some clear indications of potential effects. For example, First Bank of the Americas, a small bank recently created in a low-income, immigrant neighborhood in Chicago, created a series of reasonably priced financial services programs targeted at this market. The Bank, which has a goal of helping to build community wealth through its variety of loan products and financial services, prepared a study indicating the likelihood of their loans saving over $4 million for local residents in four years. The study compared the Bank's rates and fees for financial services, mortgages and consumer loans for all of its transactions as of April 27, 2000 to the prevailing rates and fees from other local financial services companies (check cashers, rent-to-own stores, predatory lenders, etc.). For instance, the Bank charges nothing to wire funds and there is no loss from differences in the exchange rates; this service saves substantial amounts of money compared to the other wiring services. In the two years since this projection, the savings have likely increased substantially.

Chapter 2 of this report contains an example of a hypothetical family facing the need to use available financial services in a low-income neighborhood. Unable to obtain better priced financial services from more conventional sources, they must use other sources that extract a very high cost on their incomes, their lives and their opportunities for moving out of poverty to a better life. *In this hypothetical example, the family spends almost 16% of its annual income on interest and financing charges!* When the amortization costs are included, the figure jumps to almost 28% of family income. Depending on the assumptions used, the percent of income could have been substantially higher than 16%. If the family had had access to financial services available to higher income households, the percent of their income spent for these services would have fallen dramatically.

This level of expense makes it extremely difficult for low-income people to save money or work their way out of poverty. It works against the activities of many community development efforts to date that attempt to assist low-income families in building wealth through savings programs and providing improved financial services from conventional sources and CDFIs.

DUAL FINANCIAL ECONOMY

The institutions that many low-income people have to utilize include check cashing outlets, pawn brokers, rent-to-own stores, personal finance companies, pay-day loan stores, mortgage companies and the like.

Many people are aware of these institutions in low-income neighborhoods. But the extent of their use, their number, and their impact on low-income neighborhoods is often unknown.

There is an entire set of financial institutions and practices in low-income neighborhoods that replaces the institutions that the rest of the society uses. It is not just check cashing companies or payday lenders that create issues. It is an entire range of institutions that is different from the institutions in other neighborhoods and that are much more expensive. Low-income people tend to use the full range of these institutions, not just an occasional isolated service. It is this entire range of institutions that constitutes a dual financial economy and it is the problem created by this range of institutions, which must be addressed.

Many low-income people live in this dual financial economy. In the country as a whole, there are capital markets, institutions, instruments and techniques that efficiently serve the needs of most Americans, enabling them to easily buy homes, purchase cars and other personal items, pay for their children's higher education, start or expand small businesses, obtain insurance, accrue earnings from savings and make all types of investments. These institutions, instruments and markets are quite sophisticated, efficiently serve large numbers of people at mostly reasonable costs and are characterized by frequent innovation.

This same condition does not exist in low-income communities. Low-income people tend to have difficulty obtaining credit for relatively simple "ordinary" purchases or other credit needs such as starting a business that others take for granted. When credit is available, the terms are often much worse—higher rates, rapid compounding, high service fees, shorter term, etc. (these methods will be described in later sections of this report). While there are sometimes legitimate reasons for difficulties in obtaining credit in some individual cases, such difficulties are often unjustified and ignore profitable opportunities for communities as a whole.

In trying to grapple with the possibilities available in working with conventional lenders in community development lending, it is also crucial to understand the directions of the financial services industry. The industry has been moving away from this type of activity, for both low-income people as well as middle income people. This trend has been occurring for many years. For example, a 1995 Deloitte & Touche study sees the following picture:

> Retail banks today depend heavily on their branch networks and see it as a core of their business. In the future, the branch network is but one of several channels with which the bank accesses its stand-alone client base. Indeed, the branch network is in the future a privileged channel, used only for accessing that small percentage of the client base which offers the potential for genuinely profitable relationship. The rest of humanity will have to be content with entering the lobby and dealing with technology to transact its banking. Alternatively, it will use the telephone or home-TV based system as its access to retail banks, supplementing this with other products bought on their merits direct, via retailers, or off the page.

A few conventional lenders, understanding the potential market in these areas and seeing the higher income markets achieving some degree of saturation, have begun to start some small scale efforts to provide financial services in these neighborhoods. However, they must use a different business model to be successful; the business models used in middle and upper income neighborhoods do not work well in low-income neighborhoods. And, while there have been some efforts by conventional institutions in this arena, there has not been an enormous rush of conventional institutions into the inner city market.

Furthermore, many contend that the reason for the growth of the check cashing outlets, pawn brokers and the like was the banks' earlier abandonment of these neighborhoods in the first place (e.g., Caskey). Finally, conventional lenders are being replaced in many financial areas as the field opens up to vast changes. Other lenders now are making inroads into the arenas that banks traditionally operated in by themselves. For example, many new non-bank banks (e.g., GE Capital, brokerage houses) have entered the field and are making large amounts of new loans and collecting extensive deposits. And, in credit cards, by 1997, credit card issuers were the two most popular lenders for the highly profitable small business market, outranking Wells Fargo, Bank of America and Chase Manhattan Bank; they have no branch network but offer a wide range of financial services (*New York Times*, 1999).

It is, therefore, important to recognize the very wide array of new institutions that is affecting low-income neighborhoods and to develop strategies which reflect these new realities. The times are changing very rapidly and with them may go the older concepts of what can be realistically expected in the future from the past methods of increasing capital access in low-income communities—especially the heavy reliance on the strategy of pushing conventional lenders to fill all the missing financial gaps.

PAST INITIATIVES

In response to changing conditions, the "technology" of providing credit in low-income communities has certainly grown and experienced some innovation over the past decade. However, it is still relatively backward compared to the approaches available to the larger society. It is important to the future of low-income communities—both urban and rural—to understand the full range of economic forces affecting them and to bring innovation to the capital institutions and instruments serving them that are flexible, efficient and adapted to meet their needs.

The CRA and CDFI activities have been major efforts to break this dual financial economy and to bring financial innovation to community development. But these activities represent just a beginning. The field of community development finance is in a very early stage of change and is far behind the conventional markets in financial innovation. Many new areas of innovation and change are possible.

NEED FOR NEW INITIATIVES

The lack of financial services and the existence of harmful financial institutions and programs in low-income neighborhoods work against the other efforts being made in this arena. Wealth building programs, for example, are less effective when payday lenders charge high fees or predatory mortgage lenders take large amounts of equity out of homes that the owners have worked a lifetime to build. The savings provided by affordable housing developments and/or quality child care services can be reduced when the interest and fees on financial services are extremely high that they can cancel out the housing savings. The new small business started with special financing from a nonprofit CDFI may be endangered at the financial margin due to the higher costs for financial services that it is forced to pay; the additional costs can push the business into failure.

Therefore, it is worth considering new ways, approaches and paradigms for community development financing efforts to be implemented alongside the primary existing methods described above. Community Development Finance was created to explore these new directions, among others. The purpose of this report is to describe the findings of extensive analysis in the area over the past few years.

HISTORY OF COMMUNITY DEVELOPMENT FINANCE (CDF) ACTIVITIES IN FINANCIAL SERVICES

CDF began exploring this area in 1999. The original goals were 1) reaching an understanding of the financial services industry serving low-income households and 2) creating a business plan to support various alternatives.

Most of the work completed has been framed from the perspective of developing and understanding a range of business models, their financial feasibility and finding possible new financially feasible models or alternatives. There is an increasing amount of activity and research in this field. Most of this work, which is of very high quality, focuses on programmatic and policy options. However, there is also a need for work that is aimed at understanding the business models and financial feasibility. These additional steps are necessary to understand the situation and develop new approaches to improve conditions. Therefore, the primary focus of most of CDF's Financial Services program activities has been aimed at understanding business models and their financial feasibility.

However, there is no single place or obvious group of places to research this subject. Information is not readily available. As a result, research had to look in many different areas to gather a meaningful body of information. At one point in 2001, it was thought that this might not be possible. There was great difficulty in getting hard numbers for these businesses and in understanding the business models and approaches that made them work. Without these numbers and an understanding of the businesses themselves, it was not possible to build business plans for alternative approaches.

These businesses are so obscure and out of the mainstream that there are few available sources of general information about their inner workings. Those who earn their livelihoods from these businesses often do not want to discuss this information (this, of course, is understandable). Moreover, others involved in the business in other ways (e.g., accountants, trade associations) also often have not been willing to share their knowledge.

Even in situations where there are related institutions and individuals involved, such as credit unions, it was not possible to obtain the operating and profit numbers or other details (e.g., use of technology, necessary level of scale) for running a business.

Ultimately, however, it was possible to obtain these numbers and an understanding of the business models, at least in a larger, generic framework, using a variety of different methods. A major first step was holding focus groups, which supplied extremely valuable information. Five were held—three in Oakland and two in Los Angeles— with different ethnic groups. These focus groups indicated that there were very different markets and the people had different needs that have to be addressed in different ways.

In addition, an analysis of the impact of typical financial services on a hypothetical low-income family was prepared (see Chapter 2). In the analysis, the costs of these financial services were compared to the costs incurred if the family had had access to more traditional financial services through commercial banks, savings institutions, etc. The costs of using the available financial services are substantial for low-income households. These costs make it very difficult for low-income people to work their way out of poverty when they must spend so much of their income on interest and fees. This difficulty is clearly illustrated in the analysis.

Case studies also became a key part of the background work. Nine case studies were completed.[1]

Bethex Federal Credit Union and RiteCheck Check Cashing, Inc. in Bronx, New York.

Union Bank of California in Los Angeles.

First Bank of the Americas in Chicago.

Northside Community Federal Credit Union in Chicago.

Shorebank in Chicago.

Northeast Community Federal Credit Union in San Francisco.

Compass Center in Seattle.

American River Health Pro Credit Union in Sacramento, California.

St. Mary's Bank in Manchester, New Hampshire.

These case studies, which were completed over a ten month period, were a major step in gaining a much better understanding of existing business models, the possibilities for well structured partnerships and the financial feasibility and realities of this field.

It was also possible to find professionals—accountants, business owners, software developers—who agreed to help with understanding the financial feasibility of check cashing stores, including payday lending activities, as well as some of the operating business practices of these businesses.

Moreover, it was possible to find other information by reviewing the financial statements and other materials of check cashing businesses that were placed on the market for sale. Another extremely useful method was assisting a community based organization in Baltimore, which considered various options—

---

[1] Leibsohn, Daniel (2005). *Financial Services Programs: Case Studies from a Business Model Perspective.* Manchester: Community Economic Development Press.

including opening their own check cashing store—to deal with the financial services needs of the low-income people in its neighborhood. Information from local check cashing agencies was available.

In addition to the sources noted above, there are also aggregate numbers on the Internet for a few public companies listed on the stock exchanges. Also, there are aggregate numbers for all the check cashers in New York State, where they are regulated.

Other sources also offered insights, from individual credit unions, courses, a conference held by the check cashing organizations' trade association, etc. In addition, interviews were conducted with many people, visits were made to many of the stores, articles and books were reviewed, along with various other sites on the Internet.

Part of the effort derived from consulting work for the Southern New Hampshire University Financial Innovations Roundtable, which focused on financial services. People from around the country have participated, providing much additional information. Finally, there are also other community development efforts going on around the country and many different people have additional pieces of important information and insights or produced materials that have been very helpful.

From all of this cumulative research and discussion, a reasonable understanding was pieced together of some of the different business models and the financial feasibility of these approaches. Even so, some of the information in parts of the report is based on newspaper and magazine articles, which are not always the most reliable sources. In many circumstances, no other options were possible—outside independent reports or studies or the author's direct research. There are still gaps in this knowledge. Our resulting understanding is more from research than from actually operating a business. Nevertheless, this report is basically sound.

FUNDING HISTORY

Work on CDF's Financial Services program started in the beginning of 1999. Through the time of preparation of this report at the end of 2002, the funders supporting the effort were the ARCO Foundation, the F. B. Heron Foundation, Harrington Investments, individual donors (one through the Social Equity Group), the National Council of La Raza and Union Bank of California (UBOC).

Please note that, although UBOC is deeply involved in developing alternatives to financial services, the Bank's staff never gave me any direction or forced any particular ideas into this research; they were always available and accessible for discussion.

Chapter 2

Many people are aware of the check cashers, payday lenders and pawn brokers in low-income neighborhoods. They are aware that low-income people clearly use them. But the extent of the use of these institutions, the number of institutions and the impact on low-income neighborhoods are often unknown.

There is an entire set of financial institutions and practices in low-income neighborhoods that replaces the institutions that the rest of the society uses. It is not just check cashing companies or payday lenders that create problems. It is an entire range of institutions that is different from the institutions in the other neighborhoods and that are much more expensive. Low-income people tend to use the full range of these institutions not just an isolated service on an occasional basis. It is this entire range of institutions that constitutes a dual financial economy; it is this entire range of institutions that creates problems and must be addressed.

Check cashing and payday lending receive most of the attention. However, many other elements of the financial services industry in low-income neighborhoods are not receiving adequate attention. Rent-to-own stores, car title lenders, money transfer companies, consumer finance companies and the like can have a very great impact on the finances of a low-income household as well. The check cashers and payday lenders tend to receive so much attention because they are so much more ubiquitous and visible, while the other lenders are less visible and somewhat more specialized.

This section of the report will describe the overall industry—numbers of the unbanked, numbers and sizes of the types of businesses that provide financial services, growth of the industry, reasons for the present conditions, etc. Then, several parts of this range of institutions—check cashing outlets, payday lenders, rent-to-own stores, consumer lending companies, pawn brokers, automobile title lenders and mortgage lending companies—are discussed briefly to offer an overview of the types of institutions that are available to low-income households.

Also included in these initial descriptions are some of the financial services—money transfers/ remittances, tax refund anticipation loans, credit cards and electronic funds transfer—along with information on the types of institutions that provide these services. Four of these—rent-to-own stores, consumer finance companies, money transfers and refund anticipation loans—are discussed in more detail. Finally, two others—check cashing outlets and payday lenders—are described as case studies (Leibsohn, 2005).

The impact on low-income households is discussed to show the effects of these services. In addition, a focus group report is summarized and the issue of targeting customers by some of the businesses in the industry is discussed.

THE UNBANKED

The term "unbanked" or "nonbanked" usually refers to households and individuals who do not have checking or savings accounts at conventional financial institutions—commercial banks, savings and loans, credit unions, brokerages and the like. Mostly, they tend to be poorer households who do not have adequate income to be profitable for conventional institutions. They tend to live in neighborhoods that tend not have conventional institutions' branches located in their areas. Nevertheless, all of these households are not poor; some of them may have other reasons for not having banking relationships even though they may be attractive to conventional institutions.

There are various estimates of the number of people not served by conventional institutions, or the "nonbanked" or "unbanked" population as they are called. The estimates range from 10% (Hawke) to as high as 15% (Manning) of the U.S. population. The most often quoted numbers are from a Federal Reserve study—1998 Survey of Customer Finance, which found that nearly 10% of U.S. households did not have a checking, savings, money market, mutual fund or brokerage account with a financial institution. (Hawke; Dove). Other figures quoted include an estimated 40 million unbanked consumers (Business Wire, April 2002).

The Federal Reserve Survey also indicated the following factors about the unbanked (quoted from Hawke, p.4).
- 22% of families earning under $25,000 had no bank account.
- More than 80% of families without a checking account had incomes under $25,000.
- More than 60% of families without a checking account were minorities.
- 25% of minorities did not have a checking account.

Dove Consulting described another report that showed 24% of those receiving federal benefit checks did not have bank accounts (p.11). The report further indicated that an estimated 30 to 40 million U.S. households were unbanked or were sub-prime credit risks and that 40% of U.S. households did not have an unsecured credit card.

However, the numbers of unbanked households may not necessarily reflect the exact conditions in low-income neighborhoods. It is more likely that there is some sort of mix. Some people might have savings and/or checking accounts, in addition to credit cards, but use fringe banking institutions anyway for many of their needs for a variety of reasons. It is also possible that there are many households in most low-income neighborhoods who could qualify for banking services with conventional institutions but do not try or do not want to do so.

Percentages for the unbanked population reflect the total U.S. population. The percent of unbanked households in low-income neighborhoods must be significantly higher. A substantial portion of low-income households in any low-income area without a conventional financial institution must be unbanked.

It is also possible that the percentages and numbers of unbanked households fluctuate at different times of the year and when economic circumstances vary. Dove Consulting reported that the percentage of unbanked in 1995, according to the same series of Federal Reserve reports, was 13%. In that year, the economy faced more difficult conditions than in 1998 and 2000. Manning reports that the percent reached 18.7% in 1989 (footnote 16, p. 355). In bad times, households who are on the economic margins may be less able to maintain banking relationships with more limited income. At the same time, some of the more recent efforts of commercial banks to offer limited accounts to low-income households may have offset this trend to some degree and increased the percent of households with bank accounts.

There is a range of reasons stated by people for not using conventional financial institutions. These include (Caskey, 197; Dove; CDF focus groups):

- The household does not write enough checks to make it worthwhile.
- The household does not like dealing with banks and/or banks make customers feel unwelcome.
- The household does not have enough money to put into banks.
- The service charges are too high (including monthly account fees, check writing fees, bounced check fees and ATM fees).
- The minimum balance requirements are too high.
- The household cannot manage or balance a checking account.
- The household doesn't need or want an account.
- The household has (or had past) credit problems.
- The banks do not have convenient hours or locations.
- The household desires privacy of financial transactions and status.

As part of this research, CDF held 5 focus groups in the Oakland and Los Angeles with similar results. One key finding was the difference between immigrants and native-born households. Immigrants often came from situations that had even less choice in financial services than exist in the U.S.; therefore, they sometimes had less concern than people born in the U.S. who were more familiar with the services available in the larger society. There were also differences among various ethnic groups and the ways they perceived and used fringe banking institutions. Southeast Asians, for example, often used travel agencies as a means to obtain very affordable money wiring services.

THE INDUSTRY

There is an entire range of institutions that offers financial services to low-income households. These institutions are known by many names, such as fringe banks, non-bank financial institutions, alternative financial sector, etc. Sometimes the individual types are known by different terms, such as check cashing outlets, check cashing stores, etc. In this report, these terms will be used somewhat interchangeably.

The industry is growing very rapidly. This growth is described in more detail below in the discussions of individual businesses. The growth is also reflected in the growth of chains and consolidation within various parts of the industry, such as in the Rent-to-Own and Pawn Brokering businesses. For check cashers, Dove Consulting found in its 1999 report that two chains, Ace Cash Express and Dollar Financial Group, operated about 12% of the stores in the country. There were 7 chains that operated 20% of the stores. The remaining 80% of check cashing stores were independently owned, mostly with one to ten stores (Dove). As a rule, they found the following characteristics and differences between the chains and independents in their four city study:

- Chains were open fewer hours.
- Chains had smaller stores, but had more employees and teller windows.
- Chains were often closer to major intersections and mass transit.
- The average chain generated higher total revenues than independents.
- The average chain cashed a higher volume of checks.
- The average chain charged higher fees.
- The average chain generated a higher level of pre-tax profits., but independents generated a higher rate of profit on smaller revenues.

The rent-to-own industry is more concentrated than the check cashers. One company alone, Rent-A-Center, owned over 2,300 stores out of a total of 8,000.

There were several other smaller chains, as well, adding to the concentration levels. The money transfer industry is heavily dominated by two corporations—Western Union and MoneyGram. Other parts of the industry are also concentrated to some degree. It may be likely that more concentration is possible in the future, especially as more established, larger corporations enter the market. Large new entrants will create the necessity for further growth in order to adequately compete.

There are many reasons for the rapid growth of the industry. Carr and Schuetz list several reasons:

- Restructuring of the financial services industry. Consolidation of the banking industry and banking deregulation (Silvestrini) created profit pressures that led to banks' reduced interest in low-income neighborhoods; in turn, this led to their moving from low-income neighborhoods, closing branches that did not earn adequate profits, charging for services that did not otherwise make a profit and closing down money losing services. At the same time, many of the fringe banking companies began entering the field and, later, consolidating, as noted above.

- Changing relationships between fringe banks and mainstream institutions. Wall Street activities—securitizing and secondary market sales, taking companies public—greatly enhanced access to capital and the growth of fringe institutions. Banks began to purchase subprime lenders and now own 5 of the top 10 lenders and 10 of the top 25.

- Marketing and appropriate services. The fringe banking institutions developed improved methods of marketing to the target populations and of developing products and services that met their needs.

Other factors contributed. The influx of immigrants, who may not have trusted banks or had little or no experience with banks, increased the business for fringe bankers. Also, the federal government, in its attempts to stop money laundering and to collect more taxes from those involved in the cash economy and creating the requirements for a social security number, pushed some others away from banks. The banks also started developing better risk management tools with the expanded use of computers and ways to assess different risks (Hartnack). Caskey describes the increase in people without accounts who were shut off from the mainstream financial services. Some of this trend was due to the bank branch closings and increased fees.

More recently, the economic downturn may also have played a part with declining real incomes and a rise in poverty. Layoffs and bankruptcies have been occurring at a very pace. This has resulted in extensive work for bankruptcy attorneys, distressed debt traders, accountants, bankruptcy lenders, etc. But it has placed increasing pressure on employees and laid off workers who become strapped for cash. They use pawn shops and payday lenders with increasing frequency. The profits at some of these companies are increasing as a result (AP Newswires).

However, even in these situations of falling interest rates, low-income households do not benefit, as the rates and fees that they pay for their financial services do not fall. (Scherer) In comparison, those with better access to financial services often pay less when interest rates fall. The rates—mortgages, loans, etc.—that they pay usually fall at the same time.

Fringe banking institutions began a rapid growth in the late1970s and 1980s. Manning describes some of the key forces that helped to shape the industry:

- Industry consolidation through acquisitions and mergers.
- Constant technological improvements and modernization.
- Expansion of new services.
- Use of corporate structures similar to other financial institutions.

DESCRIPTION OF THE BUSINESSES

There are many parts to the financial services industry serving low-income people. It is a range of institutions that is different from the institutions in the other neighborhoods and that are much more expensive. Core elements of this range of institutions that constitutes a dual financial economy are described briefly below.

- **Check cashing outlets.** One of the cornerstones of the fringe banking industry, check cashers cash payroll, government and personal checks for a fee, usually some percentage of the face amount of the check. In addition, they usually provide a range of other services including money transfers, bill payment and money orders. Sometimes, they offer payday loans as well. Finally, they may offer many additional ancillary services, such as faxing, copying, stamps, mailboxes, notary service, envelopes, bus passes, lottery tickets, phones and prepaid phone cards, etc. These stores are open long hours during the week and the weekends in order to provide more convenient service for their customers. Regulation varies in different states.
- **Payday lenders.** These companies offer small, short term loans of up to two weeks in length. The loans may be as high as $500, but are often less. The charge for the loans is usually in the form of some fee per $100 borrowed for up to two weeks. Many borrowers cannot repay loans on time

and have to roll them over, when they are again charged the same fee. The stores may be set up to offer only payday loans and nothing else or they may be offered by check cashing outlets, pawn shops and others. There is some regulation in different states.

- **Rent-to-Own (RTO) stores.** Major appliances—washers, clothes dryers, refrigerators, etc., furniture, computers, televisions and stereos, VCRs, etc.—can be "rented" for a short period of time or until weekly payments after a set amount of time (often 18 to 24 months) allow the "renter" to purchase the item. These transactions can appeal to households which do not need an item for a long time period, cannot afford full cash purchase at another store, have bad credit or cannot or will not save the full amount of the cash purchase. It is not considered an extension of credit, so no credit report is obtained, no reports are made to credit companies for either good or bad performance, no debt per se is incurred and there is little or no down payment required. There are also no reports made to credit companies if the rented item is not purchased. Usually free delivery and repair are included. The industry is relatively new, having begun in the 1960s and it has experienced rapid growth.

- **Consumer finance lenders.** Unsecured personal loans are available to households without adequate credit records to obtain bank loans. The lenders include companies such as Household Finance, Beneficial Finance, the Money Store, Aames, the Associates (now owned by Citigroup and discussed briefly in Chapter 4), Citifinancial (also owned by Citigroup) and others. The rates charged are high—often over 30% — and the industry is regulated. The charges may include additional types of insurance—such as single premium credit insurance—and other charges that significantly add to the costs. The lenders may not always make borrowers aware of these extra charges and fees.

- **Money transfers.** Many immigrants living in the U.S. routinely send money earned here to their relatives in their home countries. Many types of businesses provide this service—check cashing stores, payday lenders, sometimes pawn brokers, grocery stores, some 7-Eleven and Wal-Mart stores and even storefronts specializing in wiring funds. (In some European countries and Japan, the post offices are often used for this purpose while the U.S. Post Office also has a money transfer program). Large corporations such as Western Union or MoneyGram have dominated the market. They charge high fees and pay a portion of that fee to the local store. On November 9, 1998, the Gold Star Check Cashing store in Oakland, California, showed the following prices for wiring outside of the country:

0 to $50—$15;

$51 to $100—$15

$100 to $200—$22;

$200 to $300—$29;

$300 to $400—$34;

$400 to $500—$43;

$500 to $625—$50;

$625 to $750—$57;

$750 to $875—$65;

$875 to $1,000—$75.

These fees ranged up to 30% of the wired funds; the percentage decreased to 7.5% for the largest amount, still a high fee for performing essentially the same function as the smallest amounts (although higher insurance costs are part of the higher transferred amounts).

There were similar fees charged in other stores in different locations in the Bay Area and in other parts of the country visited. If a household sends $250 per month to another country, the cost is $348 annually. Coupled with the other high fees that low-income households pay, these fees can be very burdensome, especially when lower cost alternatives are available. In addition to these fees, other costs—exchange rate commissions, check casing fees, other charges at the point of receipt, etc, can eat up to 20% or more of the money sent (please see the financial impact of these fees on a hypothetical family later in this section).

Competition is beginning to have an impact in lowering costs in some areas—the Western Union fee for $1,000 was recently quoted at $46 and it has been estimated that Western Union's fees in some locations have fallen 50% in the past two or three years. (Brazil). Other factors are also having an impact—new companies are entering the field and technology is starting to become a major factor—as described below. More recently, several large banks have entered the remittance field, hoping to attract the Hispanic market in particular. However, the banks have so far had a relatively small impact, with about 3% of the market. The market is quite large at present, has grown considerably recently and is expected to continue growing extensively in the future.

- **Refund Anticipation Loans (RAL).** When households have their taxes prepared, some companies will make available an immediate loan based on the amount of the tax return. About 40% of the people who obtain these loans are receiving refunds through the Earned Income Tax Credit program, a federal tax refund program for low-income households. Several fees are associated with this process and the fees can add up to a substantial portion of the tax refund itself. The tax preparer's fee can be about $75 to $100, depending on the potential refund. The loan fee is often a flat fee of $78 or $88 and then the refund check must be cashed, often by a check casher, for a fee of up to 10%. In total, 7% to 20% of the total refund checks can be eaten up with these fees. The loans allow the refunds to be received within two to three days compared to 8 to 17 days if the borrower waits for the refund from the IRS, since the refunds are usually filed electronically. The effective rate for this loan can be from 100% APR up to as much as 700% or even higher.

- **Pawn shops.** Pawn shops make small, fixed term (often around 3 months with a grace period) consumer loans to borrowers (often with bad credit and/or high debt) who secure the loans with some form of collateral—jewelry, musical instruments, computers, watches, etc. The loan is equal to some percentage of the appraised value of the collateral—sometimes 25% to 30% or slightly higher. About 30% default on their loans; in this case, the pawn shop keeps the collateral and the debt is extinguished. There is no report made to the credit agencies, considered a benefit of this type of loan by many of the borrowers because it does not create any new problems for their credit records. (This aspect may also be considered a disadvantage by borrowers who successfully repay their loans and are not able to have this record become part of their credit histories). The others pay interest on the loans and sometimes fees; they can redeem their collateral once the principal and interest are repaid. The rates vary depending on the state from about 1.5% to 25% per month. There is regulation of pawn brokers in most states. Pawn shops have grown extensively. There were 4,850 in 1985and 8,878 in 1992. By the end of the century, there were almost 14,000 (Manning; Caskey; J. Johnson; C. Johnson).

- **Car title lenders.** Car title loans are similar to payday loans in some ways. They also appeal to borrowers who need small loans for a short period of time. However, car title lenders make larger loans than payday lenders and pawn brokers—typically up to perhaps $1,200 for a period of about one month. The rate can be from 2.5% up to 25% per month, depending on the state and its regulations. (Some states specifically allow car title lending while others allow it under pawn brokerage laws). The lender does not lend more than a portion of the automobile's worth and the borrower uses the car's title as security for the loan—like pawn brokers, but the lender usually requires that the car title is free of liens. Typically, additional insurance and other fees are added to the loan principal. The loans are made quickly without much underwriting or credit checks. The loans can be rolled over several times, like payday loans and the lenders' rate of return on capital is very high compared to banks. If the borrower defaults, the lender can sell the car and charge late fees and repossession charges. Any excess received in a sale of the auto is returned to the borrower in some states or may be kept by the lenders in other states. The repossession rate is quite high compared to prime car lenders; some repossession tactics have come under criticism. The industry is growing rapidly with strong industry lobbying pressures and political contributions to legislators in some cases. Title Loans of America was the largest company in 1999 with over 300 offices. There were an estimated 600 outlets in Florida, starting with none in 1995. Between 1997 and 1999, 34 stores opened in Oregon. While most banks and investment bankers would not make these loans directly, they are sometimes willing to offer lines of credit, help car title lenders become publicly listed on stock exchanges and package their loans for resale. Like many other elements of this industry, car title lenders have come under public scrutiny, debate and legal challenge (Cahill; Heinz; Hudson; Malveaux; Manning; Nendick; Norris). The car industry has other issues as well, including discrimination in sales of automobiles (Henriques). There is also the large subprime auto loan business. Publicly traded, Americredit is the largest lender; it also buys loans from dealers. Formed in 1988, Americredit has 250 branches in the U.S. and Canada with $15.7 billion in managed receivables. Americredit often sells its loans to the secondary market, collateralizing the sales with the receivables. One commentator described its business plan in the following way: "Their business model is to borrow at 3.5% and lend at 17%," although they recently paid 5.5%. The projected return on equity is over 25% and the earnings growth rate is 30% even in a difficult market (Shaver).

- **Credit cards.** Many low-income households have no credit or poor credit. As a result, they may be unable to obtain a credit card. Nevertheless, there are credit card companies specializing in this "subprime" market. There is a very large "subprime" credit card volume for many credit card companies; between 1997 and 2001, the number of subprime credit cards grew to 26.8 million, an increase of 215% (Koudsi). Some of the companies enter the subprime market as only a part of their business (e.g.,

Capital One Financial) and others enter it as the main focus of their business (e.g., Providian Financial). Providian offers secured credit cards to high risk individuals and charges high rates in return. While much of the focus is often placed on the rates, high fees (e.g., $100 membership fees) also can be a large component of a customer's costs and the company's profits. Although regulators are starting to look more closely at these fees, credit card companies frequently charge late fees and over-the-limit fees that can sometimes cause the balances to increase even when minimum payments are made without further charges against the card. These companies generally face higher default rates especially when the economy is troubled and unemployment rises. At one time, Providian was extremely successful. It rose to the fifth largest credit card issuer in the country in 2000. In 1997, it wrote off 6.4% of its loans while yielding a 5.2% return, compared to 3.1% for some of its large rivals. Providian used credit scoring to set different rates for its borrowers and tried to target the "low-risk segment within high-risk populations" also called the "best of the bad"—people who were more interested in low minimum monthly payments rather than high interest rates, who would take on a lot of debt but who would not default. The company was rigorous in acting quickly with any problem loans. In 1997, it had revenues of $1.5 billion, assets of $12.2 billion and net income of $191 million (Sinton). By 1999, its profits had risen 187% and its portfolio had grown to $21 billion (Koudsi). However, Providian, which had gone public a few years earlier, kept pushing to meet high growth projections and high expectations of its investors. To reach them, the company apparently started extending credit cards to people who represented greater risk, abandoning its financial and business model that had worked earlier. Its charge offs increased to about 12%; losses mounted to high levels ($395 million in the fourth quarter of 2001); the stock value plummeted; the CEO resigned (the new CEO received a $2 million "signing bonus" and a $600,000 salary with a guaranteed minimum annual bonus of $900,000); and Providian sold off over $10 billion of its best accounts. It also came to public attention that some of the company's business practices were questionable and, in two separate agreements for a class action suit and a suit from government regulators, Providian paid a total of $410 million for deceptive advertising and marketing and for inappropriate charges and fees. According to newspaper reports, internal memos from the proceedings showed how Providian (which is far from being alone in these practices) tried to dupe its customers and generate as much income as possible from low-income people through high and hidden fees and rate adjustments. The company founder, acting as a consultant after selling the company, wrote "Making people pay for access to credit is a lucrative business wherever it is practiced . . . Is any bit of food too small to grab when you're starving and when there is nothing else in sight? The trick is charging a lot, repeatedly, for small doses of incremental credit." (Leuty; Manning; Berthelsen; Koudsi; Zuckerman; Sinton; Weber). Another company, the United Credit National Bank offering a Visa card, followed this approach when it included $369 for an educational program, shipping and handling, processing and annual card fee for a card that had a maximum credit line of $400 (Manning). When Providian and other companies ran into financial problems, Capital One Financial, the country's sixth largest credit card company, ." . . swooped down and scooped up many of their customers" in the next year. About 40% of the company's 8.1 million new customers during the last year were subprime. Capital One, which also prided itself on credit evaluation techniques that had generated low losses and high profits in the past, fell on more difficult times due to ignoring those techniques; losses were expected to reach the high 6% range during 2003. Profits, though, are also higher as Capital One charges almost 16% to subprime customers compared to 8.9% for its better risks (Smith). However, new federal guidelines are likely to be proposed that will limit the fees charged on these accounts and potentially lower earnings by half (Shaver).

- **Electronic Funds Transfer (EFT).** The federal government prefers to deposit transfer payments (e.g., Social Security, SSI, Veterans Administration payments, welfare, etc.) electronically by direct deposit into recipients' accounts. Some check cashing agencies offer this service. In one service, the government sends the funds to an account that is accessed with an ATM card. In another type of service, the check casher prints the check and then cashes the check; the recipient is charged for both activities. Initially, the EFT was mandatory, but the service was not used with great frequency. The program then became voluntary. Several other institutions also offer some form of the product. Western Union agents can receive checks or the checks can be directly deposited at the Western Union Industrial Bank in Colorado. Under the second option, the recipient can withdraw funds through an ATM or an agent. Western Union charges a fee for the service. Delaware, Corus Bank, Bank of Agriculture and Commerce and others offer variations of these services, using direct deposit, card access and the like (Dove; Castaneda; E. Saunders; Smith; Aversa; Cal. Health and Human Services Department). The program is moving forward on a demonstration basis in some California counties. Citibank has been a major provider of EBT services for welfare recipients, as discussed in Chapter 4 (Barstow; Sengupta). A recent report indicated that the account has not been widely accepted by either banks, which find the program unprofitable, or the unbanked recipients, who are interested in convenience and low costs (Davenport).

- **Mortgage lenders.** Some mortgage lenders in low-income neighborhoods target highly vulnerable homeowners for high interest mortgages with additional fees. These lenders often foreclose on unwary homeowners, frequently elderly, who are forced out of their homes (and primary asset) with no equity left. One recent estimate of these costs placed the total at $9.1 billion annually to lending practices associated with predatory mortgage lending (Stein). This topic has been covered extensively (e.g., Carr and Schuetz; Gramlich; Bradford; M. Saunders; Immergluck; Peattie; Goldstein; California Reinvestment Committee) and has been the subject of many efforts to change the practices. Therefore, it will not be included in any detail in this report.

ADDITIONAL DESCRIPTIONS

It is useful to look at some of these businesses in greater detail. There will be two different levels of review. First, four of the business will be discussed in more detail: rent-to-own, consumer finance companies, money transfers and refund anticipation loans. These discussions are followed by more detailed case studies of check cashing and payday lending.

Rent-To-Own. The rent-to-own industry has grown very quickly since its primary beginning in the 1960s. It is now a $5.3 billion industry with over 8,000 stores located in every state (one company, Rent-A-Center, owned over 2,300 stores and other smaller chains also owned significant numbers of stores). The industry serves about 3 million households each year according to the trade association, Association of Progressive Rental Organizations (APRO).

The rentals are for one week or one month, and the contracts can be terminated without any penalty at that time or they can be renewed for another similar period. According to industry materials, approximately 75% of customers return the items within the first four months (it is not clear whether these customers return the items because they can no longer afford them or because they only needed the items for a short period of time). Less than 25% of customers actually end up owning the items that they rent, according to the industry. Items that are returned are refurbished and then rented again at lower rates. Furniture is the favorite item for customers with 40% of the leased items. Appliances were next (22.6%) followed by televisions (11.9%), stereos (6.7%), computers (4.2%) and VCRs (4.1%). The customers generally have incomes in the ranges of $15,000 to $23,000 (23%), $24,000 to $35,000 (36.67%) and $36,000 to $49,999 (32.17%) (APRO).

A Federal Trade Commission survey of over 12,000 households conducted in 1998-99, found that 2.3% of U.S. households had made a transaction through RTO services in the last year and the 4.9% had used the services at least once in the preceding five years. The customers were more likely to be African-American (a finding in conflict with the industry figures presented by APRO), younger, less educated, renters, with less income and live in the south. The survey also found that 70% of the customers purchased at least one item of merchandise (again in great conflict with the industry numbers from APRO). Also in conflict with the APRO presentations was the finding that purchase of home electronics was the most favored product rather than furniture. The survey also found that most users of RTO services were satisfied with the experience, although both satisfied and dissatisfied customers alike often mentioned the issue of high cost of the merchandise (Lacko, et. al.).

In buying a RTO item, the customer has the opportunity of paying a full cash price. This price seems heavily inflated from cash prices available in other stores in other parts of most cities (see example of hypothetical family later in this section). The weekly payments, if the rent-to-own option is chosen, builds on this initial cash price so that the full price that is paid is very high, usually twice or more the cost of the same item at another store in the same city. For a typical example, a 19 inch Magnavox TV had a cash cost of $195.99 at Circuit City and a cost of $231.46 if purchased through credit. The same television cost $549 at a Rent-A-Center store if purchased for all cash and $779.22 if purchased through weekly rent-to-own payments. The full cash price is apparently used to discourage customers with good credit from using the rent-to-own approach (Manning, p. 214-5; see examples of a hypothetical family later in this section). Also, the customer often pays the equivalent of the full amount of the merchandise, if purchased at a different store, in the first few months of renting. These differences can be even greater with different products in different places.

The industry figures indicate that the average store has annual revenue of $432,517. With an average of 587 items on rent at any given time, the average income per unit per month is $61.35 (APRO, Average Store Profile). The profitability of RTO stores seems to vary from that of other furniture stores, which depend more on higher gross margins (total revenue less total costs of goods sold) and higher turn rates. In other words, the profits depended on moving the furniture. The average gross margin in the furniture business was 42% and higher gross margin stores, the more profitable ones, averaged 46.6%.

RTO, on the other hand, has higher operating costs due to repair and replacement expenses, the need to continually market to new customers, etc. (APRO). This factor would cut into the gross margins. Nevertheless, the industry seems quite profitable. Rent-A-Center, the largest chain in the industry and discussed in more detail in Chapter 4, had revenues of $1,808,528,000 by the end of 2001. The operating expenses were $1,571,942,000 (Rent-A-Center). The gross margin was 86.9% (although these numbers are not fully comparable with the gross margin reported above—they include more than the cost of goods sold). Nevertheless, this is an extremely high gross margin. And it is reflected in the profitability of the RTO business. Rent-A-Center had net earnings after taxes of $97,497,000 in 2001. This results in a net income percentage of over 5.4%, after taxes (APRO reported the industry profit before tax was 4.3% in an earlier year, presumably 1999). The average for the furniture business is 3%, before taxes (Western Reporter; McCarthy).

These numbers are not fully comparable, as noted above. The numbers for one company do not necessarily reflect the performance of the entire industry. Yet these numbers are probably somewhat reflective of the industry. One conclusion is that the profits are coming from the financing of the purchases in the RTO sector while profits in the overall furniture sector arise from sale of furniture and the careful handling of inventories, turnover rates, cost controls, etc.

The financing of RTO operations may also point to the conclusion that profits stem from the financing and not the actual furniture sales or rentals. The effective rates that RTO stores charge can be quite high as shown in the example of television purchase above. However, the companies usually have bank financing for their activities at much lower rates, perhaps 7% to 9% in the 2002 market. They earn an extensive spread from this financing arrangement.

Rent-A-Center provides another example of the industry's economics. On its website (Company Information, Investor Relations, Analysis), it shows a chart called Rent-to-Own Economics.

Monthly Revenue Stream	Total Rental Revenues	COGS	Gross Margin
Buy Upfront (1 month)	$800	$400	50.0%
Rent-To-Own (18 months)	$1,600	$400	75.0%
Rent-To-Own (22 mos.: avg. contract life)	$1,780	$400	77.5%

The mainstream furniture business has average gross margins of 42%, and a 46% gross margin is considered excellent, as noted above. There are other financial differences as well. The financing for other furniture stores varies markedly from the RTO model. A 2000 Ethan Allen catalog, for example, offers a financing plan with a 9.9% APR and flexible payment terms of 12 to 84 months (Ethan Allen). There is much less profit in this type of financing and a furniture company must rely on the sales of the furniture itself for its profit. Moreover, it is possible that furniture and rent-to-own companies may sell the financing paper—usually at a discount—to financing companies.

In addition to the rates and financial issues, there are other consumer matters that exist. These include the adequacy of the information that the stores give to consumers on the terms and conditions of the purchases, condition of the item purchased (new or used), need for more information on the purchase option, collections and repossession of merchandise. For example, consumer advocates stress the need for providing information on the APR, while the industry argues that it is not needed. Many states offer some regulation of RTO businesses, while the industry is arguing for federal legislation that would override state regulations, in some cases with less restrictive requirements (Lacko, et. al.).

Consumer Finance Companies. Consumer finance companies, a very large business characterized by large companies with access to the capital markets and mostly listed on various stock exchanges, have some similar characteristics, including profitability. And the industry has attracted many financial supporters as well as many new entrants into the arena. Business Week stated this issue in the following way. "Lending to deadbeats was once regarded as barely a cut above loan sharking. Now many well healed finance companies are targeting this market." (Byrnes). And the primary reason probably is profitability.

For example, Commercial Financial Services, which managed bad credit card loans, earned $137 million on $206 million in revenues in 1996 (Zellner & Zweig). Aames Financial Corporation revenues increased 52% in the year ending June 30, 1995 and its gross profit margin was 30% (Byrnes). The per-share earnings at Household Finance increased more than 20% per year for several years through 1998 (Condon).

Another example is Countrywide Credit, a large mortgage lender for prime loans. The company also had a small amount of subprime mortgage loans; it expanded this lending in 1996. During the three months ending August 31, 1996, the company made $318 million in subprime loans compared to $9.2 billion in prime loans in the same period. Countrywide made $33.8 million in pre-tax profits during the period—an estimated 50% of this profit came from the small segment of subprime loans. The profit margin on the prime loans was

0.2% and the margin on the subprime loans was 5.35% (Ellis). In the early 1990's and well into that decade, there were very high profits that attracted many new players (Lipin & Bailey).

The business appears to operate on a principal of charging high rates that result in both high losses and profits. In the Wall Street Journal, for example, Household Finance's approach was compared to Norwest Bank in Minneapolis in the mid 1990s, during the end of a recession. Household's bad loans were $922.7 million for the first nine months of 1996. Nevertheless, net income was $375 million, of $3.68 per share, for the same time period. This amounted to a ratio of almost $2.50 in loan writeoffs for each $1 in after-tax profit. In contrast, the Bank had almost an opposite approach—it had less than $1 in losses for each $3 in net income. Even so, both institutions were ." . . about equally profitable" (Bailey). Household Finance charged rates of 18% to over 30%.

Even with these profits, the business has had many casualties since the mid 1990s. Several banks entered the field. First Union Bank, for example, purchased The Money Store in 1998 and then decided to close it in 2000, charging off $2.6 billion in the process (Sinton; Timmons). Barnett Bank, which was later purchased by Nations Bank, bought EquiCredit for over $330 million in cash. KeyCorp bought a sub prime auto lender, AutoFinance Group, Inc., for over $305 million (Byrnes).

Others also expanded in the field. Conseco, for example, bought Greentree Financial in 1998 in a purchase valued at $6.4 billion. By 2000, the company was experiencing great losses and greatly increased debt (Bailey; Sparks; Osterland). In 2002, Conseco was forced to renegotiate the terms of $1.5 billion in debt held by a consortium of major banks and remains in deep financial trouble, in large part due to the Greentree acquisition (Hallinan). The industry seems to be a victim of its own success to some degree.

The industry may also be creating some of its own problems, as the accounting practices in the industry have been questioned for years (Melcher and Osterland; Timmons, 2001). Also, the lenders sometimes compete for the customers of other lenders. This can then lead to offering loans to less and less credit worthy borrowers in an attempt to maintain revenue and profit growth (Lippin & Bailey). Other practices to expand revenue and market share include buying loans directly from appliance dealers and furniture stores

Even with these issues, others still enter the field and expand. Household Financial (now Household International) bought Beneficial Finance, although at a high premium (Condon). Household recently reached an agreement to settle a suit from several state attorneys general for $484 million in penalties. Wall Street analysts estimated the costs to the borrowers for the deceptive practices to be $3 billion to $4 billion, while ACORN, a national community organization, estimated the costs to be $8 billion to $10 billion. The accusations included charging higher interest rates than had been previously disclosed, inadequately disclosing prepayment penalties and other fees, charging excessive points and charging higher rates for people who qualified for lower rates. Household agreed to change many practices including a 5% cap on the points and fees that it charges and disclosure of the loan terms that will be clear and full. Household, which earned net income of $1.85 billion on $9.6 billion in 2001 revenue and earned an estimated $2 billion in profit in 2002, will lose an estimated $30 million to $50 million annually due to the cap on fees/points and the shortening of prepayment penalties. The stock's value, which had been under pressure due to the suit, increased 25% the day before the announcement and an additional 9.2% on the day the announcement of the settlement was made. Nevertheless, the stock value has fallen from a high of $62 to around $28 (Berthelsen; Reuters; Beckett and Hallinan; Economist).

Even so, the company continues to be under pressure. Before the agreement and the penalty were announced, Household had agreed to restate its income from 1994, with a reduction of $386 million. Household, which has made $100 billion in loans to 50 million customers, also uses different methods to assess the risk of their loans. One measure is the number and amount of past due loans. But Household often allows customers to skip payments while not including these loans as past due. As of June 30, 2002, these "re-aged" loans totaled 16.7% of total loans (Eavis).

Household is the eighth corporate issuer of debt on Lehman Brothers Inc.'s credit index with $85.4 billion of debt as of September 30, 2002 and was planning to raise over $36 billion in debt in 2003. Moody's rates Household's senior debt "A3," its seventh highest investment grade out of ten. One issue, for example, paid 5.75% for 2007 bonds (Stempel).

Household's rating improved when HSBC, a British bank holding company with $5.4 billion in net income in 2001, announced its intended purchase of Household (which was advised by Goldman Sachs Group) in November 2002 for over $14 billion in stock. The purchase will be made at some discount due to the reduction in Household's stock stemming from its recent problems. Household will be able to access the Bank's deposits in the future, which will lower its borrowing costs (Sorkin; Economist).

Citigroup purchased a large commercial lending institution, Associates First Capital Corporation, in 2000 for $31.1 billion. It has since been involved in changing a number of its lending practices and negotiating a settlement with the FTC. The Associates and Citibank's own existing consumer finance division—Citifinancial—have come under fire for some of its practices. Citigroup made certain changes in its activities, including the ending of expensive and often unneeded credit insurance (McGeehan) and recently announced a settlement with the U.S. Federal Trade Commission for refunding $215 million to the customers of Associates for activities which occurred before Citigroup purchased the company (Beckett; Ho; Oppel; Timmons). Citigroup also ended relationships with over 3,600 outside brokers who had brought loans to Associates in the past but who were improperly licensed, failed to agree to a Citigroup code of ethics and other reasons (Nol).

These businesses can be successfully operated, but they require careful attention to costs and details. At the time of Household Finance's acquisition of Beneficial, there was a large difference in operating efficiencies. At Beneficial, the overhead costs were 52% of its $3 billion in 1997 revenue. Household Finance, in contrast, spent 36% of its 1997 revenue of $5.5 billion on expenses. Household, in the meantime, had losses of 4.3% for annualized 1998 (Condon). To be successful, these businesses need to be very strategic with its marketing, very careful in evaluating credit risks, careful in monitoring risks and rigorous in its collections. Scale also may play a key role, as in any other business.

Differing business conditions significantly affect consumer finance companies. When the economy is strong, there is more employment and higher income; banks increase their lending as a result. Competitors, often in the subprime market niche, also enter the market, frequently using debt to finance new companies, expansions of existing companies and acquisitions. Profit margins are reduced with the new competition and the lenders start to take greater risks. In tougher economic times, bank lending decreases. But the bad loans and/or the high corporate debt incurred during good times by the subprime lenders create failures among the competitors. There can be mergers and consolidations. In turn, the remaining lenders can increase rates and fees as market share increases.

Wall Street has played an important role in the growth of this industry. The securitization of the loans allowed lenders to replenish their capital and expand lending for many subprime lenders such as the home equity lenders (Capel). Going public opened up the equity markets. Jayhawk Acceptance, which made loans to people with very bad credit—people with defaults and bankruptcies on their records—to purchase used cars, went public in 1995. The initial share price was hoped to be $6.50 to $8.50, but it went public at $10 and was soon at $15 a share. The owner, who had invested $100,000, soon owned shares worth $150 million ." . . for a business whose total revenues in its short life are about $14 million" (Norris).

These institutions often face legal actions and political pressure as a result of their practices. Like Citigroup's Associates, Household Finance has indicated that it will also stop using single premium credit insurance. The company also announced changes that would give more information to borrowers on the home mortgage rates, create a cap on its rates, offer a rate reduction to borrowers with good track records with their loans, etc. (Allison). Household also agreed to pay $12 million in fees to the state of California to settle an earlier suit.

Money Transfers. Remittances to other countries now play a key role in the economies of many countries, often larger than many other industries. They also are often significantly larger than the aid that the U.S. gives to many countries. For example, the value of remittances to Mexico is greater than revenues from tourism and agriculture. In El Salvador, Nicaragua, Jamaica and the Dominican Republic, the remittances are greater than 10% of each country's gross domestic product (Hendricks). As a result, remittances are now receiving much more attention both here and in the recipient countries.

There are large numbers of outlets providing this service. Close to 10,000 businesses classified their primary service as money transfer while another 40,000 stores classified wiring as an ancillary service (Dove). As a result, the market is quite large, now estimated at $23 billion in wire remittances sent from the U.S. to Latin American countries in 2001. The world wide market is estimated at around $140 billion. While the Mexican transfers are estimated at $9.27 billion in 2001 and reached over $13 billion in 2003, the Latin American market for other countries was also quite large, including remittances of $1.972 billion to El Salvador, $1.807 billion to the Dominican Republic, $1.4 billion to Ecuador and, in 1999, $1.898 billion to Brazil (Brazil). It has been estimated that 69% of Latin American adults living in the U.S. send an average of $200 back to their families about seven times a year (Electronic Payments International). This level of transfers between the U.S. and Latin America translates into approximately $3 billion in fees (Electronic Payments International).

At this time, Western Union (which recently has been the best performing division owned by First Data Corporation [Breitkopf], and discussed in Chapter 4) and MoneyGram dominate the market—comprising 97% of the Latin American money wiring market in 1996. (Brazil; Romney). The two companies earned 30% profit margins (Timmons) at least prior to competition, which has lowered the fees a great deal (First Data had first purchased Money Gram.

When the company purchased Western Union, it was forced to sell Money-Gram due to the concentration that it would have had in this market) part of the market—card based wiring—has been estimated by a Celent Communications report. The number of card-based money transfer products is projected to grow from 200,000 in 2002 to 13 million in 2006; the value of remittances made through cards using ATMs will grow from $300 million to $19.5 billion in that same period; and the revenues from these products will increase from $40 million to $2.34 billion. The market share of card based money transfer products is projected to grow from 0.2% in 2002 to 11% in 2006 (Breitkopf). Overall, the number of transactions, already 80 to 100 million, is expected to grow by 460% by 2010. The value of the transfers is expected to grow by 610% (Krebsbach). The industry has also attracted investment bankers who securitize the remittances (Druckerman).

The First Bank of the Americas began using a card based product for its customers a few years ago. The Bank issues two ATM cards for its account holders (and does not charge for the issuance of these two ATM cards). One card stores the value of the deposits and the other is sent to someone in the U.S. or to another country who can access the funds through an ATM in that location (usually for a fee of $1.50 if the ATM uses CIRRUS) without losing any funding due to exchange rate differences.

Many other large institutions are entering the market, both for the fees as well as a means to increase their customer base among immigrants. Bank of America started a new program in June 2002 in California called Safesend. Bank of America also announced the acquisition of a 25% share of Banco Santander Serfin, Mexico's third largest bank, for $1.6 billion (Berthelsen). Citibank, through its subsidiary Banamex (which was Mexico's second largest bank at the time of purchase in 2001), uses a Citibank Money Card Account to transfer money to Mexico through cards; the program began in July 2002 on a pilot basis (Krebsbach; Electronic Payments International). Wells Fargo charges $10 for sending up to $1,000 for account holders (Hendricks). The service is called Intercuenta Express Account. Credit unions have also entered in a substantial way (Krebsbach; Electronic Payments International; Romney; Brazil). Some of the credit unions are able to bring the costs down to $6.50 to $10 (Romney) while some of the banks charge more, but still less than Western Union. Smaller companies are also entering the field—several for example in Los Angeles and other parts of southern California (Romney). About 47% of remittances to Mexico emanate from Los Angeles (Berthelsen). And a Mexican bank, Banco Del Ahorro Nacional Servicios Financieros, is planning to begin charging $5 per $1,000 wired by 2003 (Krebsbach).

The increased entry of banks, which account for only a small percentage of the immigrants who send money to their home countries, may result in lower fees. An estimated $3 billion is spent on fees for wiring funds by companies, which charge up to 15% (and sometimes even more) of the wired money. (Fees and losses from exchange rates can require 25% or more from the money wired).

A recent study by the Pew Hispanic Center and the Multilateral Investment Fund indicated the potential for savings, which is especially important in allowing more efficient use of the remittances in the receiving countries (Canto; Lockyer). The receiving families often spend the money on housing or durable goods, which can generate three to four dollars in economic growth for every dollar spent *(Economist)*. The Latino Community Credit Union, the U.S. Treasury, U. S. AID, and the World Council of Credit Unions announced a new effort to reduce those money wiring costs with support through the government's First Accounts program (Ortiz; *PR Newswire*). Mexico recently passed legislation allowing credit unions to send and receive wired funds.

Technology is helping a great deal in lowering costs. Nevertheless, there are issues with the use of technology. For example, the use of the cards often requires a bank account. Many immigrants do not have accounts because they do not trust banks (or have other reasons). An estimated 56% of Mexican migrant workers have bank accounts and the percentage of immigrants with accounts falls dramatically as the income levels fall. In addition, the use of cards may take a while to gain acceptance in receiving countries as well (Hendricks; Electronic Payments International). Therefore, more expensive options may continue to be used along with other newer, more high tech methods. Some use money orders and send them by courier. Some Asian immigrants use travel agencies, which are very inexpensive. And some use the smaller companies, where they exist.

The market size and the resulting competition have lowered prices dramatically in the last few years, at least in some areas. Further inroads are expected. However, it is still a difficult business to enter. A network is needed to distribute funds in the target countries as well as sign up local stores as agents. Western Union has 101,000 agents world wide and MoneyGram has 37,000. Western Union also transfers funds in 15 minutes, a time that most other institutions cannot match (Timmons). And it has brand recognition that many new entrants, even the large banks, do not have in other countries. This strong market position makes it difficult to break into the business, but competition has nevertheless brought major changes in a relatively short period of time.

Refund Anticipation Loans (RAL). The breakdown of RAL costs, shown below, reflects the high costs to a low-income family receiving a refund of $1,000 to $1,5000 using a commercial tax preparer (Mendel).

Form 1040	$ 40.00
W-2 forms	10.00
EITC	15.00
IRS Form 8453 (filing)	15.00
Electronic filing fee	4.00
RAL Preparation	15.00
Loan fee	64.95
Total	$163.95

Some of these fees may be higher, for example, the Loan fee, which can sometimes be a flat fee up to $95. In addition, there can be check cashing fee. Many banks will not cash IRS tax returns if the person does not have an account at the bank; without an account the tax payer may have to pay a very high fee to cash the check. Fraud is the main concern for the banks and the reason for the high fee (Klees). If the recipient goes to a check casher, the fee may be high for the same reason. This fee could be up to 10% (Consumer Federation of America), which could add up to $150 to the cost of the entire package. These costs would total $314 for a $1,500 refund, or almost 21% of the total refund. For a $1,000 refund, the cost could be up to $264, or over 26% of the refund. If the check cashing fees were smaller, the costs would be 14% to 19%, if the check cashing fee were 3%, although the industry states that the total cost percentage is closer to 6%. One consumer organization estimated that these activities ." . . can cost $267" (Consumer Federation of America).

The business is growing rapidly. EITC refunds totaled over $30 billion in 1999 with about 50% of it funded through RALs (Berube, et. al.). About 19 million people receive EITC refunds. About 68% use commercial tax preparers and 4.9 million take out a RAL (Johnston). In total, about 40% of those who use RALs are low-income households receiving an EITC refund (Ha). In 2001, the ." . . nation's largest commercial tax preparation service and tax refund lenders earned $357 million from 'fast cash' products . . . more than double the approximately $138 million these companies earned on similar products in fiscal year 1998" (Berube, et. al.). The Brookings Institute study estimated that fees accounted for $1.75 billion of 1999's $30 billion in EITC refunds. Another study estimated $810 million in RAL fees in 2000 in fees for tax preparation, electronic filing, loan fees and check cashing fees (Wu).

H&R Block and other tax preparers form a key part of this business. H&R Block served 19.2 million taxpayers in 2001 through 10,400 offices (PR *Newswire*). H&R Block processed 4.5 million RALs in 2001 and, in 2000, the loans represented 8% of the company's revenue (Ha). Jackson Hewitt is another major player. Its offices have grown from 15 in 1986 to 3,800 now. It targets people in the income range of $30,000 to $50,000.

Banks are also involved in providing the loans. One small bank has set up a practice in a St. Paul laundromat where an accountant prepares the return on line and obtains a RAL from Bank One in Chicago. The filer receives the refund check and is then encouraged to cash it at the bank (University National Bank), which also bought a check cashing company six years ago (Thompson; Northwestern Financial Review). In another partnership, ACE Cash Express has placed 100 of its check cashing machines in H&R Block offices and charges 2.9% to 3.4% plus a $3 fee for first time users. (Johnston; PR Newswire).

And other companies market to check cashing companies by offering bonuses for increasing numbers of referrals for preparation of tax returns and RALs. For example, Tax Mart offers ." . . commissions from 40 to 50% of the tax preparation fees. Average tax preparation fees are $120–$150 per return . . . (and) are deducted from the Refund Loan check." This company provides the software and has the referring company send the client's tax information by computer to Tax Mart where its accountants prepare the return and deliver the loan by wire to be printed and cashed at the check cashing company.

These loans would cost relatively little to underwrite and originate. The preparer knows the income and the lender knows the repayment source will be available in a short time period, so there is no underwriting to speak of. The documents are standard and can be produced very quickly. There appears to be little staff time involved. Therefore, the fees probably represent extensive profit.

These fees can be another heavy burden for low-income people. This is even more problematic in light of the possibility of being able to avoid many of these costs. A free program available on a limited basis in many cities, Volunteer Income Tax Assistance (VITA), uses volunteers to assist with the tax preparation. When filers wait for their refunds in combination with using VITA, most of the costs can be avoided and the funds can be saved or used for key living costs. Moreover, there are other potential pitfalls with using RALs. If the IRS contests the return, the filer may receive a lower refund than anticipated, leaving the borrower with a liability to repay the full amount of the RAL.

CASE STUDY: CHECK CASHING OUTLETS

Many of the aspects of this business are covered later in this report—business model approaches in Capter 3 and the financial feasibility in Chapter 4. Therefore, this case study only describes limited aspects of the business.

Most check cashing outlets offer a full range of services to customers, including check cashing, bill payment, money orders, money wiring and often, payday loans. In addition, they typically offer a range of miscellaneous services such as faxing, mail boxes, stamps and envelopes, photocopying, notary services, lottery tickets, bus passes, pre-paid phone cards, etc. In many ways, they offer one-stop shopping for many necessary financial services. The stores have relatively fixed costs for the long hours that they are open, so adding extra services that require little cost mostly creates profit for the stores once the initial fixed costs are covered (the economic feasibility of this business concept is explained in the next two sections).

The industry is now quite large, as described in Chapter 4. According to a Dove Consulting study in 2000, using numbers from 1998, there were 180 million transactions, generating $60 billion in gross revenue and $1.5 billion in fees (Dove). These figures are probably higher now. The Dove report also discusses the growth in stores, increasing from about 7,100 in June 1998 to 9,500 in 2000 (the growth mostly occurred recently, as there were only a reported 2,000 stores in 1985 and 2,151 in 1987, according to Manning). In addition, another 1,300 stores list check cashing as a secondary line of business and another 831 stores in Illinois should also be classified as check cashing companies because they were not included due to the use of different terminology—the stores are called currency exchanges there. Also crucial in the industry is the very large, but unknown number of grocery stores and liquor stores that cash checks when a purchase is made. And there is also an increasing number of check cashing machines in a variety of locations that are not included in these numbers.

Location is always a critical issue and is discussed in later sections. However, one factor in location is the public view of check cashers, which is often negative. As a result of this perception, there may be zoning regulations which restrict locating check cashing stores to certain area and attempts to open new stores in other areas—higher income neighborhoods—may be met with stiff resistance. This can be problematic because some check cashing companies are beginning to target lower middle and middle income households.

The clients tend to come from several different types of customer. There are blue collar employees from construction and related trades, services and factories and automotive facilities; immigrants who have settled permanently or temporarily in an area; people who are newcomers and who have not established permanent residency or set up bank accounts; recipients of government transfer benefits such as veterans benefits, welfare, social security, SSI, unemployment, disability, etc.; students and tourists (*Entrepreneur*).

They sometimes have different needs and may require different services. For example, it is very useful, critical even, to have employees who can speak other languages in areas where there is a large immigrant population. Money wiring can be more important to immigrants than some other services. Bill paying and money orders may be more crucial to permanent residents while transients are more concerned with check cashing. A good market study can be very useful in determining the existing population—number of people, income levels and sources of income, ages, homeowner/renter breakdown, etc.—surrounding a potential location.

The Dove Report surveyed check cashing companies in four cities—Boston, Atlanta, San Antonio and San Diego in 1998-99. Their findings apply only to those stores and those cities, but they nevertheless give some insight into the character of the business.

- Primarily, the checks cashed were payroll checks (80%), followed by government checks (16%).
- The average size of the store space varied widely. The independents were larger at an average of 1,835 square feet total (with 1,294 square feet for the lobby and 541 square feet for the back office space. The chains were much smaller with an average size of 1,228 square feet (736 square feet for the lobby and 492 dedicated to back office space). Another report listed the average size at roughly 800 to 1,200 square feet, with about 75% of the space allocated to customer area (*Entrepreneur*).
- On the other hand, the independents had a smaller number of teller windows and fewer tellers. The chains used their existing space more intensively, spending less on rent and overhead while hiring more tellers to keep on duty.
- At the same time, the independents were open longer hours.
- The stores tended to be located in storefronts and, in San Antonio, in strip malls.
- The chains charged higher fees but, nevertheless, had higher volumes than the independents.
- The largest revenue producers were from check cashing, money wiring and money orders. There were few payday lenders in their sample.
- The chains generated more revenue per store (it is important to note that the figures may not have shown the full income for independent stores, as they are a cash business and may not report all of their income, especially in a survey of this type. There are many ways for a store owner to hide income—for example, later recoveries of previously written off bad debts. To the extent that this is the case, the results of the Dove report may be

inaccurate, especially in the areas of the revenues and profits).

- The percentage of revenue spent on operating expenses was higher for chains, especially for salaries, bad debts, corporate overhead and advertising.
- The chains had lower pre-tax profit margins.

Many states regulate check cashers. New York, for example, limits the fees for some checks to 1.40% of the face value. This regulation makes profitability more difficult to achieve. However, this regulation is tied to another that limits competing stores to a minimum distance from each other, creating small geographic areas with some degree of competitive strength. The profits are still reasonable in New York, although another regulation denies payday lending (which is circumvented in some ways, as described in the payday lending description) and thereby also limits profits to some extent. To some degree, this experience demonstrates that check cashing fees can be lowered and still offer a reasonable return to business owners.

Many other stores—grocery stores and liquor stores in particular—also cash checks. They frequently do not charge for cashing the checks as long as the customer buys some minimum amount of goods. The check cashing stores must counter to some degree by offering a wide range of products and using some as loss leaders to attract customers.

The check cashers need a large volume of transactions to succeed. The long hours that they are open and the relatively low operating costs help in that regard. And the one-stop-shopping concept also plays a key role (these concepts—business models and revenues/operating costs/profits—are described in more detail in Chapters 3 and 4).

In an interesting finding, Dove noted that commercial banks were often located more closely to the check cashers than other check cashers. This finding could indicate that the two types of institutions have different businesses and in some instances, different customers. This concept is discussed more fully in the next sections.

There is also a possible difference between check cashing and payday lending—they often attract different customers. Check cashing companies rely on customers with jobs mostly, and customers with government transfer payments of some kind, secondarily. These customers do not have bank accounts for the most part. Pay day lenders rely on people who are working and do have checking accounts. So they often serve different people; therefore, some payday lenders do not include check cashing and other types of traditional check cashing services in their stores.

There have been changes in the industry at different times that have been initially perceived as threats. Electronic Benefits Transfer (EBT) was one change that did not create a threat in the end, although it was initially considered problematic. Another is the movement of banks and other institutions in to the field. Another potential one is the move away from checks altogether. In 1979, checks accounted for 85% of noncash payments. In 2001, the figure had dropped to about 60%. Forms of electronic transactions grew from 13.5% to 37.5% during the same period. According to a Federal Reserve study, checks now account for 49.1 billion transactions compared to 30 billion electronic transactions. However, the differential in 1979 was 32 million checks and 5 million electronic transactions. The highest percentage of checks goes to businesses for paying bills. The next highest percentage is used to pay for point-of-sale transactions (Berthelsen).

However, low-income households may tend to use checks at a higher rate. There are no data on this issue that could be found, so this statement is somewhat of a guess based on some of the case studies and the slower transition to using technological methods, often due to lack of access to the technology itself.

Another threat is fraud. Check fraud includes fake checks and counterfeiting—checks can now be easily printed on computers. Illegal activity grew 25% in 2000. Mostly, this activity affects banks, which tend not to reimburse the businesses which are cheated. Banks process most of the checks by machine and do not carefully look at all of the checks (Timmons). The check cashing companies are also targets. Counterfeit checks written on computers represent one problem.

Businesses that hire undocumented workers are also problematic. Garment contractors ." . . are especially notorious for running out on creditors, stranding workers in lofts stripped of sewing machines with paychecks that prove worthless." Banco Popular, using a mobile van to cash pay checks in Los Angeles' garment district, lost $66,000 from one company alone (Millman). Check cashing stores are also targets for fake checks and other schemes, excluding people with accounts that have non-sufficient funds to pay the bills (Sarkisian). Check cashing stores have to be especially alert to fraudulent checks and be very careful with the inspections of checks as well as establishing close relationships with their customers.

Another large risk is the potential for lack of sufficient funds in an account, whether business or personal. Carr and Schuetz describe remarks from a Progressive Policy Institute analyst indicating that this risk is fairly low, at least statistically. The two largest check cashing companies cashed about $6.5 billion in checks in 2000, mostly paychecks and government benefit checks. The actual losses from bad checks totaled one quarter of one percent of the face value of the checks. With a heavy volume, these companies had excellent profits. This indicates the potential for strong profits in this business when coupled with mechanisms that lower risk to a very reasonable level.

Technology will increasingly play a role in check cashing. Although the initial capital costs may be high, some technological advances may be ultimately cut costs and allow more efficient—and lower cost—delivery of financial services to low-income households. However, there still may be some unwillingness on the part of low-income households to participate in the use of new technologies (Sarkisian) and require the need for additional steps to assist them to adopt these approaches.

CASE STUDY: PAYDAY LENDERS

Payday lending is a very controversial topic. The lenders believe that they are fairly filling an important niche and providing an excellent service to borrowers. Consumer advocates, some critics and some legislators consider the product to be outrageous, a large scale predatory approach that takes advantage of people who are strapped for money and may not be informed about the full range of alternatives. The borrowers' reactions are mixed—some are satisfied while others recognize the product as a huge mistake that started them on a downward spiral toward bankruptcy; however, there are very few complaints made to regulatory authorities by customers throughout the country.

A borrower must have a job and a checking account to be eligible for a payday loan. To obtain a loan, the borrower writes a check for the borrowed amount plus a fee. The cost of the loan, based on the annual percentage rate or APR, must be disclosed to the borrower; the cost is the fee that is charged for the loan on an annualized basis. This practice is required of the lender under the Truth in Lending Act.

The check is postdated up to a maximum of two weeks to the date of the borrower's next payday (in effect, both parties acknowledge that the check is "bad," in that the borrower does not have enough cash in the account to cover the check at the time it is written). The lender agrees to hold the check until the next payday, the date on the check, which is not longer than two weeks away. On the date of the post dated check, the customer has several options—paying off the debt with cash, allowing the check to be deposited or renewing the loan by paying another fee, typically the same one which was required for the first loan. Many repay when the loan comes due the first time or with one or a small number of rollovers. However, many borrowers cannot repay the full amount of the loan and are forced to rollover the loan many times until the amount of fees equals or far outweighs the original loan. The financial repercussions for these borrowers can be extensive and very damaging.

The financial services product itself is called by many different names, including payday loans, payday advances, cash advance loans, check advance loans, post dated check loans and deferred deposit advances. The industry itself seems to prefer "advances" of some type in the title because it tends to believe that the product is not a loan; this terminology and method allows the product to be considered a service and not a loan—and therefore not subject to usury laws (however, the terms "lender" and "borrower" are used in this report).

The fees charged are usually regulated at the state level and range from $8 per $100 borrowed to about $30 per $100 borrowed. The average tends to be in the middle, about $15 to perhaps $20, or 15% to 20%. However, this rate can be increased by lenders, which use the following methodology. The customer needs a loan of $100. The fee is 15%, presumably $15. However, the loan is computed as $100 = 85% of the total loan amount, or $117.65. So the borrower may actually pay $17.65 to borrow $100, or 17.65%.

The APR of the loans is one measure of the impact. For a single loan of $100 with a $15 fee, the APR for a 14 day loan is 391% (or 782% for 7 days). For loans with higher fees—20% for example, the APR is higher—521% and 1042% for 14 day and 7 day loans in this example. The adequacy of APR as a measure is discussed further later in this section.

In addition to this fee, other fees are sometimes charged. For example, some lenders may also charge a one-time administrative fee of $10. And, whenever a check bounces, the lender is entitled to charge a non-sufficient funds fee; in addition, the bank will typically charge a fee for the bounced check.

History of Recent PayDay Lending

Although variations of these loans have been available for well over 100 years in the U.S. (Caldor), the real growth began in the 1990s. (Kilborn, Lynch). In the beginning of the decade, there were few lenders making these loans. And that was part of the problem. Conventional lenders do not want to make small loans because of the cost and low returns that are controlled by the usury laws. The waves of bank mergers and resulting branch closings, combined with a new focus on fee income, provide a new set of incentives and profit guidelines for financial services. Other institutional lenders such as credit unions have tended to stay away from this type of lending as well for somewhat similar reasons; in addition, credit unions do not have the geographic coverage that banks and thrifts do, so their impact is lesser. Many consumer finance companies that might have served the subprime market with these loans in the past apparently moved into other areas such as larger secured subprime mortgage lending (Heinz).

There was a vacuum and a need that began to be filled by these new lenders. There were just a few lenders in the early 1990s, about 300 in 1992, according to one report. By 2001, there were an estimated 10,000 lenders in the country as a whole making roughly $14 billion in loans and collecting about $1.6 billion per year in fees (one source, Consumer Federation of America by Fox and Mierzwinski, in a November 2001 report titled "Rent-A-Bank Payday Lending," indicates that there are 12,000 to 14,000 payday loan stores making at least 100 loans per month with another 8,000 to 10,000 lenders with smaller volumes in 2001. CFA indicates that industry statistics show that there are about 65 million transactions for 8 to 10 million households resulting in fees of $2.4 billion). This is clearly a substantial industry.

Most individual states also show the rapid growth. For example:

- Utah had 14 stores in 1994 and 96 in 2000 (Fattah); Utah leads the country in fraud and mortgage foreclosures.
- Idaho went from 360,776 loans totaling $ 96.746 million in 1998 to 442,901 loans totaling $136.181 million in 2001 (Heinz).
- Wisconsin had 17 outlets making 80,000 loans totaling $11 million in 1996 and 175 lenders making 850,000 loans totaling $200 million in 1998. (Harris).
- In North Carolina, there were over 40,000 loans totaling over $84 million with $12 million collected in fees in 1999 (Thompson).
- California had 2,011 licensed lenders making over 1 million loans in 2001. The product was not legalized in California until 1997 (Sais).
- In Colorado, the amount of payday lending grew from $86.4 million in 1999 to $106.1 million in 2000 (Heilman).

Structure of the PayDay Lenders

There are many different types of lenders involved in the industry in many different ways. The direct payday lenders include check cashing outlets, stand alone payday lenders, pawn brokers, banks that operate through some of these other lenders and, in at least one case, banks directly making these loans. In some situations, other lenders, such as pawn brokers, will make similar loans. For example, car title lenders will make small short term loans, often collateralized by the title of the borrower's automobile. The rates charged by car title lenders are also very high and may also include other items, such as credit insurance (Nendick).

Some of the payday loan companies are single stores or a few stores. Some are businesses involved in offering other financial services such as check cashing stores or pawn brokers. There are also some chains of stores that provide multiple financial services and other chains that offer only, or primarily, payday loans. Ace Cash Express, headquartered in Texas, which combines check cashing and payday lending, has 1,000 outlets in 30 states. Other chains in both businesses include Dollar Financial (Pennsylvania) with 700 stores in 24 states and QC Financial (Kansas City) with 200 outlets in 11 states. Check N Go in Ohio, a stand alone payday lender, has 650 outlets in 26 states; and Advance America (South Carolina) has 1,375 stand alone stores in 30 states. Other large stand alone companies include Check Into Cash (Tennessee) and United Credit Services (Tennessee).

Another more recently used vehicle for payday lending has been partnerships between payday lenders and some smaller banks (Fox and Mierzwinski). The local non-bank (payday lender, check casher, pawn broker) originates the loan on behalf of the bank. The bank then sells back all or most of the loan to the originator, which continues to service the loan. The payday lender actually advances the funds, takes the risks and services the loan.

The legal basis for these loans lies in a 1978 U.S. Supreme Court decision. Some banks with certain types of charters are exempt from usury laws in their home states. These banks in the deregulated states enter agreements with other agencies—payday lenders—and claim the right to export the deregulated rates to other states. This involvement of a bank has encouraged the payday lenders to state that any local state laws that restrict payday lending (e.g., prohibiting payday loans entirely, setting caps on amounts and rates, etc.) are pre-empted (e.g., AP *Newswires*, 4/29/02; *Business Wire*, 1/04/02; Jackson 8/05/02). As a result, they have even entered New York, a state that does not permit payday lending (Cox; Guart).

The banks involved include Eagle National Bank in Pennsylvania, which has partnered with Dollar Financial Group and others in different states; People's National Bank (Texas) which has partnered with North Carolina lenders; Goleta National Bank (California) with $317 million in assets partnering with Ace Cash Express; Brickyard Bank (Illinois) which has partnered with Check 'n Go; BankWest, Inc. of South Dakota which has worked with Advance America in Virginia; and County Bank of Rehoboth (Delaware), First Bank of Delaware, First National Bank (South Dakota) and First Bank of Washington. These lenders are both national and state chartered banks; they tend to be fairly small. Eagle National Bank, for example, has about $70 million in assets (although it made about $400 million in payday loans in 2001 according to newspaper reports).

Some of these arrangements have been recently prohibited (Duran; OCC). For example, the Office of the Controller of the Currency stopped Eagle National's arrangement with Dollar. Eagle had charge offs on its loans of 17.21% in the first three quarters of 2001—far above the industry norm of .27% for banks of similar size; however, Eagle had a return on equity of 18.07% compared to 8.49% for its peer group.

The OCC has also moved to stop People's National Bank of Paris, Texas (OCC). The $103 million asset Bank had maintained a loss reserve of 1.14% of its $82.9 million loan portfolio. The Bank charged off $1.8 million in losses in the first half of 2002, compared to $255,000 the year before. However, its interest earnings grew from $6.3 million in 2000, the year before it entered into the payday lending business, to $29.4 million in the first half of 2002. The profit for the first half of 2002 was $2.2 million, making it the most profitable small bank in Texas, according to the Independent Bankers Association of Texas (Reosti; Duran).

The OCC made these moves against both Eagle and People's National based on safety and soundness issues (e.g., inadequate reserves, inadequate oversight of underwriting and lending, overbalance of one type of lending, lack of qualifying delinquent loans, inappropriate reliance on third parties to make loans, etc.), although acknowledging the inappropriateness of, in essence, renting its bank charter to payday lenders. The regulatory pressures are increasing.

This pressure resulted in the ending of the relationship between Goleta National Bank and ACE. It was prohibited by the OCC, the bank's regulator, in late 2002. The reasons did not include a judgement that payday lending is illegal or inappropriate. The ruling was based on ACE's throwing away over 600 client files in a Virginia dumpster and other unsafe and unsound practices by ACE which included excessive exemptions to the Bank's policies and procedures (Beckett; Jackson and Reosti).

Brickyard Bank recently announced that it was leaving the industry due to regulatory requirements necessitating $1 of reserves for every $1 of payday loans. This requirement, imposed because of the higher risk of payday loans, makes the lending too costly for the Bank. The change was due, again, to banking issues—lack of capital protection for the type of lending, rather than a ruling that payday lending is illegal (Jackson, 9/02).

Another lender, Crusader Holding Co. of Philadelphia, stopped this lending when it was sold to Royal Bank of Pennsylvania. This change was due to a CRA rating of "needs to improve" from the Office of Thrift Supervision when the sale occurred; the low rating was due to the payday lending program (Jackson, 9/02). However, a U.S. District court judge in Indiana recently ruled that the loans made by ACE Cash Express and Goleta National Bank did not violate Indiana law (Dallas). While these practices are still occurring at this time, their future seems unclear.

As a response to the legal issues and other legislative concerns that have arisen around the country (and described later in this section), one payday lender is attempting to buy a bank (Jackson 7/9/02). Presumably, the parent company of Ohio's Check 'n Go, CNG Financial, created a bank holding company and applied to the Federal Reserve Bank of Chicago to purchase Bank of Kenney in Illinois for $1.3 million. The one-branch Bank is located in a small town of less than 400 people and has assets of about $5 million. High rates are permitted under Illinois law and some people (including at least four members of the state's congressional delegation) fear that CNG will try to export these rates through its payday lending business. Check 'n Go has 670 outlets in 24 states, including 57 in Illinois.

Other companies use the internet and fax to make the loans. For example, the County Bank of Rehoboth (Delaware) uses multiple web sites (e.g., BadCreditBanks.com; eFastCashLoans.com; MoneyByPhone.com; Webfastcash. com; 911CashMoney.com; 500Cash.com; LoanFastCash.com; etc.) to make loans through different trade names that are advertised in the phone book. In some cases, the lending has apparently moved off shore. The companies approve loans over the computer and wire the money into the borrowers' accounts, just as the U.S. based web sites do (Fox). There are other websites as well, such as www.paydayandcheckloans.com, which offer payday loans as well as all sorts of support to the industry, including training, sales of businesses, new technology, etc.

In other situations, other types of mechanisms are used. For example, some lenders will "sell" consumer certificates in catalogs. Others say that they are "buying" an item from a consumer who then "leases" it back. In Georgia, payday lenders "buy" a household item from a borrower and then lease it back. The borrower writes a post dated check that includes the amount of the sale plus the lease fee that is due on the next payday. In other cases, the lender states that the cash is leased, not lent.

Roles of Conventional Lending Institutions and Other Financial Institutions

Conventional institutions are involved in payday lending in different ways. A few are directly involved. For example, Union Bank of California (UBOC) is using two different vehicles to reach low-income households with a variety of financial services. Cash and Save is a traditional bank branch in some ways— offering all UBOC bank products. Cash and Save also offers check cashing and "transitional" bank products—e.g., the Nest Egg savings account (with six free money orders per month), which can be started with $10 and a monthly deposit of $25 that can be automatically drawn from paychecks without monthly fees; Benefit Transfer Service; and basic checking—that help check cashing clients transition to more traditional banking products. The branches are very small, in some cases about 250 square feet. UBOC has tried them in existing branches, stand alone check cashing stores, retail and warehouse grocery stores and a laundromat/multi-retail setting. Started in 1993, Cash and Save now has 12 branches in Los Angeles, San Diego and the Central Valley (7 are in traditional branches and 5 are in supermarket/retail venues).

In 2000, UBOC entered into another approach to reach low-income households. It purchased a 40% equity interest (with an option to purchase the remaining ownership in 10 years) of an established check cashing company, Navicert Financial, Inc., known as Nix Check Cashing. Nix, a 34 year-old company with 600,000 customers, has 47 branches in the southern California region (after selling 23 branches, mostly in northern California in 1998 in an effort to consolidate its business). All UBOC products—including ATM, consumer deposits, loans, and small business products—are available in the Nix stores and Nix agreed to modify its pricing for some of its products.

Payday loans are also offered. Payday loans require payment of a 15% fee for the initial loan with a 10% fee thereafter. Nix also agreed to modify its payday loan product to limit the number of rollovers, offer consumer education information, offer descriptions of all alternatives to payday loans, discuss the risks and problems with the applicant and provide a one day waiting period to decline taking out the loan with no costs. Neither UBOC nor its Cash and Save division offers payday loans.

The Bank has tried to address some of the issues associated with payday loans. The Bank did make adjustments to the product to try to reduce some of its worst features, as noted above. And the Bank also tried to create a new product recently as a replacement to the payday loan. It was a short term loan product which they tried with a six month pilot. Unfortunately, it did not work and resulted in an extremely high default rate on the initial payment (Interviews, Richard Hartnack). However, credit unions in different parts of the country seem to have made this type of short term loan product work and may offer a model for other institutions to follow in the future. Finding payday loan alternatives is crucial and all institutions involved in providing financial services to low-income people should be encouraged to institute viable programs, if possible. However, it is also clear that the payday loan alternatives as presently utilized do not represent very strong financial returns nor are they without substantial risk.

Wells Fargo Bank has also tried to create an alternative to payday loans. The

Bank's loan product is capped at $300. Wells Fargo requires a direct deposit of the borrower's pay check into a Bank checking account. No rollovers are permitted and the rate is capped at 5%. Wells Fargo is able to tightly control the use of these loans through these methods (Wells Fargo has been involved in other aspects of the low-income financial services markets and is apparently is also an investor in the parent company of Goleta National Bank of California, which generates a 20% of its profits from its payday lending relationship with ACE Cash Express).

Others have tried to create alternatives to payday loans. These alternatives are short term loans that structured very differently than payday loans. Mostly, the institutions working on these alternatives are credit unions; these approaches will be described in more detail later in this section.

In contrast, some banks—FleetBoston, for example—and other institutions such as Household International, MBNA and Capital One, are now offering 0% cash advances to their higher income credit card customers with strong credit ratings. The term of the advances averages about seven months before high interest rates begin; there is also an initial fee for the service. If the loan can be repaid within the term, the consumer benefits; however, the banks are assuming that the loans will not be able to repaid within the time period and that there will be excellent profits available. Other banks—Chase and Wachovia—are offering low interest rate cash advances (Higgins).

Other companies have played an important role. Some have helped the payday lenders go public and join stock exchanges as well as financed their expansion. Some banks have helped to finance payday lenders with lines of credit and loans. While many financial institutions do not want to be directly involved in the business, they are willing to play behind-the-scenes roles that are very lucrative.

Payday Lending Niche

The payday lending industry, as many related financial services for low-income people, has many critics. Nevertheless, it has either created or filled an important niche for many low-income and working families. There are very few lenders making short term, small loans up to $500. These loans are expensive and do not offer reasonable profits under most existing banking business models. And banks, as a result, do not make these loans. Even many credit unions do not make these loans, for the same reasons.

Consumer finance companies do offer these loans. However, they tend to prefer to make larger loans, such as the range of $2,000 to $3,000—again for the same reasons that other financial institutions do not like to make smaller loans. They have also seemed to move away from these loans, instead preferring home loans. And these companies are not very accessible to low-income people and their neighborhoods in the way that multiple bank branches were in the past and check cashing/payday stores are now.

Other alternatives also may not be available to households needing a short term loan.

- Borrowers may have credit cards but they are at the spending and borrowing limits, a condition often experienced by low-income people trying to pull every possible resource together.
- They may have bad credit or no credit.
- Their family or friends might not have money to lend to them or they might not want to borrow from family or friends.
- They will have checking accounts but the use of checking accounts as alternatives to payday loans also have negative repercussions if there is an inadequate level of funds in the account to cover their financial needs. The fee for a bounced check is generally $29—which would be equivalent to borrowing $200 at a payday lender for $30 for two weeks—and the bounced check still does not solve the immediate problem of needed cash. Also, banks tend to clear checks by starting with the highest amounts first, so they can collect more fees from a higher number of bounced checks (Brooks). In this case, there might be more than one bounced check, sending the costs much higher than $29 for the specific bounced check.
- Pawn brokers, another alternative, require collateral for a loan, and the amount of the loan is usually a much lower percentage of the actual value of the collateral. So the potential losses are higher.
- Another avenue would be savings, which would be an excellent possibility if people in these tight situations had much savings to cover these events; typically, they do not have much savings, if any at all, and that is why they need a payday loan in the first place.
- A late fee for paying some types of bills may also be an alternative. However, late fees are also often higher than the fee for the first payday loan. Late fees for rent, for example, often cost $50 or some percent of the rent that is higher than the payday loan fee. And the payday fee does not immediately jeopardize the borrower's housing.
- Illegal loan sharks are possible sources, but are not reasonable alternatives in this situation if there is any other possible option.

There is also the issue of time and convenience. For busy people who need money quickly to cover debts, payday loans (and car title loans, which do require collateral, but only in the form of a piece of paper) are very convenient. There is a clear demand, as evidenced by the incredible growth that has even caught the attention of mainstream banks and Wall Street investment banks.

There is some disagreement on the characteristics of the payday loan borrowers. The industry itself commissioned a study through Georgetown University (McDonough School of Business Credit Research Center), which found that payday loan borrowers are mostly middle income (between $25,000 and $50,000 income) with an average income of $33,187. 36% own their own homes. The very large majority said they have other options but chose payday loans over the other options. 35% of borrowers in the study reported taking out a payday loan to pay off another payday loan (Heilman; Lynch). A Utah study found even higher incomes than the Georgetown study. The Utah study also reported that most people were very satisfied with the services (Fattah).

However, studies in California and Illinois found households with lower average incomes (Said). Similarly, a Woodstock Institute study found a high percentage of very low-income people using payday loans. A Consumer Federation of America report described a Wisconsin state government study indicating that the average customer was a 39-year-old female with a gross income of $24,673 who tended to be a renter. A Filene Research Institute (which supports credit unions) reported that payday loan customers use the product because they feel it is the best alternative for meeting small cash needs (Caskey, 2002). In most states, there are very few complaints recorded against payday lenders.

The problems of using payday loans are compounded for low-income households. The poorest households in the country tend to have the highest debt burdens and the lowest wealth levels. A 1995 study reported that the median U.S. family had $1,000 in financial assets. The poorest households were found to have very large debt, averaging over 50% of the median income (which was $7,779 for the lowest family income quintile) and 27.9% for the second quintile ($12,940-$23,138) (Manning). The poor are the least able to afford high rates due to their already high debt burdens and lack of financial reserves and other assets. The rates they pay for any additional debt becomes crucial and payday loans, especially those that must be rolled over several times, have very high rates.

Some of the Mechanics of the Business

For a potential borrower entering a payday lending business, one key is to obtain great convenience—and this usually means a fast approval. The underwriting of the loans is, therefore, fairly minimal. There appears to be a range in the levels of underwriting that occurs. At a minimum, the applicant needs to demonstrate an active checking account (usually for some minimum time period) and a job (also for some minimum period. Some lenders want to see verifications, again with different levels of due diligence. Therefore, some of the types of verification include pay stubs going back for some minimum period, bank statements, utility bills, etc. Other verifications might include proof of residency and proof of income levels. The payday lender will then call to verify at least some of the information, such as employment and determining whether the checking account is still open.

An Eagle National Bank application ("Cash 'Til Payday" application, which is a registered trademark for Dollar Financial) is fairly extensive. It includes social security number, driver's license, telephone, information about the employer and the job (date of last paycheck, number of paychecks per month, monthly income, time with employer, contact information) and the bank (account number, ABA number, branch location and address, bank phone). The application also includes a requirement for at least two references. It also asks a series of questions concerning bankruptcy, legal actions and judgements, and whether the applicant has filed all required income tax returns.

The application also asks if the applicant has any post-dated checks outstanding and if there are any garnishments against the applicant. Besides the personal checking account and employment information, the applicant is asked to bring a recent phone bill showing that it is in working order (and whose name the phone is registered under) and a valid photo identification. The application also states that "special qualification requirements" will need to be met for loans over $300, but does not specify what these requirements are.

Eagle National Bank's application also includes requiring the borrower to sign the agreement with the knowledge that any misinformation on the application will be a criminal offense, that the initial application may be used for future loans if nothing has changed and that the information provided becomes the property of the Bank. The applicant also authorizes the Bank to charge any of the applicant's accounts for unpaid amounts, interest, bounced check fees and all costs and expenses of collection.

An application from Money Mart, also owned by DFG, requires somewhat less detailed information, but looks at the same basic information and the borrower signs a similar set of understandings, except that binding arbitration is required in case of disputes. An application from a payday website (www.quikpayday.com) also asks similar questions but with somewhat less detail than the Eagle National application. Quik Payday will deposit money into the borrower's account through wire transfer and withdraw the loan amount plus a fee ($20 per $100 borrowed).

The emphasis in the loan processing tends to be on speed. The borrowers, often in a difficult position, need cash quickly. The lenders use the simplified underwriting process to offer fast approvals. They typically approve and disburse loans the next day if the applications are received before 3:00 p.m. on the preceding day.

The lenders do not use credit checks for the applicants. The cost involved would significantly reduce the profit potential. The lenders feel that they can obtain adequate information without credit checks and many of their customers might have poor credit anyway.

The post dated check also offers some degree of security for lenders, at least more than an unsecured personal loan. Most of the other alternatives are purely unsecured loans, increasing the risk to these lenders (such as banks or credit unions). The tie to the pay check does create some added security, although it has its flaws as well. To date, the payday lenders seem to have accurately assessed this issue, as there are strong profits even with high losses.

When a borrower applies, the lender is required to discuss the Annual Percentage Rate (APR) of the loan, under the Truth in Lending Act. However, the APR is not shown very obviously in much of the printed information, if at all. The employees of the lenders supposedly explain this information to the borrower, but some surveys have reported that some lenders omit this information in the process (Fox). The website lender noted above does include a long detailed description, but the borrower must find the material by clicking on a separate link to access the information.

Chains often use a computerized listing database of all clients to share information. This allows the customer to use any store but also protects the owner who can see if the borrower is merely going from one store to another to pay off the earlier payday loans. This frequently occurs. When there is a state requirement for the data base, any lender can track the outstanding loans for any borrower. However, without this requirement, only the chains with this internal capacity can track this pattern, but only for its own stores.

If there are defaults, many of the smaller stores may try to collect the loan themselves. Some may also use agencies, but the margins are often too thin to make payments to the collection agencies unless they are working on a percentage of funds recovered. Default is considered a civil matter and not a criminal one. There have been reports of heavy handed collection methods being used, but that does not seem to be of great frequency, although collections are the biggest area of complaints.

Marketing for all kinds of fringe banking services—check cashers, pawn brokers, payday lenders, wiring money—seems to be expanding in recent years.

Advertisements are now seen on television and billboards, in the newspapers and back covers of the yellow pages, heard on radio and appear in other mainstream sources as the businesses gain more acceptance. There is even a move into "branding" for check cashers recently (Storey). Former professional football coach John Madden has done a television commercial for a rent-to-own chain. Flyers, telemarketing and other similar methods are also used.

Electronic marketing is the most effective and allows a new store or company to achieve scale more quickly. However, smaller stores usually cannot afford electronic marketing. The most efficient marketing comes from owners with several stores that have enough revenue to support electronic marketing for all of the stores. They also offer the most efficient means for centralizing collections (FISCA conference, 2002).

Location is critical, as it is in many businesses. The market comes from a radius of roughly three miles or less around the store. The store's profitability will depend on the traffic, visibility and competition. The demographics of the surrounding area should contain large numbers of people who are working but without very high incomes. The chains can be at somewhat of a disadvantage as they may lose efficiency at larger sizes, often see a leveling off of revenues, tend to attract more litigation, etc. However, their total gross revenues and profits are obviously higher.

Financially, the lenders either have to have their own capital to lend or they raise it from other sources. The banks sometimes offer lines of credit to the payday lenders. There are also investors. One website advertises the sale of ARAs (Accounts Receivable Acquisitions) with 30% returns to investors, paid monthly. The investment is listed as conservative and low risk. The Security and Exchange Commission shut down a North Miami Beach, Florida payday lender which had raised over $800,000 from investors claiming 360% to 720% in annual profits (Burns).

In addition, lenders can apparently charge off unpaid loans as an expense, even if the collected fees are greater than the principal in the aggregate. This can be a valuable tax advantage (Wenske).

PayDay Loan Profits

Critics of payday loans often refer to the very high Annual Percentage Rates (APR) to describe the impact of payday loans. However, this measure may not be fully adequate as a means to evaluate payday lending. APR's for small loans are always going to be high. It is also important to evaluate whether the profit level is exorbitant by some measure. Some key aspects of understanding the profits from payday loans include an understanding of the level of losses incurred, the mechanics of rollovers and their contributions to revenues, and the operating

64

costs involved in making the loans and collections for delinquent loans.

It is difficult to find information concerning the level of losses incurred by payday lenders. The primary justification for the rates they charge is the reported risk associated with this type of lending. However, direct evidence is difficult to find and the information appears to vary widely. One knowledgeable source lists the national average of losses due to non-collectable loans at less than 4% of the gross loan amount. (B.E.S.T. Inc., "Show Me The Money!") In Colorado, one of the few states to collect information on payday lenders, the state's Attorney General's office indicated that payday lenders wrote off 3.9% of their loans in 1998 (*Consumer Reports*).

However, others involved in the business indicate much higher losses. A San Francisco owner, for example, listed his losses at 10% to 30% in 2001 (Said). One highly respected banker indicated that over 25% of payday loan transactions, including rollovers, are not repaid (Hartnack). In North Carolina, payday lenders reported losses of about 12% of fees generated in a recent year, more than double the rate of the preceding year (Skillern). Other industry estimates show writeoffs equal to 5% to 17% of fees (FISCA conference). These measures obviously differ; some use a percent of fees and some use a percent of the total loan amount.

Nevertheless, the mechanics of the rollovers indicates the growth potential for revenues with this product. Most of the revenue is made from borrowers who roll over their loans many times. For example, in North Carolina in the year 2000, payday lenders generated about $123 million in fees. However, the borrowers who took out 13 to 24 loans in that year accounted for over 40% of the total revenue while constituting slightly less than 20% of the borrowers. Those borrowers who took out more than 25 loans in the year accounted for about 10% of the revenue while constituting less than 3% of the borrowers. The borrowers who used the loans four times or less were over 40% of the borrowers but accounted for slightly over 10% of revenues (Skillern).

The keys to payday lending are the short term—14 days or less, typically—coupled with volume and the need to pay a new fee when the loan is due and the borrower cannot repay the loan. Although each renewal should tend to increase the chances of default and lower the possibilities of repayment, the greater the number of renewals can also be thought of as decreasing the chances of loss—the fees paid quickly increase the revenue to equal or exceed the actual amount of principal.

After 7 rollovers with a 15% fee, the amount of principal is exceeded by the amount of fees paid. If the loan is defaulted at this point, however, there would be still be a loss due to the costs associated with originating and servicing the loan. Most likely, principal and costs approximately could be covered with eight rollovers. Profit for a defaulted loan would probably not occur until nine or ten rollovers, depending on the level of collection efforts and related costs.

Overall, these fees generate extensive revenue, as noted above. By 2001, there were an estimated 10,000 payday lenders in the country as a whole making roughly $14 billion in loans and collecting about $1.6 billion (or more) per year in fees. However, one source, Consumer Federation of America in a November 2001 report titled "Rent-A-Bank Payday Lending," indicates that there are 12,000 to 14,000 payday loan stores making at least 100 loans per month with another 8,000 to 10,000 lenders with smaller volumes in 2001. CFA indicates that industry statistics show that there are about 65 million transactions for 8 to 10 million households resulting in fees of $2.4 billion.

The average number of rollovers for customers is not clear, as there are somewhat conflicting reports. One analysis showed an average of ten rollovers per customer in Indiana (Harris). A 1999 state Commissioner of Banks survey in North Carolina showed that 90% of payday borrowers who took one loan made at least 5 rollovers (Serres). Woodstock Institute found that the average is 13.8 rollovers in minority neighborhoods, 38% higher than in white neighborhoods. Others put the figure at 30% of borrowers who receive rollover payday loans (Berthelsen). Whatever the actual numbers, which probably vary around the country, the number of borrowers receiving rollovers is apparently high—and high enough to generate adequate profit for the lenders.

However, the focus on rollovers, fees and revenues only partly explains the issue. A more complete analysis also includes costs and profits, which are derived from subtracting revenues from costs. Here, too, the information is difficult to obtain. However, estimates can be derived.

For example, it might require 1 to 1.5 hours to make a $200 loan with a $30 fee, including intake of the application, running the necessary checks on the applicant (phone calls to verify bank accounts and employment, etc.), preparing the paperwork, explaining the loan (including the APR, when that is done) to the borrower, disbursing funds and then doing the necessary paperwork to book the loan and continue to track it. If there are any payment problems, the time and cost can increase significantly. There is also some supervisory time for the entire process that is required. These activities may be done by several different staff people, depending on the size of the operation, with different pay scales. For this example, assume an average pay rate of $12 to $15 per hour, excluding the owner's time and rate of pay. Also, assume losses of 25% of the fee, as an average, plus rent, overhead and other costs of perhaps $5 to $10 per loan. From this basic analysis, the lender would probably lose money on a $100 loan, break even on a $200 loan and make up to $15 on a $300 loan. If the high end of the costs is assumed, almost all of the $45 fee is used up by the costs of making the $300 loan. (This is a very general analysis and the reality may vary considerably depending on the actual costs such as staffing, owner draws, volume, rent, etc.).

If the loan is repaid on time and the customer does not need to borrow any more, the lender makes nothing to perhaps up to $15 profit on a $300 loan. However, if the loan is rolled over, the associated costs for the rollover are lower than for the initial loan. The first rollover generates another $45 of revenue and probably generates a great deal more profit, perhaps up to $30 or more the second time, rather than up to $15 from the first loan. This cycle is then repeated many times and, each time the profit increases for little work but increased risk, as the threat of default grows until the cumulative amount of fee income approaches or surpasses the original loan amount.

The key here is also volume. The more loans that are made at higher amounts—i.e. the amount needed above breakeven, or $200 to $300 in this example—the greater the profit generated, even if there are relatively few rollovers. However, this is true primarily if there are relatively few losses. The losses cut into the profits, of course. The roll-over borrowers, however, make up for the losses on both the high and low volume roll over borrowers. The high number roll-over borrowers generates revenues that make up for the principal losses among all borrowers, including those who use only a smaller number of rollovers and those who have a much higher number.

This cost structure can also be seen by looking at the revenues of a typical check cashing store with multiple products, including payday loans. Show Me The Money, prepared by B.E.S.T., lists the income for this type of business from check cashing, money orders, utility bill processing, wire transfers, money order float and miscellaneous items (bus passes, stamps, copying, phones, etc) as just under $400,000 per year. When payday lending is added at an appropriate scale for this store of 20 new and renewed loans per day (some stores make up to 200 per day), the annual revenues increase to just over $672,000, a very large increase for one financial service product, with relatively low increases in operating expenses (See Chapter 4, Feasibility Analysis, Stabilized Revenues).

Of course, there would be losses and some added costs, but including payday loans in a business may increase the profits more than for a stand alone payday store. Adding payday lending increases costs only modestly. The risk is potential losses. This increase in revenues does depend on the product mix and the mix used in the above example could be substantially modified depending on the location; substantially higher check cashing fees could be targeted with much lower payday loan fees than those in the above example.

On the other hand, payday lending and check cashing often attract two different types of clientele. People who need checks cashed typically do not have checking accounts while payday borrowers do have checking accounts but need interim cash. Sometimes the same location may not appeal to both types of customer.

Payday lending can be very profitable, especially with several rollovers. One of the concerns of the OCC in its ruling against Eagle National Bank was its high concentration in the payday loan business. Eagle National apparently generated nearly half of its revenues through its arrangements with Dollar Financial Group, according to a January 2002 article in American Banker (Jackson).

Other characteristics also need to be considered. Key areas are the startup capital needed and the time period needed to reach breakeven and then profitability. Some stores can become profitable in a matter of a few months whereas others may take over a year, depending on volume, cost structure, etc. The initial capital needs to include losses during the startup period as well as the capital needed to rent and equip a store, as described in Chapter 4. It may take some time before there is an adequate return on capital. The rate of return, therefore, also needs to be considered in analyzing the rates charged by payday lenders.

The payday lending business appears to have similar characteristics as other elements of the fringe banking business, such as subprime credit cards and commercial lending. They are all businesses with higher risk, higher losses and higher fees or interest. The results are, often, higher profits. The growth of this business in the last decade, as documented earlier, is another indication of the potential profit.

Impacts of Payday Loans on Borrowers

Most of the fringe banking industry appears to maintain that their customers have full knowledge of their options for financial services and the impacts of these different options. They believe that the customers make reasoned and thoughtful choices among available options. This perspective assumes that the customers understand financial conditions in general, know how to deal with their own financial situations (budgeting, saving, etc.), understand their options, have the time to look into all the options, perhaps even during a crisis, and that the types of information required of the lenders to give to the borrowers gives them all the information they need.

Some legislators, regulators, advocates and others believe the opposite—that many people, especially low-income households and immigrants—do not fully understand the economic context, the necessary ways to manage their finances and do not understand the full range of options available to them or the impacts of the financial products used by the fringe banking industry.

There may be many borrowers who do fully understand the financial situations, the options and their impacts. However, it is also likely that there are many—possibly a much larger number—who do not understand all of the issues and implications and/or do not have the time to find out. Surveys have found lenders who do not tell borrowers about the APR and other legally required information while other lenders may make it difficult to reach or understand this information, as noted above in the discussion about the website lender.

It is clear that the impacts of the fringe banking in general and the payday loan industry in particular can be either very helpful or harsh. For many of those borrowers who borrow and are able to repay the loan within the two week period or with one or two rollovers, the payday loan may, in fact, be their best option. However, for those who fall into the trap of repeated rollovers, the impacts can be very harsh and problematic. Some of these potential impacts could include:

- Harassment of the borrower and the borrower's employer if there are repayment difficulties.
- Further damage to the borrowers' credit.
- Mounting costs from the fees and any bounced checks.
- High court costs of judgements for defaulting borrowers. In small claims court, some lenders seek triple damages plus bounced check fees, legal fees and court costs under the civil code. For example, a $300 loan with a $45 fee could result in a court award of $1,035 for triple damages, $150 legal fees, $60 court costs, $29 bank bounced check fees and $20 lender bounced check fees—all in addition to the original costs of the rollovers of $45 for one rollover to $450 for 10 rollovers (Kilborn).
- Some lenders try to take borrowers to criminal court under criminal code bad check provisions and seek criminal penalties, even though it is clear to all parties that the check is "bad" at the time it is written and that most in the industry frown on the practice, including the industry's own trade association.
- Bankruptcy becomes an option and some bankruptcy attorneys have noted the increase in bankruptcies from those who use payday loans. For example, a study of the 2001 bankruptcy filings found cases in the Northern District of Indiana increased at the fourth highest rate among the 96 U.S. districts. According to the American Bankruptcy Institute, which analyzed information from the Administrative Office of the U.S. Courts, filings in the region rose 34%, a rate almost twice the national

average. One Ft. Wayne attorney, who also works as a bankruptcy court appointee, believes the culprits are payday loans and predatory mortgage loans in the area. Fringe banking lending products can be the last step before bankruptcy for many people (Frazier).

- Another area, often overlooked, is the potential for invasion of privacy. The payday lenders receive a great amount of personal information and it is not clear how well trained their employees are or what protections exist for this information.

For some of the borrowers, the payday loans can become "debt traps" that they have great difficulty escaping from. The negative impacts of defaulting on their loans and the relatively small cost and ease of obtaining each rollover create incentives for the borrowers to continue to extend their loans. This process can occur without the borrowers' being able to pay down the original, relatively small loan principal.

Existing Legal Framework and Requirements

Many states have some type of registration or certification requirements for lenders (e.g., Hazard). payday lenders avoid some of the lending regulations by charging "fees" instead of "interest." Nevertheless, most states require registration and some minimum level of certification. A few collect information on payday lenders, but most do not seem to. Since the lending is made by a non-depository institution using its own capital instead of depositors' capital, the requirements for the entire regulatory framework, including reporting and licensing, is considered to be less important than for conventional depository lenders such as commercial banks and savings institutions.

And, since the fees are not considered interest, the usury laws in many states are not used as guidelines for payday lending. The loans are called deferred deposits or are considered to be check cashing fees. In some states, payday lenders have been statutorily granted an exemption from usury laws.

Nevertheless, there have been extensive recent attempts at additional regulation of payday lenders. The federal government has attempted some intervention. The regulatory approach of the OCC with the involvement of national banks was discussed above. (However, the courts are now reviewing the rulings and have not reached clear decisions yet). The Federal Reserve began requiring the implementation of Regulation Z, Truth-in-Lending Act with payday loans in 2000, in which lenders must now disclose to borrowers information about the APR on their loans (NCRC/Morton; Paskind). There have also been attempts at federal legislation to control the national bank/payday lender relationships and some discussion about the need for federal regulation of the payday business in general (Duran; Jackson). However, Congress has not approved any legislation and it is unlikely to occur in the present environment.

As a result, the states, and to a lesser extent, courts have become battle-grounds for the payday lending issues. Many states have considered legislation and several have passed laws regulating and occasionally outlawing the practices over the past two or three years. In those states where laws have been passed, guidelines for the maximum loan amount, total number of rollovers, caps on the interest rates charged and similar steps have been taken.

For example, Oklahoma now has a 240% APR cap on small loans based on its 1997 law. The short biweekly or semimonthly payment schedules were disallowed. No collateral (car or boat) is allowed to be taken on loans under $300. As one result, the number of stores has decreased from about 700 to 650 from 1997 to 2001. However, some contend that the law has made little difference, as the payday lenders use out of state banks to avoid the law's requirements (AP Newswires, 1/28/02).

California has seen at least two major attempts to pass legislation in the past three years. In one of the proposals, the state Justice Department would have overseen licensing, bonding, record keeping and reporting. The maximum loan amount would have been capped at $300 with a maximum fee of $15 per $100 borrowed. Presently, the State Department of Justice checks fingerprints and requires an annual application. There is no checking on how much is lent or whether consumers are being adequately informed. There is no cap on roll-overs. Another proposed law would have capped the lending rate at 12%; if rollover were needed to repay the original loan, it could be repaid over 4 payments. Later proposals softened some of the original measures; however, they were not approved either (Anderson; Berthelsen; Hendren; *Los Angeles Times*; Pyle, Said). In 2002, legislation was approved that gives authority to the state Department of Corporations to audit payday lenders, collect information on the loans and conduct a comprehensive study for the legislature (*San Diego Union-Tribune*).

In Florida, a borrower cannot borrow from one store to pay off a loan from another one. The lending rate is capped at 10% and lenders cannot use the borrower's car as collateral for short term loans. The maximum loan amount is capped at $500 and the borrower must wait 24 hours after paying one advance to get another one. Companies must register with the state and can be tracked. There is a statewide database on customers with loans so the lenders can track who the borrowers are and conform to the law's rollover provisions (Mathosian).

There have been long, hard fought battles in many states over these issues.

Jean Ann Fox of Consumer Federation of America, in a 2001 report called "Rent-A-Bank Payday Lending," categorizes states into three types: states that prohibit payday loans due to small loan interest rate caps, usury laws and/or specific prohibitions for check cashers (19 states plus Puerto Rico and the Virgin Islands), states with no small loan/usury cap for licensed lenders (6 states) and states with specific laws or regulations that permit payday loans (25 states plus the District of Columbia).

The requirements in different states are changing as the issue receives more attention, as noted above. However, even where there are laws and regulations governing payday lending, they are not always effective in muting the worst excesses of the process that the laws are supposed to address. For example, many of the state laws can be circumvented in different ways.

- Where rollovers are limited, a borrower brings in cash and pays off the loan and then applies for a new loan and receives the cash again.
- Borrowers may go to one payday lender to pay off another loan. Borrowers sometimes have simultaneous loans from several payday lenders.
- Some payday lenders have used commercial banks, as described above.
- One company, Check 'n Go, is trying to buy its own bank as a means of circumventing the local laws, as noted above.
- Some lenders shift to "other" services, such as "renting" or "leasing" cash.
- Some lenders use the internet or may move off shore.
- Some lenders have been reported to just ignore existing laws or regulations.

Passing legislation to create improved frameworks for payday lending has been difficult. One of the reasons for the difficulty is the strong lobby that the payday lenders and the fringe banking industry as a whole has created. In California, for example, state Senator Don Perata, who has sponsored unsuccessful legislation for the past few years to try to limit payday lending, noted in 2000 that "The payday lending industry is pretty powerful, and it's an election year."

In a *Los Angeles Times* editorial (May 14, 2001), the paper noted that one key state legislator had received over $44,000 in contributions from the payday industry in 2000. *Mother Jones* reported that the first attempt at regulating payday loans in the state resulted in a $528,000 lobbying and political contribution campaign (Koerner). This level of political activity is difficult to match for opponents and advocates for the poor. The payment of campaign contributions and the lobbying by industry representatives have made the industry very powerful across the country.

Nevertheless, the battles have been fought in several state legislatures across the country. Maryland outlawed payday lending (AP Newswires, 5/20/02). In addition, there have been several law suits. For example, Ace Cash Express settled a suit brought by the state Attorney General's office in Colorado by ending its relationship with Goleta National Bank and agreed to pay $1.3 million in refunds to customers who rolled over loans more than once (Jackson; Pankrantz). National Cash Advance agreed to pay $1.4 million to refund some its customers to settle a class action suit in Wisconsin; initial federal court approval has been obtained (AP Newswires 3/9/02).

Proposals and Guidelines for Changes: Existing Payday Lending

There have been many statutory changes at the state level for payday lenders. There have also been other proposed statutory changes and guidelines for change. For example, Community Financial Services of America (FISCA), the trade association for the check cashing and payday lending industry, issued guidelines called "Best Practices for the Payday Advance Industry," as printed in 2001. The guidelines specify various procedural aspects of the lending practice; for example, full disclosure of information in line with the state and federal statutory requirements; compliance with all laws; truthful advertising of services; encouraging responsible use of payday loans as they are intended; compliance with any state's statutory number of allowed rollovers with a maximum of four; offering customers a right of rescission; use of appropriate collection practices that are not intimidating or harassing; no threat of criminal actions for nonpayment; self policing of the industry; support for legislation that incorporates the best practices; and use of banks to make payday loans that follow the best practices.

The National Consumer Law Center created a proposal called the Model Deferred Deposit Loan Act, with many more specifics, including licensing (minimum requirements including past criminality and minimum capital assets per location of $25,000), bonding (minimum of $50,000 per location for damages that might have to be paid to consumers), reporting on various aspects of lending activity, minimal accounting requirements and disclosure requirements. There are also civil and criminal penalties for breaking the law. The Model Act also specifies that the loan minimum is $50 and the maximum is $300, with a minimum term of two weeks. There is an annual rate cap of 36%, or 1.38% per two weeks (thus, a $200, two-week loan would cost $2.76 interest and $5 for the administrative fee. The APR for this loan would be 100.88%). An administrative fee of up to $5 is also permitted. Bounced check fee maximum charges are $15 per check in this model legislation.

Union Bank of California, when it purchased an ownership share of Navicert (Nix Check Cashing), instituted new policies for the company's payday lending. Potential borrowers were given consumer education information and descriptions of alternative borrowing possibilities, and they were told of the risks and problems of payday loans. Once a loan is made, the borrower had a one-day rescission period. Finally, the number of renewals was limited and partial, scheduled pay downs over a period of time were allowed for borrowers who had more than one renewal.

As noted above, many states have attempted to build in some protections against abusive payday lenders. The Florida and Oklahoma legislation was described along with proposed legislation in California. Generally, this type of legislation looks at maximum loan amounts, caps on rates and numbers of rollovers, and similar guidelines. These steps are usually far more generous to payday loan companies than other proposals, such as that of the National Consumer Law Center.

Alternative Lending Programs

Some alternative lending programs have been created in various parts of the country, usually through credit unions. Based on its analysis of two community development credit unions, ASI Federal Credit Union in Louisiana and the Faith Community United Credit Union in Cleveland, the Woodstock Institute developed a Model Affordable Payday Loan structure. With a loan maximum, Woodstock's model loan suggests an annual interest rate between 15% and 20% with a loan fee of $10 to $15. Other allowed fees included bounced check fees and fees to cancel direct deposit. The term should not be longer than six to eight weeks, including rollovers, but no rollover fees should be charged. There were also provisions for minimum tenure as a credit union member (one to six months), direct deposit and appropriate borrower documentation. The Model Loan also suggested special loan loss reserves for these loans, the inclusion of a savings program for the borrowers in which some portion of the loan repayment went into a savings account, and encouragement to attend financial literacy training (Williams and Smolik).

Some of the site visits included institutions that offered alternatives to payday loans. The Northside Community Federal Credit Union in Chicago, for example, has been offering a payday loan alternative since 1994. Northside offers a loan called "Hot Funds, Cold Cash." The CU offers this short term loan product, but the rate and fee structure is much more reasonable for the borrowers and does not force extremely difficult choices caused by the constant rolling over of fees every two weeks or so if the loan cannot be repaid. The loan program offers up to $500 and is repaid with equal monthly payments over a one year term.

Partial payments are allowed and there is no prepayment penalty for early repayment. In the past, the program had required that the borrower be a member of the credit union for at least one year with an income of at least $1,000 per month. It also required that the applicant had no current loans or rejections in the last year.

Recently, the credit union obtained a grant of $20,000 from Northern Trust Bank to act as a segregated loan loss reserve for this program. As a result, starting January 1, 2002, Northside will be able to make these loans without the one year membership requirement. The applicant will need to demonstrate an up-to-date work history if the membership record is not met. The term will be shortened to six months. The rate of 16.5% and the initial loan fee of $10 will remain the same. The credit union will run credit reports (not for loan approval but to understand the credit background and history of the borrowers) and ask the purpose of the loan under the new program, which it did not do under the old program. With some of the employer groups, Northside will obtain repayment through direct payments from the borrower's paycheck.

Beginning in 1994 and running through 2001, Northside had made 1,779 loans in this program totaling $889,500. These loans comprised 34% of the number of outstanding loans at the end of 2001—the largest single loan type; however, the outstanding loan amount for this loan product equaled only 3.23% of the credit union's total outstanding loan portfolio. The loan application process is very simple with a brief application form (account number, date, social security number, name, address, home and work phone, employer, position, work address, gross monthly income, date hired, residence—own/rent/other, and purpose of the loan). There is no real underwriting of the loan applicant as there would be with a personal signature loan.

The credit union has an historic rate of charge offs in its portfolio of 1.55% of total funds lent, as of 1-31-02. At the same date, the write offs for the Hot Funds/Cold Cash program were 3.01% ($26,829.61), or roughly twice the rate of write offs of the total portfolio. The average loan amount written off under this program was $282.41. The total number of loans written off under the program is 95, or 5.34% of the total number of loans disbursed. Delinquencies have also run at a higher rate historically under this program, roughly three times more. The credit union had delinquencies of 2.44% on its total portfolio at 1-31-02. While the performance of the Hot Funds/Cold Cash program is below that of its general lending, the performance record is, nevertheless, very good. A larger organization with greater financial cushion would be able to more easily absorb this risk.

The economics of this loan vary dramatically with that of payday loans. As described above, the latter keep rolling over high fees roughly every two weeks if the borrower cannot repay. Pay day lenders do not allow partial repayments; this often forces borrowers to keep rolling over the loans and incurring continuous fees. As a result, the APR can reach well into the high hundred percentages on an annual if the borrower requires a full year or more to repay.

In contrast, Northside earns $82.50 in interest and a $10 fee for a $500, one year loan at 16.5% if the loan is repaid at maturity. If the loan is repaid prior to maturity, the earnings are even less. The loans require at least 10 minutes of staff time and probably much more, even though the process is very simple, and the time increases greatly if there are any collection problems. The loan must also be accounted for in the bookkeeping, reporting and auditing. The situation is worse for a smaller loan even though the amount of work is the same. For example, a $300 one year loan would generate $49.50 in interest if repaid at maturity.

The credit union hopes to break even on these loans and not create financial damage for its members. But the loan product does not generate profit although it is a major part of the organization's activities (234 of these loans were outstanding at 12-31-01 out of a total of 693 total outstanding loans for the credit union). The default/writeoff rate of around 3% is relatively low, but is nevertheless twice as high as the default rate on the credit union's other loans (see below) and can still strain the credit union's resources. If the volume increased, these economic factors would not change—increased scale would still not generate additional profit. However, the program has been beneficial in some other ways for the credit union, as some borrowers have improved their financial condition over time and have moved on to take out car loans at a later time.

As described above, the income generated by the Hot Funds/Cold Cash program is minimal. Over the course of a year, one of these loans might break even if there were no problems and it is repaid on time. It is difficult to estimate whether the program as a whole achieves break even, however, it is likely that it generates a small operating loss in addition to its actual loan losses.

Other credit unions are also employing a similar type of loan. Bethex Federal Credit Union, a Bronx-based community development credit union, is beginning its own alternative to payday loans, called "Cash in a Flash" (It appears that the lender must have an unusual name for this type of loan). In May 2002, the Credit Union announced a pilot program totaling $10,000 that would serve as an alternative to payday loans. The program offers loans of $200, $300 and $500 to members, depending on the length of time of their membership and the availability of payroll deductions. For example, if the member can receive payroll deductions, the loan can be $500. Moreover, if the member has a proven borrowing record with the CU (i.e. the loan is at least the second one taken out by the member), then the loan can be set up as a revolving line of credit rather than a loan with a set due date. The term of the loan is six months and the APR is 17%, yielding $9.64 in income for a $200 loan for six months and $24.10 for the six-month $500 loan—the CU will certainly not generate earnings from this loan product. There is no origination fee and no prepayment penalty. No account is required. The application form and process are relatively simple. Loan proceedings are available on the same day if the request is made before noon and on the next day if the request is made later. The program will also tie into financial counseling. Implementation costs were minimal at $250, excluding staff time for program development.

Ohio's largest credit union, Wright-Patt Credit Union in Dayton with over $717 million in assets, is now offering a payday loan alternative as a means of helping the community, even though it is not a community development credit union. The charge for the loan, which is called a bridge line of credit, is $2 to $3 per $100. (Bohman) Ed Gallaghy, president of a Tampa credit union, stated that about 100 credit unions in the country are now offering equivalent payday loans (Bohman).

Another credit union, Landmark Credit Union in Milwaukee, now offers a new program. Implemented as a demonstration, the program offers qualifying customers unsecured loans of up to $1,000 at 18% for 12 months. Another loan is also offered—$1,300 for 12 months at 13.9% interest. In this loan, which is designed to help members develop increased savings, the borrower must put $300 into a savings account. The loans, available only at one of the credit union's branches, requires a credit check (Gores).

As noted above, Union Bank of California attempted its own version of a payday loan alternative. It was a small installment loan with three payments over a 90 day term. The underwriting was simple, but there were problems with loan processing and the processing costs were higher than expected. The losses were very high and the Bank was not interested in continuing the program.

Analysis

The payday lending industry is complicated and is not simple to analyze. The conclusions drawn from this research indicates the following:

- There is a demonstrated need for a short term loan product. Many people need a short term loan to cover a variety of emergencies in their lives.
- The existing product can be very profitable for the lenders. The business seems to be based on high volume and sustaining relatively high losses

with relatively low operating costs. The main segment of the profits depends on repeat fees from borrowers who rollover their very short term loans more than once or twice. From a borrower's perspective, it would be a better structure to have a longer term loan or some variation of an installment loan. However, these types of loans are unsecured—and are, therefore, even higher risk. Part of the key of the payday loan is that it does offer at least some security to the lender and is able to lock in many borrowers, who fear the repercussions of not paying.

- Viable options to payday loans must be developed. There is a major effort throughout the country at present to eliminate or restrict these loans. This effort is very appropriate. It is crucial that many continue to advocate for changes in existing laws and that other options be created for low-income households and other borrowers, including additional financial literacy training. However, if payday loans were to end or be rendered ineffective due to political and/or regulatory pressures, many borrowers could be forced to find other lenders who could be even worse.

- Therefore, it is also very important to try to develop viable alternatives. Community development credit unions offer one such possibility, although with limitations: for example, this option requires credit union membership (although North Side Community Federal Credit Union in Chicago is beginning to offer these loans to non-members), a credit union or similar institution willing to offer these loans, adequate capitalization to be able to undertake the risks, and geographic coverage to make it reasonably accessible for many people to obtain these loans. It would be important for the credit union trade associations and other interested parties to publicize this option and others more widely and to help interested institutions implement these new approaches where the right conditions exist. Additionally, other options need to be developed for locations without interested credit unions or other similar institutions. Finally, alternatives for people who do not want to join credit unions or other institutions need to be developed.

- There are at least two kinds of borrowers. The first does need the short term loan and can handle repayment within the term or within a small number of rollovers. This borrower would be better served by a term loan. The second type of borrower needs the short term loan but may be a gambler of sorts, may not know how to handle household finances and/or just does not make enough money to cover all the costs that exist no matter how much financial education is available.

- There are borrowers, included in the second type, who "abuse" the financial service. They need to be screened out more effectively. Payday lenders don't seem to want to do this, probably, because they tend to be the most lucrative customers; but the loans do not offer much help to this type of borrower and, often, may create additional and even more profound problems.

- There are also "abuses" structured into the payday loan product. These can be adjusted, as described below.

- In other words, it may be possible to segment the market and its risks and to offer a reasonably priced short term loan product to the borrowers who are most likely to repay and to screen out the borrowers who are least likely to repay after a few rollovers. Another product could be developed for this second category of borrowers or they could be screened out altogether; their problems may be less with short term borrowing needs than other issues.

- APR may be an inadequate measure to evaluate payday loans, at least when discussing the initial loan and the first or second rollover. The rate and its resultant APR are considered in this analysis through the loan's revenues over time. However, it is also important to include operating costs and profits in any analysis. The amount of revenue is one important part but not the entire picture. The costs of making a loan and the level of profit also need to be considered, along with the risk. It is not an accident that there are few institutional lenders willing to make small short term loans. Short term loans are always expensive because some minimal amount of work—and therefore, cost—is involved in making the loan. And payday loans also represent a lack of security and some degree of risk that is above "normal." Lenders have to be able to cover costs and make some profit, even if the APR is high—as in this case. This is necessary to attract lenders into the business to meet the identified need. As a rule, for example, banks do not make these loans. Bankers tend to talk, in general when there is a choice and "all other things are equal," about their preference for a larger loan over a smaller loan. In this comparison, roughly the same amount of work goes into both loans, but the larger loan produces greater profit for roughly the same amount of work. The smaller the loan size, the more difficult it is to make profits. Many of the payday lenders, check cashers and other fringe bankers use a business model that relies on lower costs than banks and other lenders, and have an easier time of making the lending financially viable. However, the profits are generated from excessive rollovers over a short period of time, and this aspect needs to be curbed to create a fairer product for the consumer. Some balance is needed that will allow adequate profit without taking advantage of the borrowers.

- The lender argument—that the payday loan is merely a short term loan—is also not the appropriate basis for evaluation because, all too often, it is not a short term loan. The short term loan is rolled over many times in some cases and becomes a longer term loan. The profitability of payday loans depends on lengthening the term through repeated rollovers.

- Multiple approaches to addressing these issues are possible. (1) Legal and regulatory is one approach, assuming that there is adequate enforcement. (2) Another approach is the encouragement of more participation from existing institutions, which can be strengthened and assisted in providing this service. (3) Another approach, which can be independent of the others or part of an overall effort to address payday loans, is a major effort to encourage the creation of new institutions, new loan products and approaches.

- Another aspect of finding alternatives is creating competition. In some other parts of the fringe banking industry, institutions and businesses have demonstrated that competition can be effective in lowering prices and providing better services. While this has occurred in some locations with check cashing and money wiring costs, it has not yet occurred in payday lending. Creating competition on a level adequate to impact prices and services requires extensive capital, knowledge and technical assistance.

- Another related issue for creating payday loan alternatives is scale. Pay day loans and other fringe banking institutions and products have spread with remarkable speed across the country. Therefore, it is equally important to not only develop payday loan alternatives but also to find ways to achieve scale in these efforts. Moreover, it is also important to find ways to make them more accessible to a wider range of people. All credit unions, for example, only lend to their members (and cash checks, usually, only for their members). The check cashing outlets accommodate everyone. Similarly, the check cashing stores have many more branches convenient to their customers and they are open for much longer hours during the work week and on the weekends as well. To compete on a larger scale and meet these financial needs, the alternative lending solutions and institutions will have to find ways to expand their coverage, locations and hours.

- To be successful with these alternative approaches, there will be a great need for capital, technical assistance, organizational development, business assistance, etc.

Options: Legal and Regulatory

There are many ways to structure legal parameters for operating payday lending establishments. Many have already been proposed or are in use. However, no matter how sophisticated and useful the system is, it must also have adequate penalties and enforcement powers to be effective.

- Some possible guidelines for a viable statutory and regulatory framework include the following concepts:
- Some form of maximum loan amount, which exists in most places. The cap is usually $500 or less in many states.
- Scale the loan size to income and household size. Someone who takes home $1,000 per month would be eligible for a maximum loan of $100, for example, with a $200 loan available to someone with the same household size who takes home $2,000.
- A rate cap is useful up to a point and a maximum should be established. This cap might still have a relatively high APR and serve to continue to attract businesses into the industry, but it would also be more reasonable to the borrowers.
- Also useful is thinking about the fees from the perspective of profits. If the lender's costs are covered with the first loan, then the fee on future rollovers can be lowered to reduce the incentive for the lenders to keep rolling over the loans. For example, if the rate for the first loan is $15 per $100, lower the fee to $10 or $12 for the first rollover, $8 or $10 for the second rollover, and so forth. This could allow some profit but would reduce the absolute profit level substantially and lower the burden on the borrowers.
- Use a term that is longer than 1 to 2 weeks. For example, a four week term, as used in Oklahoma, would be a great improvement without turning the loan product into an installment loan. And it would still offer the lender the security of the pay check so that it does not become an unsecured loan.
- Alternatively, allow the borrower to repay through several post dated checks in pieces over a longer period of time. For example, the borrower could repay 25% or 33% of the loan after two weeks with a post dated check, another similar amount after 4 weeks with another post dated check, and the remainder after 6 weeks with another post dated check.

- Cap the number of rollovers, after which the borrower would be allowed to repay through some form of installment loan plan with low fees (that cover costs) for recasting the loan.
- Create a computerized data base of all payday borrowers available to all lenders. Place strict limits on the number of other payday loans from other lenders that any single borrower can obtain. Create effective penalties for any lender who does not follow the guidelines.
- Limit the rollover escape in which a borrow repays the loan with cash and immediately borrows the money back with a "new" loan by requiring a waiting period of several days or weeks before a borrower can obtain a new loan. Create effective penalties for any lender who does not follow the guidelines.
- Separate out the problem borrowers through the data base and prohibit lending to some people who have shown that they cannot repay the loans. In general, stability is the best indicator of repayment, including length of time on the job, length of time at the present address or one recent address and length of time as a bank customer. Create effective penalties for any lender who does not follow the guidelines.
- Licensing, reporting, bonding and minimal capital requirements should be instituted for lenders.
- Prohibit out of state banks and internet lenders from avoiding the regulations. Create effective penalties for any lender who does not follow the guidelines.

Some combination of these methods would create a much more reasonable loan product. However, any legislation must include appropriate civil and criminal penalties and allocate adequate enforcement resources.

Options: Lending Institutions

One ideal solution for this problem is installment loans. However, these loans are more difficult and costly to service than payday loans. In addition, they have even less security. Available lenders are fairly rare and do not have much geographic coverage to make it reasonable for borrowers to use them. The profit level is so low that costs are barely covered, if at all. They may sometimes require different licensing.

Therefore, the lenders willing to make these loans should be allowed a greater return. Although the rate seems very high at 16% or 18%—just as the APR for the payday loans seem high—that is not really the issue. A 16% rate charged by a credit union does not allow the lender to cover the costs of origination, reserves, bookkeeping, reporting, delinquencies, defaults and collections. In addition, there is certainly no profit involved.

A rate of 20% to 25% should be allowed, perhaps even higher, even though it sounds very high. A rate of 25% on an interest only $300 loan with a balloon payment will generate $75 in earnings over the course of one year—and even this rate will probably not cover costs (one estimate of credit union costs for any loan is in the $100 to $150 range). Therefore, some small fee should also be allowed. Compare the cost on a loan of $75 interest plus a $10 fee for a one year loan to a payday loan with a rate of $17.65 per $100. For the $300 payday loan, it would cost $52.95 to borrow the money on the first day; with the first rollover, the total cost would be $105.90 after only 2 weeks, $158.85 with the second rollover in four weeks, and so on.

Options: Alternative Approaches

There are other possible ways to address this issue. An example of an interesting approach is now being developed by Mastercard and E-Duction as a payroll deduction program. An employee of an enrolled company may obtain a "Clear" card for an annual fee of $29. The employees can make purchases wherever Mastercard is accepted with a line of credit based on income (with a salary between $20,000 and $75,000, the extended line is up to 2.5% of gross salary and it increases to 4% above that amount). All of the purchases made in this manner are not charged any interest. The loan is repaid in four equal installments from payroll deductions over two months (Blassingame).

Another entirely different approach is to create an organization to assist community based organizations around the country to develop their own alternative institutions that would provide a range of financial services to low-income neighborhoods. This possibility is described in the business plan.

Other political approaches are also possible. One of these is pressing for the use of Community Reinvestment Act (CRA) ratings for banks that are involved in this industry in an inappropriate way. Brickyard Bank has already come under this type of pressure directly and others will in the future. Some advocacy organizations have already requested that bank regulators use this method generically with lenders involved in this industry.

It should be noted that conventional lenders are involved in other ways than as lenders to payday companies as means to avoid existing payday lending laws. They are also involved in financing them through lines of credit, underwriting their initial public offerings, packaging and selling their loans on the secondary markets, clearing their checks (if there is check cashing involved), and so on. Financial institutions involved in these ways may also be susceptible to legal and political pressures.

Conclusion

The payday industry is changing very rapidly in a short period of time. The high profits from some approaches, capacity to reach new markets, advances of technology, availability of credit, changing consumer values, financial innovation and sometimes, financial chicanery—all have combined to create some positive effects on the industry as well potentially negative ones. The old fashioned pawn shop is one example. Some believe it is losing favor due to payday lenders, among other influences, although they appear to be growing or holding steady in terms of numbers of stores. Customers prefer the convenience of payday loans and the lack of a need to offer collateral—much different conditions than needed for obtaining a loan from a pawn broker. And, as described above (and further considered below), changing regulations and political and legal pressures prompt many in the industry to devise different techniques to circumvent the new restrictions. Some have indicated that there are fewer lenders as a result of the increased attention and attempted regulation of payday loans, but the volume of loans has not seemed to decrease. A game of financial cat and mouse, which does not necessarily lead to improved financial services for low-income people, has been the result.

There are other examples of improved delivery of financial services to low-income people. For example, by 1999, there were 10 payday lenders in Kokomo, Indiana, an industrial city north of Indianapolis. The state allowed a maximum fee of $33 per $100 at that time and most lenders charged at least $30. Carol Brenner stepped into the market with her company called Quick Cash in 1998, and by June 1999 had 350 customers. However, she made some changes in her lending practices. She charged $20 per $100, less than most other lenders in the area (although still a high rate). She charged $10 for the next $100, or $30 for a $200 loan. She allowed her clients to make partial payments on their loans instead of requiring them to choose between a complete repayment or a rollover. She did not lend to anyone who had more than two loans with other payday lenders (Kilborn).

Ms. Brenner's approach illustrates that more reasonable practices can be used in the industry while still creating a viable business. In fact, it would seem likely that her clients were possibly more loyal and appreciative than the clients of other lenders.

IMPACT ON CONSUMERS

Many of these services that the fringe banking institutions provide are essential for low-income households. Without them, they might have to pay even more or find other even less efficient methods to address their needs for financial services.

The footnotes contain a description of typical interest rates for several categories of financial services institutions along with descriptions of some of the terms, prepared by Jack Northrup and the author. It is based on different types of financial institutions and the services they provide to low-income households. The format tries to emphasize the overlaps and gaps in services among institutions and offers a means of comparison among the more traditional depository institutions and fringe lending institutions. Interest rates, fees, and levels of services vary widely among institutions and services. Many low-income households must pay high rates and fees for these financial services.

There also have been some attempts to determine the actual impacts these existing financial services on low-income households. For example, First Bank of the Americas, in Chicago, attempted to quantify the impact of its programs on the people in their neighborhood and the savings compared to the use of fringe banking institutions.

This analysis indicates that the Bank appears to be successful in its goal of helping to build community wealth. Many loans have been made to local small businesses and the commercial strip appears to be doing well (there are no vacancies, there is activity on the street, stores are busy and appear to meet the needs of local residents). The Bank has also impacted the families as well. The Bank prepared a study indicating the likelihood of their loans saving over $4 million for local residents in four years. The study compared the Bank's rates and fees for financial services, mortgages and consumer loans for all of its transactions as of April 27, 2000 to the prevailing rates and fees from other local financial services companies (check cashers, rent-to-own stores, predatory lenders, etc.). For example, the Bank charges nothing to wire funds to another country and there is no loss from differences in the exchange rates; this service saves substantial amounts of money compared to the other wiring services. In this study, the Bank found that they had most likely saved over $4 million for local residents. In the two and one half years since this projection, they have likely increased this figure substantially.

This study demonstrates how the Bank and its products have helped to meet their goal of building the wealth of local residents. Local residents were able to keep this level of income and use it to provide basic services for their families and perhaps buy homes, start savings accounts, build businesses or other efforts that build the wealth of the families in the neighborhood. It also gave them more disposable income to be spent on necessities and non-necessities, some portion of which was most likely spent with local businesses that tended to keep the income within the neighborhood and helped local merchants also build wealth through a multiplier effect. This impact is felt not only in the U.S. but also in Mexico, as the Bank is working with the Mexican government to have a small part of the wired remittances used for economic development in Mexico.

There are other measures as well. John Hawke, Comptroller of the Currency, stated that "Over the course of a lifetime, estimates suggest that a person without a bank account could incur fees of more than $15,000 for cashing checks and paying bills."

Mr. Hawke quoted another study showing that ." . . low-income families with bank accounts were 43% more likely to have positive net financial assets than families without" accounts (Hawke).

Federal Reserve research indicates that the costs of check cashing and bill payment would cost a household with $20,000 annual income about $86 to $50 per year. These same services would cost about $30 to $60 per year at a bank if the customer were eligible for a low cost account. This amount of savings per year is very significant when compounded over many years and the loss of savings is considered (Caskey; Carr and Schuetz). The capacity to build assets and escape from poverty can be severely hampered by the costs of fringe bankers.

Other estimates also exist showing how these costs have greatly increased. In the early 1990s, the cost of check cashing, obtaining money orders and paying bills was estimated at $199 for a household with take-home income of $10,000 and $444 for take-home income of $24,000. These costs have increased substantially as described above. However, the costs of using alternatives—in particular, banks—for holding accounts below minimum balances in a bank have also increased. For example, the cost of an account of less than $300 has increased from $60 in 1991 to $100 in 2000 while ATM fees and high bounced check ($29) fees have also been instituted (Manning). An Aberdeen newspaper tried to quantify the capacity of a single woman living on the minimum wage and indicated the need for some assistance or a 50 or 60 hour work week. Otherwise, the woman would need to use credit cards or payday lenders to cover all the needed expenses. And, when this debt is incurred, other problems emerge (*Aberdeen American News*).

IMPACT ON A HYPOTHETICAL FAMILY

An analysis was prepared of the impact of fringe banking services on a low-income household to try to gauge a fuller sense of the effects of these fees. The implications of this institutional framework that low-income people depend on are stark—the rates and fees charged by these institutions make it very difficult for low-income people to escape poverty. They represent one more significant challenge for poor people.

This discussion will demonstrate the financial impact of some parts of the financial services industry—check cashing, rent-to-own stores, automobile loans, remittances, and sub-prime consumer finance companies—on a hypothetical family. It will show the immense impact on their lives and indicate how difficult it can be for low-income people to escape poverty when they are caught in the framework of these institutions. It will not include all the potential components of this industry, just the ones listed above. If all parts of this industry were included, the results would be even worse.

This discussion is based on a hypothetical family of five with a series of activities and expenses that are probably reasonably representative—on a composite basis—of the conditions facing low-income households.

The Family

Juan and Maria Gonzalez have two young daughters, aged 10 months and $3^1/2$ years, and a son 8 years old. They are legal immigrants from Guatemala (or Russia or the Philippines or Ireland or Nigeria or China) and have lived in the United States for six years. They live in the Fruitvale neighborhood of Oakland, California (or New York or Miami or Chicago or Cleveland or Los Angeles or Kansas City).

Juan is 28 years old and Maria is 27. Neither graduated from high school, but both are smart, energetic and ambitious, especially to better the lives of their children. They are somewhat knowledgeable about financial alternatives. They also understand that the costs are significantly higher at the institutions that they use. However, they are unaware of what the actual differences are because they do not have the time to fully research the costs and because they have had some negative experiences with conventional institutions in the past. They feel that they have few other alternatives than those that they have chosen.

Both Juan and Maria hold at least two jobs and work very long hours. From 4 a.m. to 7:30 a.m., Juan works as a janitor on a call-in basis at a small, local shopping center. He works an average of 25 weeks annually, although he does work some hours each week of the year. The wage is $6.50 per hour; he has no benefits and the crew is non-unionized. He earns $2,843.75 per year from this job. From 9 a.m. to 6 p.m., he works for a small repair/handyman company doing odd jobs, earning $7.50 per hour. While he does work every week, he averages 40 hours per week for 50 weeks, earning $15,000 per year. Here, too, there are no benefits.

Maria takes care of the children while Juan is at his janitorial job. Then, from 9 a.m. to 6 p.m., she splits her time between a small house cleaning company and a fast food restaurant; while she works every week and most days, she averages full time work for 40 weeks of the year, earning $8 an hour. There are no benefits included with either job.

Maria and Juan are also starting their own small company for house cleaning, handyman work, painting, moving and similar tasks. They perform these jobs in the evenings from 6 p.m. to 10 p.m. and on the weekends. Juan earns $12 an hour and Maria earns $10 an hour. Juan averages 10 hours a week over 50 weeks and earns $6,250 from this source while Maria earns $6,000 from 12 hours a week over 50 weeks.

In total, Juan earns $24,093.75 per year while Maria earns $15,600. Together, they gross $39,693.75 in income for a year.

Borrowing and Finance Costs

This section describes the borrowing and financing costs for this family. The analysis uses a moderate or mid-level of costs faced by low-income households using these institutions. It is difficult to use an average or exact number because the costs vary greatly by neighborhood and region. These costs may also vary greatly for specific families depending on their individual circumstances. The costs shown here are based on research obtained from visits to stores in San Francisco, Oakland and Los Angeles, discussions with people in the field, focus groups and research from available written materials. The costs shown here therefore represent a rough approximation of the moderate/middle costs as determined from these sources. Higher or lower costs could be used. More important, however, other costs could have been used based on the assumptions for this family. There are many other institutions that exist in low-income neighborhoods and charge very high rates—e.g., mortgage companies, pawn brokers, "payday loan" institutions, etc. These and other institutions were not included in this example, although they could have been easily worked into the assumptions.

The Gonzalez family may or may not qualify for an account with a bank or S&L. They might not qualify due to bad credit, a bad checking account history, or other reasons. On the other hand, they could qualify but they do not have adequate information about the banking system. Or, a branch is not close enough to them or is not open during the hours that they need to use it. And there may be additional reasons for their avoiding use of a conventional financial institution—for example, they may not feel comfortable in these institutions.

Therefore, the Gonzalez' use a variety of very high cost, local financial institutions instead. This assumption is representative of many families in low-income neighborhoods. However, there is an additional reality. Many families are part of both financial worlds. That is, they use some of the mainstream institutions and some of the low-income financial institutions. To the extent that some of the mainstream institutions are used, the actual financial costs may be lower, although the costs in time and transportation may be greater when these institutions are located farther away than the local institutions.

They cash all their checks at a local check cashing store. They are charged 2% of the face value of the checks. They pay a total of $66.16 per month or $793.92 per year to cash checks totaling $39,693.75 (in southern California, the costs have been reduced to about 1.75% in recent years due to competition. However, elsewhere, such as northern California, these costs may be higher— 3% to 3.5% for government or employer checks—although lower costs are sometimes available).

Because of a lack of credit, along with some small slips due to the very heavy debt burden they bear in order to survive, the family had to buy some furniture from a rent-to-own store. They purchased a 32" television set, a couch/loveseat, a refrigerator and a washer/dryer (all other furniture—stove, beds, dressers, tables, chairs, etc.—was purchased second hand, repaired by Juan and is fully paid for. The family bought only those new items that seemed absolutely necessary from the perspective of cost efficiency, repairs, usage and the their desire to provide a dignified setting for their children). The cost for these items is $485.65 per month and $5,827.92 per year.

They purchased a small used truck from a local car lot for $9,000. They borrowed the $1,000 down payment from a friend at 10% for two years and pay 27% over three years on the remaining $8,000. The monthly and annual payments for the two loans are $46.14 and $553.68 for the down payment loan and $326.60 and $3,919.20 for the purchase loan (purchase loans range up to 40% to 50% and often include a series of other very high cost extras that are sometimes forced on the borrower. Neither these extra costs nor the extremely high rates were used in this analysis).

Each sends $175 per month to their respective families, who are living in other parts of the United States, each month through the local remittance service. They are charged $22 for each remittance; by sending 24 checks per year, they pay $44 per month and $528.00 per year.

The family also took out a personal loan to begin their businesses. A local branch of a personal finance company made the loan for $3,000 at 28% for 5 years. The cost of the loan is $93.41 a month and $1,120.92 per year.

The family shopped well for its financing and avoided the highest cost financiers and companies that charged excessive and hidden fees. They were also able to avoid some of the highest cost loans, particularly the pay-day loans, that can be so damaging.

Total Financing Charges

The total financing costs paid by the Gonzalez family were as follows:

	Monthly	Annually
Check cashing	$ 66.16	$ 793.92
Rent-to-own	485.65	5,827.80
Car loans	326.60	3,919.20
	46.14	553.68
Remittances	44.00	528.00
Personal loan	93.41	1,120.92
TOTAL:	$1,061.96	$12,743.52

The costs shown above include principal payments for the furniture, the personal loan and the truck. The finance charges without the principal payments are as follows:

	Monthly	Annually
Check cashing	$ 66.16	$ 793.92
Rent-to-own	263.81	3165.72
Car loans	104.38	1252.56
	4.48	53.76
Remittances	44.00	528.00
Personal loan	43.41	520.92
TOTAL:	$ 526.24	$6314.88

The annual cost of $6,314.88 for interest charges and fees alone represents 15.9% of the family's total annual income. If annual amortization costs of $12,743.52 are included, these costs represent over 32% of the family's annual income.

The Potential Range of Borrowing and Finance Costs

The above analysis uses a moderate of level costs faced by low-income people for financial services in low-income neighborhoods. In this analysis, neither the highest costs nor the lowest costs are used in most situations.

However, it is very possible that low-income people face substantially higher costs in many situations. The primary areas where the costs would most likely be different are check cashing and the car and personal loans. The rent-to-own costs would be roughly the same unless the purchases were all converted to a similar term (these stores vary the term of the purchase, presumably in order to keep the weekly costs at a psychologically affordable level) or in a situation where less competition existed.

Similarly, the remittance costs would not increase unless more funds are sent each time or the location changes; it is less expensive to send money outside the U.S., depending on the location. Western Union charges higher fees as the amount wired increases. In this example, these costs are not increased. However, it should be noted that lower remittance costs are available from Western Union if the family were sending funds to Central America. There are also services that are considerably less expensive than Western Union; for example, in certain situations, there are travel agencies serving some Asian countries, which charge substantially less. Competition in the last few years has also been changing the fees to Mexico, the largest market. Now, up to $1000 can be sent for $15 and a $300 wire can cost less than $10 from some U.S. locations with some different, newer companies.

The check cashing at many stores costs 3% to 3.5% in many locations for government or employer checks (and much higher—10% for example—for other types of checks such as personal checks). In this example, it would have been very reasonable to use the 3% or 3.5% rate, which would have resulted in monthly costs of $99.23 to $115.77 and annual cost of $1,190.81 to $1,389.28 (these costs, in reality, most likely would be much higher because much of the family's work is normally paid by personal checks, which require a much higher fee, often 10% or more, as noted above).

The general cost for obtaining unsecured personal loans is about 28% to 32% at companies such as Household Finance and Beneficial Finance. These numbers may be significantly increased with the addition of various kinds of insurance (e.g., credit life, "non-file," tangible property, accident and health, etc.) and other charges (e.g., monthly maintenance fee, loan fee, etc.). For smaller loans, the rates with all costs included can be as high as 90% to rates in the 100%-200% range, depending on the state, the loan amount and the loan's specific characteristics. In this example, 28% was used, although the rate could have been much higher. Secured loans from the consumer finance agencies are running are about 22% at this time (year end, 2000). In comparison, Bankrate.com recently listed the range of personal loan rates in California (for people with acceptable credit) as 12% to 21.5% on 8-24-00. Store credit is often in the range of 20% to 22%, a roughly similar range as credit cards, which are sometimes lower—offering rates in the 15% to 20% range.

Automobile loans seem to run a similar range of rates. For a credit union member, the rates are approximately 9% to 11%. Bank loans may be roughly the same or slightly higher, depending on the applicant's credit (Bankrate.com listed the rates for used cars in the U.S. at about 10%-11%). On the other extreme, rates can be far higher, especially when the various types of insurance are included.

If higher (but still realistic) rates had been used in this example, the family could easily be paying well over 20% of its income on interest and fees alone. Alternatively, the family could make different decisions for items that may be somewhat discretionary in order to reduce this burden. The rent-to-own costs are the highest, followed by the car costs; both have some discretionary elements to them. For example, the family could choose to buy fewer new items (e.g., couch, television) and purchase used items instead or not purchase a television set at all. Similarly, the family could buy a lower cost used truck.

The likely result of some of these choices, however, could be higher repair costs and earlier replacement requirements, e.g., the truck and the television. The family could also choose to buy used appliances (washer/dryer) or use a neighborhood laundromat. This choice could be counter productive with three children and the very tight work schedule that the parents must maintain; in addition, the purchase of used appliances could also result in higher repair costs and earlier replacement.

By making some of these alternative choices but still using the prevailing non-bank financial system, the family could reduce its financing costs to perhaps the 10%-12% level, although there would probably be a negative impact on the rest of the family budget.

Comparison of Dual Economy Costs

If the family had had access to more reasonable financing from a commercial bank, savings institution and/or credit union, it would have paid substantially less. For example, there would be no check cashing fees. Furniture would have a lower purchase price in many stores and the rates would be dramatically lower, perhaps 22% on the high end and as low as 9% to 12% through a credit union on the lower end. The remittance costs would be lower as well; assume for example, a charge of $15 for this family for each remittance in this case. Car loans would range from 9% to perhaps 15% and personal loans could fall into the same approximate range.

Using different rates that are available for households with good credit and bank accounts would result in the following annual costs for interest and fees, excluding principal:

Check cashing	$ 0	bank account; no fees
Furniture	$ 188.21—356.75	lower purchase costs ($2900 total); 12%-22% interest
Truck loan	$ 53.74	DP loan is the same
	$ 521.91	purchase loan @ 12%
Remittances	$ 240.00	$10 per remittance
Business loan	$ 275.45	@ 16%
TOTAL	$ 1279.31—$1447.85	

These differences in the rates and fees have a clear impact on the family's finances. The resulting payments are 3.2% to 3.7% of family income in this example. Even assuming higher rates in many instances, the payments would still be well under 10% of this family's income.

Discussion

The income of this hypothetical family is fairly high and is sometimes not thought of as low-income. Although this income level clearly meets HUD's qualifying definitions for low-income (their income is slightly over 54% of median income for this family size in Alameda County in 2000), it is still somewhat high compared to the perception of what a low-income family earns.

Nevertheless, this income level is useful to illustrate the difficulties that a family with this income level faces and the role that non-bank financial institutions can play in their lives. It is the extra income from the extra jobs—their evening efforts, which are going toward establishing new small businesses—that create whatever financial "cushion" that exists in their lives.

However, this "cushion" is minimal, at best, and most likely non-existent. The analysis does not include rent, utilities, food, clothing, child care, medicines and health care, insurance, taxes, gasoline, and the like. Assume rent could easily be as high as $1,000 per month with utilities averaging $100 monthly (these are low numbers for a two or three bedroom apartment in the San Francisco Bay Area as well as many other regions around the country). Food could cost a minimum of $750 (equal to $5 per day per family member). Repairs, gasoline and insurance for the truck could cost $300 per month minimum. Including only these expense levels along with the financing charges illustrated above, the family used almost its entire income, with nothing left each month for the remaining necessities in their lives!

This discussion puts an entirely different context on the funds they must spend on financing. They spend over $12,700 per year, or over 32% of their income, on amortizing finance charges and other related fees; considering only finance charges and related fees, the family spends over $6,315 a year, or almost 16% of their annual income!

This is a staggering burden to bear with the income that they have to live on. It clearly demonstrates the impact of non-bank financial institutions in low-income neighborhoods. It can also serve to demonstrate the lack of a direct role played by conventional financial institutions. However, many conventional lenders are involved in providing lines of credit and other financing for many of these businesses (consumer finance companies, check cashers, pawn brokers, etc.), and some of their counterparts on Wall Street are involved in securitizing their receivables and even the remittances to other countries.

Finally, it also demonstrates the potential that changed policies by existing institutions, implementation of new programs by existing institutions that do not presently operated in many low-income areas, and/or more reasonable programs developed by new institutions could play in drastically reducing these costs and the impact these reductions could make in the lives of low-income people.

For example, if these costs were cut in half, the loans could be repaid much more quickly and/or there would be much more cash available for essential household items or other crucial needs such as child care or a computer for the businesses and for the children (note that a family could also make very poor consumer choices with any additional income that might accrue from lowered financial costs. For example, they could purchase more rent-to-own furniture or stereo equipment, take trips to Reno to gamble, etc. However, in the present situation, they do not have the options of making either sound or poor consumer decisions). Although the expenses associated with the financial services industry are not the only problem in the financial struggles of low-income people, they do play a very crucial role, especially if the costs are considered exorbitant—by containing a great deal of profit—and potentially could be reduced substantially.

TARGETING

Many observers have indicated that the fringe banking industry prefers certain types of consumers to generate its high level of profits. For example, payday lenders tend to thrive on borrowers who roll over their loans several times compared to the borrower who leaves a store with a $300 loan and repays it fully within two weeks (Fox; Skillern). The credit card industry may also operate somewhat in this fashion, as the discussion on Providian Bank indicated. The rent-to-own industry also has some elements of this approach. For example, one observer stated

> Inflated *cash* prices are a carefully designed industry policy for discouraging potential consumers who have alternative sources of financing . . . The credit worthy are undesirable customers because they are not desperate enough to accept the costly terms of a lease-ownership contract. Instead, the rent-to-own industry seeks the most financially distressed. (Manning, p. 216)

The impacts on these targeted consumers can typically increase the financial problems that they are facing.

Certainly, the business relies a great deal on customers who cannot or do not want to enter into banking relationships. However, the industry does not always have to target the most stretched households in order to be profitable. Check cashing does not necessarily need to follow this model. And rent-to-own stores also reach people who do not necessarily want to own the items, only needing a short term use of products.

The industry presents figures showing that the income levels of their clients is relatively high; both the rent-to-own and payday lending industries have generated these figures, also indicating that there is not the absolute need to target the most desperate consumers (however, some of these numbers are disputed by other studies, so the income levels of typical customers may not always be clear).

While these industries may not necessarily have to target customers in more difficult financial condition, it is likely that the higher levels of profit do come from the more distressed customers, such as some of the repeat payday loan borrowers, as discussed in the material presented above. And more distressed customers may likewise support the profits in the rent-to-own industry and others as well.

FOCUS GROUP REPORT

In 2000, CDF hired Andre and Associates to hold focus groups with households involved with fringe banking institutions. Three were held in Oakland and two were held in Los Angeles. These focus groups, held with different ethnicities, corroborated much of the understanding that already existed. But they also highlighted some other issues as well. For instance, each different ethnic group tended to have different perceptions of the issues, different levels of acceptance or hostility toward different types of financial services institutions, and different types of financial needs. There are many submarkets among low-income households and, to some degree, they need to be approached differently.

Many of the focus group participants had bad credit or no credit, worked in low paying jobs, had a lack of information about alternatives and, in some cases, were hampered by a lack of understanding of English. They needed lower costs for all of the services and many were very aware of the high costs that they were paying compared to others with access to banks and other institutions with lower cost financial services.

Many feel that they are being taken advantage of and feel resentful, although there are others, many immigrants for example, who do not have the same expectations in regards to financial services. They also wanted a clearer explanation of fees, rates, total costs and other options, and ATMs with lower denominations of the money so they would not overdraw. They needed the long hours and the convenient locations of most fringe banking institutions, although they would travel farther for better rates and fees for some of their larger transactions if better terms were available. And the need for "respect" from the financial institutions assisting them was very high on their list of desires, as they often felt slighted at banks and much more accepted at the fringe banking institutions.

Chapter 3

OPERATIONS OF FINANCIAL INSTITUTIONS IN LOW-INCOME NEIGHBORHOODS

Many different types of financial institutions operate in low-income neighborhoods. Commercial banks and savings and loans have been moving out of these neighborhoods for some time. However, some have remained, and sometimes new branches or new institutions appear. There are also credit unions, sometimes Community Development Credit Unions. Insurance companies, mortgage companies and other mainstream financial companies operate in low-income neighborhoods, although with nowhere near the frequency that they exist in middle and upper income areas. Then, of course, there is the whole range of specialized institutions/fringe banking institutions that have been discussed in this report in Chapter 2: check cashing outlets, rent-to-own stores, car title lenders, consumer finance companies, payday lenders, pawn brokers and the like.

Each type of institution, as well as each individual institution within each generic type, generally has a different way of looking at their methods of operation in low-income neighborhoods.

- They view risk differently and handle risk differently.
- They have different views of costs and the structure of the costs they incur.
- They have different ideas about what level and types of fees and rates to charge.
- They have different mixes of financial products that they offer.
- They have different needs for volume of transactions.
- They have differential access to capitalization, capital markets and startup capitalization needs.
- They vary in their approaches to staffing.
- They have different ideas about profitability and how to achieve profitability

These factors vary depending on the generic type of institution—credit unions will approach these issues differently than banks or check cashers. They also vary within types. A large bank will view these issues in a different way than small ones will. Likewise, a national chain of check cashing stores listed on the New York Stock Exchange will view many of these issues in a different way than a local owner of three stores that does not offer payday lending. The locations may also create differences; rural areas will create different approaches than urban areas. Likewise, the types of clients—income levels, immigrants, age, ethnic backgrounds, employment levels and types of employment, etc—will dictate differences such as variations in financial services products that are offered.

Nevertheless, certain generalities about the different approaches—or business models—can be detected. This section views some of these generalities, while attempting to account for some of the differences—for commercial banking institutions (banks and savings institutions), credit unions, Community Development Credit Unions, and fringe bankers. There will also be a shorter discussion of some nonprofit efforts as well as the growing presence of other new entrants into the field such as large, national chains of retailers, convenience stores and grocers.

One of the key information sources for this section are the nine Case Studies developed from site visits (Leibsohn, 2005). In addition, extensive research contributed to the knowledge base of this section. However, these conclusions are based on limited information. While it is considered accurate, the background work has not been exhaustive.

ELEMENTS OF BUSINESS MODEL ISSUES

On the site visits, the following issues were reviewed for each case study: description of financial services provided, startup costs and funding sources, legal form of ownership, phase in plan (services, staffing, offices), pricing, revenues by financial service product, timing of revenues, operating costs and breakdown, losses (nonpayment, theft, embezzlement), net income, profit, rates of return, volume and scale, subsidies needed, staff training, technology, legal issues and certifications/licenses, regulatory issues, market study, location/hours, marketing, partnerships, etc.

Some of the key issues emerged in the form of business models for different types of institutions.

- Conventional lending institutions had the highest operating cost structure due to their reliance on more costly branches, greater use of technology, higher paid staff and central administration. Credit unions also had relatively high operating costs, although Community Development Credit Unions usually had much lower costs than traditional, employer-based credit unions. The check cashing/payday lenders probably have the lowest operating costs, although the chains probably had higher costs than the smaller operations.

- Fringe banking institutions depended more on volume and receiving smaller levels of payments from many transactions. Banks and credit unions depended more on loans, deposits and investments for generating revenues. They had less interest in a high volume of low margin transactions.
- In part, long store hours are needed to achieve the necessary volume for fringe banking institutions.
- As a result, each type of financial institution tends to prefer prioritizing certain financial products.
- Each type of financial institution tends to use different fee structures as well.
- As a result, different types of institutions have different profiles of profitability; and, different institutions stress different products and different fee structures in order to achieve profitability.
- They are different institutions that, basically, are different businesses with different business models.
- Fringe bankers probably tend to take more risk with some of the financial services that they offer—check cashing and payday loans in particular—than the more conventional institutions.
- Achieving scale on a regional or national basis requires access to the capital markets in some fashion. The larger banks, credit unions and larger fringe banking institutions (usually chains that are listed on a national stock exchange) had reasonable access to these markets.
- The more traditional institutions that are beginning to look at low-income and immigrant populations are beginning to modify their business models, which they must do if they want to successfully reach their target markets.
- Changes are needed to offer improved financial services to low-income households at lower costs.
- Some sense of what are realistic, financially viable prices for the various services needs to be developed, if possible, that will satisfy the customers, potential business partners and advocates and yield some minimum, acceptable level of profit or cash flow that will bring appropriate, affordable services to the neighborhoods and keep them there.

BANKS, SAVINGS INSTITUTIONS AND OTHER CONVENTIONAL INSTITUTIONS

Neighborhoods need banks and other banking institutions, such as credit unions. There are many types of community development activities such as social services, grants, income supports, IDAs, workforce development, community development efforts (e.g., CDFIs, micro loan programs, etc.) and other efforts that are extremely important and need to be continued and expanded. However, a bank or bank-like institution is also crucial as a means of creating wealth for people in any neighborhood, if it is managed appropriately. This is not a new observation, but may be one that has been forgotten in low-income neighborhoods as fringe banking institutions replaced banks and, in too many cases, drained wealth out of the communities through high fees and rates. Banks, in combination with the many other evolving approaches, are still needed. It is incumbent on community development efforts to find ways to ensure banking activities are available in all neighborhoods in the country.

Generic Business Model Issues

Conventional lenders—including banks and savings institutions—of all sizes tend to depend on the float that they earn on deposits and the interest rate spread from loans as the key elements of their revenue and profit base. Many also depend on fees for some of their financial products, as well. They generally look for financial products that have lower risk and lower volume than check cashing businesses or payday lenders. These are two different businesses, in effect. As the industry is presently structured, banks are not very interested in cashing large numbers of small checks or making numerous small loans.

They are less interested in such volume businesses. They cannot charge fees high enough to make a reasonable profit from check cashing or from making very small loans. Banks do not want transactions that take a lot of time. Fringe bankers, in contrast, depend on services that often do. They have a high volume with spreads (that may range from low to very high) on each transaction and they make their profits from this volume of transactions.

A bank's competition in a low-income neighborhood is often thought to be a check casher or other fringe banker, even though the product lines, fee structures and operating approaches can be very different. These institutions have a much different cost structure. The stores of fringe banking institutions are frequently small, sometimes run down and unattractive, and certainly basic, at best, in terms of available amenity and comfort. The staff is often low paid and works long hours. The owner often works even longer hours and frequently steps in to service the long lines when there is a large rush at the store. These businesses work on high volume and charge relatively low fees (typically for some of the products such as money orders and bill payment), at least compared to what a bank might have to charge (many large banks around the country are now charging $5 to cash checks for people who do not hold accounts at the banks, creating a flurry of challenges). The fringe bankers are interested in cash transactions, so they are willing to provide services that take a lot of time, such as preparing money orders or bill paying.

A bank tends to be more interested in saving time and lowering the cost of services per customer, and therefore is less interested in offering services that take a lot of staff time. A bank also prefers making larger transactions that generate higher spreads through lending or obtaining deposits. Often, a larger loan can take roughly the same amount of time as a smaller loan but generates higher earnings. Similarly, a deposit can also generate strong income, although a larger deposit will earn more than a smaller one even though they may take roughly the same amount of time to service. And, very practically, banks are open for considerably fewer hours each week and pay their employees higher wages, making high volume products requiring extensive time as poor efforts to produce adequate revenue and profit. And banks are increasingly using technological approaches that usually require a large initial capital outlay but are much lower cost over the long run than paid staff.

Due to this competition and to the low-incomes of their customers, banks or other institutions in low-income neighborhoods cannot charge high fees in low-income neighborhoods that could cover their higher costs and generate some profit. Combined with other factors that push people away from banks toward fringe bankers (i.e. lack of trust, less convenience), high bank fees tend to encourage poorer people to use other, non-bank institutions.

Types of fees that exemplify this issue may be the overdraft and bounced check fees, often associated with "free checking accounts." However, these accounts have become a major revenue source for many banks. These and other fees now account for a large portion of revenue, apparently as much as 25% to 33% in some cases, and has raised questions that some banks may be encouraging these fees through their product structures. Some banks have reported an average of $150 per account per year from these fees. The average overdrawn check is about $80. The bank allows a grace period of one week to cover the overdrawn amount and charges a fee of, perhaps, $30. The return on this $30 loan is thus 1,955% to the bank on an annualized basis. While overdraft fees can save money compared to bounced check fees (which can incur up to three separate fees instead of just one), they clearly create excellent profits for banks. Banks have been using software to determine which account holders are good risks for overdraft accounts (Atlas; Irwin; Sloan).

However, these fees, which have been called a type of disguised payday lending, also represent a reason that many low-income households avoid using banks and prefer using check cashers instead. For this reason, savings accounts may be simpler and a better answer than checking accounts for many low-income households as well as the banks, which would experience fewer transactions, and therefore, lower costs with savings accounts than with checking accounts (see discussion on payday lending in Chapter 2).

But conventional institutions are generally less interested in small accounts, especially ones that turn over frequently. Based on the findings from some of the case studies, most of the financial services, including checking accounts, apparently tend to break even or lose money for many commercial banks in low-income areas; some may earn a profit, but they may be unusual. low-income customers tend to be associated with higher cost accounts due to the relatively short length of time funds are left in the accounts, lower account levels and relatively high numbers of transactions, all of which offer little opportunity to earn income from spreads of their accounts and/or generate additional costs that could result in reduced profits.

For example, it is likely that monthly float earned from federal benefits recipients' accounts is probably pretty low, as a rule, and the accounts are used frequently to pay basic bills. American Banker (Anson) reported in 1997 on a U.S. Treasury Department study that estimated that banks would earn 19 cents per month per account for federal benefit recipients. The article also quoted a Consumer Bankers Association spokesperson as saying that an institution needs $6 to $10 of float income per month to cover costs. The three month study was performed on 22,000 benefits recipients with Citibank accounts in Texas in 1996. It also showed that the average daily balance per account was $46 and that more than half the funds were usually withdrawn on the first day of the deposit. (The Treasury Department admitted various weaknesses in the study—short term, use of conservative interest rate, etc.).

Just opening a new account can be very costly. A recent study on the use of technology in financial services (Weissbourd) discussed sources that placed the cost as high as $40, which was an average "customer acquisition" cost for all customers and included marketing and advertising costs. Another estimate included only direct costs and totaled $13. However, even the costs of only opening an account probably are not covered by the interest earnings from small, frequently used accounts.

Therefore, there is little opportunity to generate income from the accounts of low-income households—from opening an account as well as the ongoing servicing of the account. The accounts tend to be small to begin with and there is a high use of the account, creating added costs for the institution. Even when a customer has a reasonably sized account such as some of the accounts created by deposits from Earned Income Tax Credit (EITC) returns, low-income households may use their accounts to pay bills and maintain the household. If there are frequent transactions in the account, especially if the transactions begin soon after the account is opened so that there is little time to earn income from the new account, this activity can cause losses for the institution. If possible, savings accounts should not be used for liquidity purposes that are more suited to checking accounts.

In practice, it is likely that there is no exact formula for these issues in creating profitability, especially for these smaller accounts. There are several variables that, in the end determine if the small accounts will be profitable. These variables include the size of the account, the length of time the funds are left in the account and the number/frequency of transactions made in the account. There can be an enormous variation in these variables that will create losses in some cases and break even or small profits in others.

For example, Shorebank's Earned Income Tax Credit program (EITC) includes new accounts that were probably larger than the accounts that most low-income households could normally open. Furthermore, not all Shorebank's EITC accounts had a high number of transactions; a large number did not. In addition, some of the larger accounts were profitable if the funds were left in for a short time before some or all was withdrawn. It is possible that Shorebank's accounts in this program broke even or even made a small profit. However, in general, it may be appropriate to conclude that the smaller accounts—checking and savings—of low-income households tend to be problematic in creating profitable financial service activity.

Nevertheless, banks are increasingly involved in this line of business. Some of the stimulus comes from the Community Reinvestment Act requirements. However, conventional institutions are increasingly involved because of the long term profit potential from untapped markets, such as immigrants and other upwardly mobile but presently low-income populations. This is especially true as more competition is created from other institutions such as brokerage houses (Coleman and Higgins). And it may also be stimulated by the heavy competition for the (presently, somewhat-depleted) middle and upper income markets, which may be on the verge of saturation (Sullivan).

As the economy slows and bankers of all kinds look for new markets (Jones; Kelley), some banks also may become increasingly involved with the unbanked. They also may see the results of the fringe banking industry and start to re-evaluate their approach to this market. And, as the capacity to charge higher fees falls and as the number of ATMs increases while the profit potential falls due to a glut of the machines (Marlin), banks may start to look at other uses of technology and cost saving methods to reach low-income people. "Downscale" markets have been appealing for a long time (Bremner).

To make this shift effectively, however, it is essential for a bank to meet a key goal: a high conversion or transition rate of check cashing customers to conventional bank products. Generally, this goal is a mutual one for both a bank and low-income customers, as it would be beneficial for both.

Union Bank of California (UBOC) has been successful in converting a large percentage of its check cashing customers into using more mainstream financial products. The Bank reports that there has been a conversion rate that has risen to 43% of those who have been repeat check cashing customers at Cash and Save (smaller full service branches located in low-income neighborhoods) into customers using some traditional bank products. This rate started at about 3% in 1992, when Cash and Save began operations, and has increased every year since 1993. The rate of increase seems to have leveled off in the last two years, increasing only one percent in the last year (2001).

However, it is not clear what percentage that the Bank considers to be a positive outcome, although the staff are clearly pleased with the results to date. Neither is it clear what percentage could be expected as a reasonable target under any circumstances, although there is probably too little experience to date to reach any conclusions about this issue. It is likely that there will always be some large percent of people who will not qualify under any circumstances and some who will not want to establish a relationship with a conventional institution.

This 43% conversion rate is probably higher than many other lenders with low-income financial services programs. For example, Harris Bank, in Chicago is targeting a 25% conversion rate after its one year pilot program achieved an 8%-10% conversion rate (Jackson). The Bank considers this rate to be very successful, probably due to the profit level that is now generated by these customers, and it seems to be a very reasonable one, especially if the Bank can continue to increase it even at a moderate pace. And, it may be impossible to set a goal because it is not possible to have any realistic idea of what is possible in these circumstances at this time.

On the other hand, the rate which is considered successful for the Bank—one that creates financial viability for a branch or the program as a whole—may not represent an adequate rate for the community as a whole, which could still prefer, and need, a higher conversion rate. In this case, additional steps may be needed.

Approaches such as UBOC's Cash and Save appear to be working and providing excellent models for conventional institutions with a desire to enter into this market. (Recently, some banks are beginning to open branches again, although smaller and lower cost, while looking to sell higher profit services such as mortgages and investments. (Calvey)) However, it represents a different model and a significant modification from banks' more traditional approaches. Generally, this more traditional approach is more geared to a middle and upper income market. It is a much higher cost model:

- The range of financial products is different and often greater and more complex.
- This often requires more skilled and better trained staff.
- Many of the salaries are substantially higher.
- There is a reliance on cross selling opportunities for the different products (which may be one reason for banks' opposition to privacy legislation), which are often absent in many low-income communities.
- The bricks and mortar for the branch offices—they are typically well appointed and have amenities—are more costly and make achievement of profitability more difficult in low-income neighborhoods.
- The hours are short compared to check cashers and payday lenders.
- There is a much greater dependence on the use of technology.
- There are high, central administrative overhead costs.

Perceptions of both high risk and potentially low profit tend to keep most conventional institutions from entering low-income neighborhoods, especially since they have been closing branches in these areas for some time. However, the experience of the First Bank of the Americas (FBA) in Chicago and other lenders is beginning to show that both parts of this perception may be inaccurate with a different business model. FBA has shown their risks to be relatively low so far, as demonstrated by their low losses and their low loan loss provision (which is required by FASB to be based on expected losses and past history). Profitability is also being demonstrated by FBA, although the Bank is operating under a different business model using a different cost structure. The initial profit levels may not reach the targets that many banks are looking for, at least in the short run.

However, conventional institutions are beginning to recognize the importance of branding in low-income neighborhoods over the long run. As the unbanked and fringe banked start becoming bankable and looking for conventional institutions, they may tend to look for those institutions that assisted them when few others would. Many of these communities are known to be very loyal over generations and the conventional lenders are beginning to understand this possible impact.

Examples from the Case Studies

There are several examples of these issues and trends, and of conventional institutions entering this market. For example, Union Bank of California is attempting to develop a different business model to reach low-income people. The traditional bricks and mortar model is rarely effective in most low-income neighborhoods, especially for larger institutions that compare the financial results of a branch in low-income neighborhoods to branches in middle and upper income communities. The results will not demonstrate comparative viability for these branches.

Lower cost banking options need to be created, and that is what UBOC is attempting to achieve in using two different approaches. Cash and Save, the first approach, is a traditional bank branch in some ways—offering all UBOC bank products. Cash and Save also offers check cashing and "transitional" bank products—e.g., the Nest Egg savings account (with six free money orders per month), which can be started with $10 and a monthly deposit of $25 that can be automatically drawn from paychecks without monthly fees; Benefit Transfer Service; and basic checking—that help check cashing clients transition to more traditional banking products. The branches are very small, in some cases about 250 square feet. UBOC has tried them in existing branches, stand alone check cashing stores, retail and warehouse grocery stores and a laundromat/multi-retail setting. Started in 1993, Cash and Save now has 12 branches in Los Angeles, San Diego and the Central Valley (seven are in traditional branches and five are in supermarket/retail venues). In addition, a nonprofit partner, Operation Hope, Inc. (OHI) now features Cash and Save check cashing and Nest Egg programs in three of its inner city Los Angeles locations.

In 2000, UBOC entered into another approach to reach low-income households. It purchased a 40% equity interest (with an option to purchase the remaining ownership in 10 years) of an established check cashing company, Navicert Financial, Inc., known as Nix Check Cashing. Nix, a 34 year-old company with 600,000 customers, has 47 branches in the southern California region (after selling 23 branches, mostly in northern California in 1998 in an effort to consolidate its business). All UBOC products—including ATM, consumer deposits, loans, and small business products—are available in the Nix stores and Nix agreed to modify its pricing for some of its products. The third partner is Operation Hope, Inc., a local nonprofit which offers financial counseling and education in addition to home ownership counseling and computer training, and has been authorized by UBOC to offer some of the Bank's financial services at some of its locations and to cash checks.

The Cash and Save is a lower cost alternative to a more typical branch and, after a slow start up period of several years, is now profitable. On the other hand, its costs are higher than a check cashing store, but it also combines other financial vehicles not available through the check cashing stores that are now generating strong profits. This appears to be a very viable business model—both financially and socially.

The partnership approach is another way of reaching low-income households, although this approach may not be as effective as the Cash and Save, depending on how success is measured. The partnership with Nix Check Cashing still contains certain elements that may be considered objectionable or difficult by some, the payday loans in particular, although it may be profitable and also create important opportunities for mainstreaming low-income people into more full scale banking relationships. All successful approaches will have trade offs that will be part of the structure that need to be addressed. It is also important to give time for new approaches to evolve. The Bank did institute some structural changes in Nix' payday loan product. UBOC also tried a payday loan alternative that was not successful, but other institutions around the country are trying other approaches that have worked and may offer models in the future to other institutions trying to make changes.

The First Bank of the Americas, in Chicago, uses a different approach. The First Bank of the Americas ("Bank" or "FBA") is a small community commercial bank in a low-income, distressed neighborhood with a large influx of immigrants on the southwest side of Chicago, Illinois. It is a wholly owned subsidiary of FBA Bancorp, Inc., a one bank holding company. Begun in 1997 as a state chartered bank by David and Pamela Voss, the Bank now has three branches after opening the main branch in January 1998. The founders purchased a savings bank branch serving mostly Polish immigrants with roughly $30 million in deposits that was no longer very responsive to the needs of many in the community. FBA focuses on the immigrant community, particularly those from Mexico, which is living in the immediate neighborhood.

The Bank's mission statement is instructive: "To be the primary financial institution for the unbanked and fringe-banked citizens of the communities we serve while building capital for our shareholders. We define our stakeholders as our investors, employees, customers, and citizens of the communities we serve. We will nourish our deep roots in our service area and be a primary source of community development by offering financial products and services responsive to the needs of the community at fair prices. We are a for-profit entity with a social focus and our success depends on serving the local community. Therefore, as our communities succeed, we succeed."

The Bank believes it can succeed both socially and financially serving a low-income community that almost all other conventional institutions have abandoned to fringe banking financial institutions. It tries to be an agent for change in the inner city and it has a major goal of trying to build the wealth of the local residents through its banking programs and partnerships.

It appears to have created a viable financial and social model that can actually meet these goals and supplant some of the fringe banking businesses for its customers at reasonable costs while still generating a profit.

And, as noted above, the experience of FBA and others is beginning to show that their risks to be relatively low so far, as demonstrated by their low losses and their low loan loss provision (which is required by FASB to be based on expected losses and past history). Profitability is also being demonstrated by FBA, although it is being administered under a different business model using a different cost structure. The profit levels may not reach the targets that most banks are looking for in the short run.

FBA is pioneering its new business model based on its own understandings of its customers. It charges low fees on financial services with earnings coming from spreads on savings accounts and loans. Like any other bank, it relies on these products for the core of its revenues and profits. And, The resulting income/earnings are good, but not the highest possible. It has both a different cost structure and different profit targets than most other lenders. It seems to require a unique blend of banker, entrepreneur and community development activist. However, it is based on a new philosophy of banking that seems to be working.

The Bank uses a "high touch, low tech" approach (greater use of direct staff contact with customers rather than use of technology to interface with customers) that relies on a lower cost approach than most other conventional institutions; it appears to work well for them and would be a essential to any banking approach in low-income neighborhoods. This also approach flies against the prevailing methods used by most banks—which increasingly tend to be "high tech, low touch"—based on lowering costs and increasing profits. At the same time, the Bank is using some technological approaches—such as the cards to send money—that are quite up-to-date and have had problems gaining acceptance in other places. (Interestingly, there is a Citibank branch on the next block but Bank officials believe that it is much more capital intensive and dependent on technology and, therefore, may possibly be reaching a different, somewhat higher income clientele born in the U.S.). However, the use of machinery and high technology may be difficult to implement in low-income neighborhoods, at least in the beginning. Over time, it will probably become more of a necessity, especially if the issues of higher costs and replication are to be confronted. However, the use of the technology should be implemented after an institution has operated in a neighborhood for a while and gained the trust of the residents.

In contrast, Shorebank, which is also located in Chicago and has worked for decades in some neighborhoods, similarly is trying to create a new model that is more grounded on the use of technology. The first and most successful of the "community development banks" in the country, Shorebank's approach is more focused on using technology than some of the other approaches. Shorebank began a series of interconnected programs for unbanked and fringe banked households in some Chicago neighborhoods, starting in 1999. These programs focused on finding ways to encourage the use of technology, increase savings through free tax preparation and linking tax refunds from the Earned Income Tax Credit (EITC) to savings accounts, and finding ways to use check cashing as a bridge to using conventional institutions and increasing savings.

Under the first program, Shorebank instituted training in the use of ATMs in one of its branch lobbies, encouraging people to sign up for accounts and receive an ATM card. A major focus has been placed on their existing IDA account holders. They have coupled various incentives with this program including entry into a raffle for using ATMs or direct deposit. The Bank also created an "Express Banking Center" in the lobby of one of its branches that includes free internet access to accounts, an ATM and access to 24 hour phone banking services. Training in the use of the mechanisms available in the Center was provided.

The Bank had a number of goals including the following—helping low-income households to increase their savings as a means to increasing their wealth; finding ways to encourage unbanked households to use banking institutions; and using technology as a way to more cost-effectively deliver financial services to low-income people in ways that will allow the Bank to at least break even. The Bank also wanted to find mechanisms to encourage people to keep funds in their accounts for a longer period and to reduce the number of transactions. The Bank also wanted to test the use of different types of incentives to encourage the use of both technology and the various savings and checking accounts that were provided. And, finally, the Bank wanted to increase customers' understanding of financial services and the options available to them.

Shorebank's approach in these demonstrations has been to focus on the use of technology and other entry points—i.e. the EITC and free tax return preparation assistance—to address these issues. The Bank is not contemplating a major overhaul of its cost structure in order to compete with these other institutions, although there are some cost reductions in some of their products and programs. In comparison, other institutions may also look at some types of cost reductions as another means to become competitive while offering more affordable financial services products.

The Bank is developing a strategy that seeks to increase the use of technology to offset a bank's inherent market weaknesses. And training in the technology also assumes an important role in the ultimate effectiveness of the use of technology to create a more profitable approach to financial services. At the same time, it is combining technology with other approaches—especially the EITC—intended to help low-income households enter the banking arena with accounts and products designed to give them incentives to help them build wealth while reducing the Bank's costs and making it more feasible to assist them.

Other examples

Many other lenders are involved in various ways to reach lower income households. For example, Wells Fargo Bank has given its banking customers with direct deposit of their paychecks the choice of borrowing against their next paycheck. The charge is $1.50 per $20 that is borrowed (Jackson).

FleetBoston Financial has created a new, free account, called Access Advantage, which allows account holders to use direct deposit for their paychecks and receive a debit card to withdraw funds. However, account holders cannot write checks or deposit other checks, creating different tiers of banking customers. Fleet, which normally cashes about 1.1 million non-customer paychecks checks per month, appears to be able to use direct deposit and debit cards to cut the costs significantly enough to make the product financially viable: "Fleet has structured the offering in such a way that it will not cost the bank too much to administer" (Waldman). The Bank hopes to register 8,000 accounts by the end of the year, thereby reducing the number of non-customer payroll checks that it processes by 216,000 in 2002 (Harlin). Certainly, it will cost less than tellers' having to manually deposit and/or cash large numbers of checks and will make the operations at branches much smoother.

Fleet also has another account for electronic transfers of government benefits. The account is called Electronic Transfer Account and has no minimum balance, includes an ATM card/debit card and carries a $3 per month fee (Harlin). Fleet also has enhanced its ATMs, using seven different languages; participated in Individual Development Account programs; introduced workplace banking for direct deposits; and is exploring "affinity" marketing for specific groups such as Hispanics and recently divorced or widowed women (Distribution Management Briefing).

In contrast, Bank One has created a program with more features, in partnership with the Woodstock Institute in Chicago. The program is called the Alternative Banking Program and has the following features for checking and savings accounts (Williams; J.M. Williams):

- $10 minimum opening deposit amount, compared to $250 for a traditional account.
- Low or no minimum balance.
- Low or no service fee.
- Unlimited check writing.
- Unlimited use of Bank One ATMs.
- Some free teller transactions, depending on the account.
- Free financial literacy training.

Called the Alternative Banking Program, it is considered a "starter" account. The accounts limit daily withdrawals to $50 (compared to $300 for the standard account) and require three days before funds are available after a deposit (compared to two days). Also, many customers with no credit or bad credit may qualify for accounts and be able to improve their account relationship with a solid, demonstrated track record. This program, which was developed when Bank One purchased First Chicago Bank in 1998, may not cover costs. However, the average balances for a checking account in the program is $1,100 and $1,600 for a savings account. These account levels may help the Bank breakeven on the accounts or even earn a small profit (see Chapter 3 discussion).

From the Bank's perspective, the number of accounts may not be too great a burden as most of the branches are probably not located in low-income neighborhoods. The Bank has other programs, such as use of the matricula card and localized demonstrations such as financial literacy training, stored value debit cards, free checking with direct deposit, etc.

Harris Bank, also in Chicago, opened Harris Express, a free standing check cashing outlet on the south side, after a one year pilot at three branches. The store will offer check cashing, bill paying, prepaid debit cards, money orders and money wiring in addition to ATM services. It will also take applications for opening accounts and make referrals for loans. The new store, aimed primarily at the Hispanic population, also accepts Matricula identification cards. The goal is to convert 25% of the customers to Bank clients (Jackson; PR Newswire).

Banco Popular, based in San Juan, Puerto Rico, is another bank, which has made significant efforts to reach the unbanked, especially Latinos, at least in the program's startup phase. It now has about 100 branches in California, Florida,

Illinois, Texas, New York and New Jersey with roughly $5.5 billion in assets. In addition, it also has opened over 75 retail centers for its Popular Cash Express (PCE), which offers check cashing, wire transfers, bill payments and money orders. PCE also offers insurance and travel services and is looking into offering other products such as credit cards, personal loans and other services.

There is also a mobile van service providing check cashing services in southern California on paydays, charging 1.1% of the face amount of the check plus twenty cents per check. Partly through its competition, wiring costs have decreased in the region. The Bank hopes to attract the unbanked and then convert them into bankable customers. The Bank now also has ambitious expansion plans for immigrant populations as well as non-Hispanic households and hopes to double its presence in the near future (Allison, Jackson, Millman, Riera).

Many other banks are entering the market as well. A new bank, El Banco de Nuestra Communidad, is geared toward Atlanta's Latino community. It will be open for extended hours, offer 24 hour ATM access, affordable wiring, international phone cards, prepaid legal services and insurance products. It will also use different documentation to allow easier opening of accounts and will offer literacy training (Businesswire).

Westamerica Bank, in northern California, has opened a chain of check cashing stores, called the Money Outlet (Community Reinvestment News). In the last year, most large banks have made opening accounts for immigrants without proper documentation much simpler.

Smaller banks are also starting to enter the field, as exemplified by First Bank of the Americas. TCF Financial in Minneapolis demonstrates another approach for a small bank. Now the third largest bank in Minnesota with $12 billion in assets, TCF is one of the most profitable banks in the country, overcoming a negative tangible net worth value of $35 million in 1985, when new ownership took over. TCF offers free checking, free ATM service and bonuses such as airline tickets and long distance calling minutes.

TCF focuses on middle and lower income customers and works substantially in lower income neighborhoods. It uses a lower cost model for all of its branches and even the main office. Employees, who are relatively low paid (e.g., tellers earn $9 to $12 per hour), fill multiple roles. Branches were opened in a large number of subsidiaries of Albertson's grocery stores, and ATMs and tellers were placed in other supermarkets and convenience stores. The latter are open 73 hours a week. They offer limited services including deposits, withdrawals and check cashing. These branches cost about $300,000 compared to the industry standard of about $2 million for typical new bank branches.

TCF pays little or no interest on most of its core deposits. On the other hand, TCF charges an average of 8% for its interest rates; in addition, another 3.3% is collected in fee income. There are gross earnings of about 4% on the deposits after interest paid (3%) and overhead (4.4%), which is kept low, are subtracted. Most of the loans are secured on housing and the resulting losses on loans was very small, about .15%. TCF collects fees, even though checking and ATM use are free. TCF averages about $210 per year per free account in other fees such as bounced check ($30), check printing ($14.25) and use of debit cards at non-TCF ATMs or at stores. TCF also acts somewhat similar to check cashing agencies in that it is interested in volume and generating its profits from many transactions with smaller levels of revenue and profit that add up as volume increases (Tatge).

Located in New Jersey with operations in New York and Pennsylvania, Commerce Bancorp has had excellent financial performance, seeing its stock price rise from about $15 in early 2000 to about $46 in November 2002, and growing by 278% in the previous five years, starting in 1995. Its 2000 non-performing loan rate was 0.18%. In 2000, its earnings were growing at a 16% annual rate. The growth is produced by a large increase in new branches as well as by increased deposits in existing branches. The $14.7 billion asset Bank has grown from $11.3 billion in early 2002; assets were under $3 billion in 1995 and just over $7 billion in 2000.

While most banks were cutting costs, pushing customers to ATMs and other technological answers and increasing fees of all kinds, the Bank used an entirely different business model based on volume, customer service and aspects of franchising. It maintains extended branch hours every day of the week (including Sundays from 11 to 4), offers free checking accounts, carefully screens and trains its employees, especially in customer service, and tries to clear out of state checks very quickly. It offers all services for free in the first year and then requires only a $100 minimum balance to maintain free services. Instead of merging and cutting branches and other services to cut costs and generate increased profit from the merged entity, Commerce Bank expands through opening new branches—from new construction rather than buying and remodeling some other company's branch. It uses the same rough design for each one, creating a recognizable brand for its bank. As other banks try to move customers on line and into the use of machinery, Commerce Bank is increasing its bricks and mortar presence; nevertheless, the Bank has a very high on line presence—but without the fees at the branches.

The key to Commerce Bank's success is a straightforward trade off. Customers receive few fees and obtain excellent service, but they also receive lower returns on their accounts. For example, the checking accounts do not pay interest and recent CDs paid 1/2 percent less than competitors. In 2000, the Bank paid 3.24% for its new deposits, compared to the 5.6% paid by local competitors First Union and Summit. These wider profit margins pay for the increased service costs and result in a much faster growing bank with strong profits (Sapsford; Heintz).

Other Key Business Model Issues

The cost structure, as noted, varies for different institutions. First Bank of the Americas, for example, is very cost conscious. Its cost structure is lower than many other banks, but probably still above the check cashing outlets' cost structure. This type of a cost structure appears to be necessary for a bank to be successful in most low-income neighborhoods. However, the resulting pay structure for employees may be somewhat inadequate to support the work that is needed to establish a traditional bank in a low-income neighborhood.

The earnings do not completely support the extra work that is required to make this business model work. Therefore, it is possible that they may struggle with turnover and finding qualified employees who will stay with the Bank for a long time. It may be more difficult to attract many staff who will be interested in traditional banking approaches. It will, in fact, require a unique blend of banker, entrepreneur and community development activist. This problem is similar to the one facing many nonprofits working in community development. It is one that exists in community development work and is part of the environment that must be addressed in many institutions working in low-income areas.

Capitalization and scale are other key issues. Union Bank of California has access to capital markets and large scale resources to enable it to employ the tools needed to reach scale and profitability. UBOC also had internal resources necessary to plan these programs and to stay with them—even when there were losses and uncertainty over several years—until they were able to prove their value. UBOC also had the capitalization necessary to purchase a major interest in a very large check cashing business. This access and long term financial backing needs to be replicated by other efforts if appropriate scale and profitability is to be achieved. Without this access and the resulting scale, the impact and profitability might be threatened.

The model used by First Bank of the Americas uses a different approach to capitalization. It depends on external "patient" capital, at least for some of its equity. The Bank received a good portion of its capital from the CDFI Fund and institutions such as the Bank of America, which can afford to wait and, in the case of Bank of America, have other objectives—such as meeting their Community Reinvestment Act requirements. Shorebank has also depended on this approach. In this type of situation, all shareholders must be willing to forgo profitability for the initial period of operations. Unfortunately, there are limited sources of this type of capital available for community development efforts at this time.

If the community development efforts in the U.S. want to seriously approach these issues, they will need to find ways to address these replication issues—through training and TA, deeper study of workable models such as the FBA, additional capital (the CDFI Fund would not be able to support a major expansion of community banks on a large scale with its present capitalization), creating the capacity to adapt models to local conditions, etc. Nevertheless, the CDFI Fund assistance was essential to the Bank's success in several ways and would need to play a central ongoing role in the future (two keys to achieving break even for FBA were the CDFI Fund grants and the purchase of the branch with its deposits at a very reasonable cost. The grants allowed the Bank to maintain its capital structure as required by the regulators. The reasonable cost of purchasing the assets allowed the Bank to generate decent net income and allow profits. If the purchase had cost more, fewer assets would have been able to be purchased with the available funds and the Bank would have required more time to reach break even).

Many other factors have an influence on the successful development of reasonable financial services for low-income households.

The interest rate environment also has an impact on these conditions. For example, as shown in a later example of a community development credit union, the existing level of below market interest rate investments in 2001-2002 produced lower income than it might in a higher interest rate environment—even compared to the rates that existed $1^1/2$ years ago. With greater income from higher rates, the Northeast Community Federal Credit Union could cover a larger part of the negative cash flow that it must otherwise pay out of its own operations. This assumes that investors would not ask for an increased return in keeping with the increased economic environment; if the requested returns increased, then the credit union would not be able to benefit much from an increased interest rate environment.

Scale, likewise, is equally crucial to these efforts. They can begin on a smaller scale and can phase in over a period of time. But some vision of scale is necessary in most of the future efforts both to achieve a real impact and to generate profitability. UBOC has many Cash and Save branches and partners with Nix on 47 other locations; this scale is crucial in reaching a large number of customers and in generating profit.

Location is also a critical element. UBOC experimented with a variety of types of locations to find the best possibilities. Los Angeles has more of a "car culture" than some other cities, but there are still key locations and density points that can be targeted. Again, check cashers often understand the important locations in many areas. It is also important to note that some states regulate this matter to some degree, for example in New York, where there is regulation over the minimum distance between check cashing stores.

Exit strategy and succession are also important issues. For example, the officers of FBA have an exit strategy of selling stock to the community members and exiting the venture at some point. It is crucial that succession planning take place and qualified people be brought in soon to learn the business thoroughly. Many businesses can falter when the initial visionaries leave. Moreover, the sales price must be one that allows the new community owners to be able to carry on without jeopardizing the operational cash flows of the Bank.

Adaptation to the local market is also crucial. For example, First Bank of the Americas may be partly dependent on a real estate market that is somewhat unique. People can buy affordable homes with low-incomes and small down payments in the nearby neighborhoods in that part of Chicago. There is not extensive appreciation that outstrips the increases in income to afford the housing in the neighborhood. Since the Bank's profitability depends extensively on its lending, this model would need to be applied in similar neighborhoods. If the Bank were to try to apply this model in Los Angeles, however, it may be more difficult to find low-income borrowers in their target markets and neighborhoods who can afford the higher housing prices. And this Chicago market may have worked because racial discrimination may have kept minorities in certain neighborhoods and capped the housing values in those neighborhoods. But other steps are possible (e.g., working with local governments to create homebuyer subsidies) and other types of loans/deposits can be substituted—such as car loans, small business loans and furniture loans—to create a business plan that meets local needs and also satisfies profitability requirements.

Therefore, it is crucial to have a better understanding of the local market for financial services. There are many different markets in many neighborhoods—different immigrant groups of many kinds with different interests and goals, individuals, families, seniors, working poor, people with government assistance or social security, etc. Each of these populations tends to relate to financial service needs differently. To successfully address these needs, an institution needs to understand these differences. This is not easily accomplished. Generally, it requires some funding support to obtain this market data—through focus groups, surveys, interviews, market studies, etc.—in order to support the appropriate product design and a business plan which incorporates these understandings.

Clearly then, creating new institutions and programs requires careful planning and evaluation. This step also costs money that is mostly not in the system at this time. To adequately address these issues will require allocating an appropriate level of resources for these functions.

The design of new products is another key ongoing feature of the industry at this time. Many institutions have made important contributions in this area, but much more can be done. However, it also may require external financial assistance to support this change, as well. For example, the incentive approach, tested by Shorebank on a small scale, could be an important element of future approaches that has potential for helping to change financial behaviors. However, it certainly adds costs, at least in the short run.

FRINGE BANKING INSTITUTIONS

Generic Business Model Issues. This topic was discussed extensively in Chapter 2 and partially in the earlier discussion in Chapter 3 above. Here, a summary will be presented rather than repeat the discussion, with the addition of related new material.

These institutions have a different product mix than banks. They focus on a core product—check cashing or payday lending, for example—and then build other products around them. These additional services include related products such as bill payment and money wiring in addition to less related products such as the provision of bus passes, lottery tickets, stamps and envelopes, phone cards, faxing, copying, laminating, etc. Banks provide almost none of the latter category and have relatively little interest in the check cashing, bill paying, payday lending, etc.

Fringe bankers make their money from a volume business with a range of fees from relatively low to high. Although the fees on check cashing and payday lending can be very onerous to low-income people, as discussed throughout this report, they are relatively low and, individually or in small numbers, would not generate great absolute levels of high profits. However, with a high volume of activity, these smaller transactions can generate excellent profits, as will be shown in Chapter 4.

High volume of relatively small fees coupled with low operating costs and long hours (on top of fixed costs that do not change much with the extended hours) are the core of the model. The employees are often not paid very well, the stores have few amenities and are sparse, the rents are usually low due to their locations in low-income areas, there is little central administration until several stores are owned by a single entity, and the owners are often heavily involved in the business. Moreover, the startup costs are reasonable.

There are fixed costs that exist and must be paid—rent, interest if there were any loans, security, etc. But many of the variable costs are relatively small and higher volume sales can far outweigh these costs of salaries, utilities, etc. The revenue from added volume from cashing checks and products such as selling phone cards and money orders generates mostly profit after a certain level of revenue is reached.

Banks rely on income from deposits and larger loans along with fees on certain financial services. They also have higher central administrative costs, which are not shared by fringe banking institutions for the most part, unless they are larger chains.

In certain situations, however, these trends are losing some strength. For example, fringe banking chains face higher costs, including central administrative costs, although probably still not at the level that banks face. And, increasingly, some of the fringe bankers are trying to change their image with fancier quarters and even efforts at "branding" to make their stores more visible (Storey).

Other Key Business Model Issues

Many fringe banking institutions are now listed on the stock exchanges. As a result, they often have relatively easy access to capital markets. These companies include payday lenders, pawn brokers, rent-to-own stores, money wiring companies, consumer finance companies and check cashing companies. They also rely on their banking relationships for large lines of credit to finance their operations. And check cashers must rely on banks to clear checks for them as quickly as possible.

Location is an important key to fringe banking success. They need to be in relatively high traffic locations with large numbers of relatively low-income and working households. In some states, there are regulations on the siting of these businesses, usually prohibiting more than one store within a minimum radius. This type of legislation can create a strong market for stores in those areas. Multiple locations with adjoining or overlapping of these areas can create a monopoly position if the stores are owned by the same entity.

Check cashers may offer the possibility of an excellent partner for community development efforts. They cover many of the areas that make potential projects viable—volume and scale, lower operating costs, existing investment of fixed costs, customer familiarity, many locations in the target markets, a capacity to add on additional services and features, etc. They are also less regulated than conventional institutions and are less expensive to set up. However, the check cashing company would need to be willing to share certain goals with its partners; for example, it is not clear how many of these companies would be willing to enter these partnerships. Several case studies (Leibsohn, 2005) illustrate examples of some successful partnerships and some of the key conditions needed for success.

Many fringe bankers may not be taking advantage of some technological advances. Card based products, for example, could help both the check cashers and banks interested in offering savings and checking accounts. For example, the check cashing outlets could give their customers access to accounts through a bank or credit union partner. Check cashers also have access to important information—about their customers and the market as a whole—that they are presently not utilizing, for the most part. Technology could also give all parties a better understanding of the market and the needs, in turn enabling better design of products to meet those needs; and being able to obtain this market information would create greater incentives for banks and nonprofits to seek them out as partners.

Most of the critical elements of the business model for check cashing companies were discussed in Chapter 2 and the financial feasibility is discussed in Chapter 4.

COMMUNITY DEVELOPMENT CREDIT UNIONS

There are different types of credit unions. One is founded on a membership base that is connected to one or more employers or industry groups. Historically, credit unions were founded on assisting low-income households. However, this goal may have become submerged over many decades. For example, a recent report concluded that credit unions in the Chicago metropolitan area are not meeting their statutory responsibility of assisting "persons of modest means" (Jacob, et. al.). Now, however, they typically serve moderate and middle income households. They tend not to target low-income households with their services. Their branches are often located near the employers and in commercial areas and/or downtowns. Increasingly, these types of credit unions are seeking new charters, which allow them to seek members throughout a larger geographic region to serve anyone living or working in that area.

Another type of credit union is called a Community Development Credit Union (CDCU). Like the employer based credit unions, they are deposit-taking, nonprofit, tax exempt institutions owned by their members. However, they differ from employment based credit unions in that they are usually created in low-income areas to serve low-income people. Their core goals are economic self help and community reinvestment to help low-income communities control their own financial destinies.

As a result, their programs, emphases, goals and products are often different than the mainstream credit unions. There are also far fewer CDCUs (over 300 CDCU's are member of the National Federation of Community Development Federal Credit Unions, the trade association for the CDCUs, compared to a total of over 10,000 credit unions in the country as a whole) and they tend to be small and not well capitalized. The NFCDCU members, for example, ranged in assets from $100,000 to $50 million with an average of about $3.3 million in 1999 (NFCDCU). Since then, a few substantially larger CDCUs have evolved.

Nevertheless, many credit unions serve low-income areas. In 2000, a reported 36% of credit unions were located in low-income areas compared to 20% for banks and 19% for thrifts (Brown).

The federally-chartered credit unions are regulated by the National Credit Union Administration, while state chartered credit unions are regulated by various state agencies.

The CDCUs tend to know the low-income neighborhoods and the needs of low-income households well. While the more mainstream credit unions do not know the issues in low-income neighborhoods as well as the CDCUs, they have much greater size and there are many more of them. It is therefore important for these credit unions to become more involved in offering financial services in low-income neighborhoods. Some CDCUs have created partnerships with the other CUs and these are very important and encouraging. More of these partnerships are needed and deepened assistance from existing partnerships will be essential in the future. Together, both types of CU can increase the effectiveness of programs designed to assist low-income neighborhoods.

Generic Business Model Issues

CDCUs are usually relatively small, undercapitalized regulated financial institutions. Their business model is a variation of the larger financial institutions serving the middle and upper income neighborhoods, but many also seem to contain elements of nonprofit business model approaches. Like most other organizations serving low-income people, a CDCU typically has a much lower cost structure than other types of financial institutions. Because it is regulated, its cost structure nevertheless is higher than many check cashing operations, but lower than traditional credit unions and most likely lower than most banks. The costs are kept low for salaries, offices, amenities, employee benefits in some situations, equipment and the like.

On the other hand, a CDCU is structured more like a bank or similar financial institution in its financial product mix and sources of profits. That is, a CDCU usually makes its profit from spreads earned on loans and the float from deposits. Since its goal is assisting low-income people, a CDCU cannot charge high fees or high interest rates or it will hurt its customers or lose them entirely.

There are other differences with fringe banking institutions. The CDCU rarely stays open during the hours that a check cashing company does. It also may not have the range of services available: bill payment, money wiring and some of the lesser products such as stamps and envelopes, bus passes, lottery tickets and the like.

However, if the members do not have income levels needed to borrow heavily enough and supply an adequate level of relatively stable deposits, then the CDCU may not generate adequate income to break even with its costs or generate any profit. It will remain poorly capitalized, with inadequate equity and reserves, unable to offer adequate salaries or an appropriate range of needed financial services for the people in the region. This situation could remain even when other cost cutting mechanisms are used, such as volunteers and low or free rent. The CDCU's success in developing an adequate range of services, creating a viable marketing plan to reach out to members, and meeting the actual level of income and borrowing needs of its members and other supporters (e.g., friendly depositors) will determine its level of financial strength.

It is important to note that the CDCUs have been very successful over time. Few have gone out of business. However, it is also difficult for them to grow as quickly, supply as many additional financial services or have the breadth of membership as some other financial institutions have been able to achieve.

Examples from the Case Studies

Bethex Federal Credit Union, located in the Bronx, New York, was created in 1970. Joy Cousminer, then an adult education teacher working with welfare mothers, was the primary organizer of Bethex, which has grown from 600 members to over 8,000. Bethex is a Community Development Credit Union, a geographically based credit union owned by its members and is therefore democratically controlled. As a credit union, it is also regulated and insured by the federal government. With its mission of empowerment for low-income people, Bethex now has assets of just under $10 million after merging with several other smaller credit unions that were having problems. There are 6 full time branches and an additional six "teller stations" which are open for one or two days a week. Bethex operates on a philosophy of low cost services and low cost operations so that members will have the opportunities of building their own assets and escape poverty.

Bethex uses a business model that allows it to compete effectively with both check cashing stores and banks. It is a lower cost model that relies on lower rent and salaries in its branches. And it utilizes the check cashing companies to help its members and its own institution as well as the check cashing businesses. This model appears to be effective in most ways, especially in a situation in which most of the members are low-income and little net income is generated. However, it has thin margins and a small asset base; therefore, the Credit Union must look for other ways to reach low-income people cost effectively and to increase its asset size in order to begin to reach greater scale. Increased scale could result in improved net earnings and give Bethex some cushion in its efforts to create new programs and approaches.

To address some of these issues, Bethex Federal Credit Union has entered into an unusual partnership with a check cashing company as a means to provide additional services to its members in a cost effective way. RiteCheck, an 11-branch check cashing business with locations mostly in the Bronx, has agreed to provide the following services at its stores to Bethex Federal Credit Union members:

- Make cash deposits to their credit union accounts.
- Make withdrawals from their Bethex savings and checking accounts at the check cashing stores.
- Cash Bethex checks at the Paynet rate (with fees paid by Bethex).
- Cash non-Bethex checks with a discount (with fees paid by the member).
- The credit union will be able to distribute information and membership and loan applications at the stores. The credit union members will not be charged for the services except for non-Bethex check cashing; the credit union will pay fees incurred by members directly to RiteCheck at below market rates to cover the costs of these activities.

Part of this program is not necessarily new. Existing networks in New York allow check cashers to cash bank payroll checks from some of the banks' large clients (known as Paynet), and permit banks to cash each others' checks for a fee and to accept deposits for another institution for a fee (known as NYCE, which is similar to Cirrus, Star, Interlink, etc. in other parts of the country). However, the check cashing feature among check cashing companies through Paynet appears to be unique to New York and most New York banks seem to have chosen not to use other banks for placing deposits, although the practice is more widespread in New Jersey. Bethex and RiteCheck are therefore using existing systems.

At the same time, there are several unique aspects to this partnership. Although Bethex has joined both of the networks, few other community development financial institutions have joined these networks. The use of these systems to help low-income people is an important new step, as is the partnership with a check casher and a community development credit union. The goal is to assist low-income people through the use of these systems, which does not appear to have been attempted in this manner before. The capacity for low-income people to make deposits at a check cashing company is also a very crucial step, which adds the ability to increase savings and build wealth for low-income credit union members as well as making it much more convenient for them. It also creates the possibility of increasing the credit union's deposits and increasing the check cashing business for RiteCheck through taking deposits. Moreover, Bethex has decided to offer most of these services without cost to the members, as the credit union will pay most of the fees associated with these transactions.

The program meets goals for all involved. The credit union has few branches and wants to meet the needs of a large low-income population in its area. Opening branches is a very expensive proposition. Check cashers are much more prevalent. Bethex wants to make it significantly easier for its members to access its services and reduce the very real costs that are now present for many members in reaching its branches (transportation costs, logistical problems with their children and time issues involved in reaching the branches). Bethex also wants to offer increased savings and lending opportunities to low-income people who do not have lower cost options; Bethex would like to increase its membership and hopes that check cashing customers will be encouraged to open new accounts. Working with RiteCheck offers Bethex the opportunity to meet all these goals at a relatively low cost to the organization compared to opening new branches.

RiteCheck will benefit by increased fees from the transactions of Bethex members, increased volume from other services that the members may purchase while in the check cashing store, assisting low-income people gain access to banking services that it cannot provide and enhancing its image as a community partner.

The community expects to benefit from increased numbers of households with increased savings and stronger credit records. They also expect improved access to credit will lead to more loans that could assist the borrowers with key financial needs and stimulate the local economy at the same time.

However, there is an inherent risk for Bethex, in particular of not achieving breakeven results for this program. The income earned from new deposits will have to cover the cost of the Bethex payments for the services by an increased volume of new deposits that would have not otherwise occurred. The costs are not too great, however, so not achieving break even would not create devastating or dangerous losses for the credit union at the present scale.

The figures below show some of the possibilities for at least break even operations for Bethex with this project. The actual numbers may be very inaccurate, but the methodology may have some use.

Assumptions:

14 stores in the program		
checks cashed, 0 to $600:	1000	cost: $4,500
checks cashed, $601 to $1,000:	500	cost: $2,750
checks cashed, over $1,000:	250	cost: $3,750
withdrawals:	3000	cost: $1,140
deposits:	2000	cost: $2,000
Total cost		$14,140

In this scenario, Bethex would need to take in deposits from new members or existing members who would not have made the deposits without the program. They would earn a spread on them equal to some weighted rate of the returns from spread on investments and the spread on loans. Bethex has a projected 2001 loan to assets ratio of roughly 38%; the credit union charges between 6% and 16.5% on its loans, depending on the type of loan. And it pays 2% on savings and more for CDs. With over $8 million in assets in early 2001 (before the merger with another credit union) and with 8,000 members, the average deposit would be $1,000. However, this would not account for all the outside accounts from nonmembers. Therefore, assume that the average daily account balance per member is $500 and that the new accounts average $250. An average net yield on the loans and investments might be anywhere from 2% to 5% or even higher, depending on the type of loans and investments that were made. Using 3.5% as an average spread, Bethex would need to attract over $400,000 in new deposits, from 1,600 new accounts, just to cover the costs of $14,140, projected above (in addition to these costs, there will also be marketing costs—credit union staff members will have tables in the check cashing stores to try to increase membership—and other costs, but these are not included in this analysis).

If the actual costs were higher due to higher volumes of check cashing and deposit/withdrawal activity, then the amount of new deposits would need to be higher. The converse would also hold true. If the earnings from new deposits could not cover the costs, then Bethex would have to pay those costs out of its net income, which was $7,028 in 1999, but projected to be over $200,000 in 2001 (Bethex usually receives some grant income and the net income projection figure probably includes some grants). Therefore, if these net income projections are accurate, Bethex would be able to cover any losses from the program, on a worst case scenario, from other net income.

However, there would be an opportunity cost; the credit union could use these funds in any number of ways, including increasing its own equity position, increasing salaries, which are presently quite low, etc. On the other hand, if the net new deposits were greater than $400,000, Bethex would generate some net income for other uses, if these assumptions are accurate.

Northside Community Federal Credit Union in Chicago also is working on creating a new business model for providing services to the unbanked and fringe banked. Their also model varies from conventional bank approaches. Commercial banks are very dependent on fee income for their retail operations. In fact, Chicago has been the site of the beginnings of this approach, as First Chicago (now part of Bank One) began charging a $3 teller fee in 1995. It was among the first large banks to try to make its retail services pay for themselves.

However, a community development credit union cannot charge high fees if its clients are mostly low-income people. First, they cannot afford it. Second, they will go to the fringe banking institutions, even if they are more expensive. Therefore, the Credit Union, like other financial institutions trying to serve low-income people, is creating a new approach.

It is centered on low cost operations, very low fees on its financial services and generating break even or slightly better cash flow from its accounts and its loans.

This highlights another difference between conventional business models and one addressing the needs of low-income households. For banks, another benefit operating in a middle or upper income market is the capacity for cross selling. Banks want their customers to use as many of their products as possible—checking and savings accounts, loans, credit cards, etc. While they may not make money on some of these products—such as checking accounts, banks use fees and machines (ATMs, online banking) to generate lower costs with some profit and also have the higher margin products to generate additional profit. This cross selling is much more difficult in a low-income community. Residents have a lower level of funds to put into various types of accounts or utilize additional products, making cross selling less realistic. They also tend to have worse credit, making lending more risky.

Therefore, the economics of the business model used by Northside and other institutions working in low-income areas are difficult. According to the Director of Northside, who came from the commercial banking world, most banks tend to be loosely structured on the "80/20" rule, in which the bank makes little money on 80% of its customers while most of its profit is derived from 20% of its customers. For this Credit Union, there is a much worse ratio—a 90/10 ratio or worse, in which it makes most of its profit from 10% of its members and breaks even or literally loses money on the remaining 90%. This approach nevertheless can result, overall, in breakeven or low profit operations, although the financial viability can be very delicate.

For example, about half of the credit union's accounts have less than $100 and about 75% have less than $250. These accounts are expensive because there may be many withdrawals as well as some deposits, which require time to administer while yielding little spread income, especially if the institution is not charging high fees for these transactions for low balance accounts. High numbers of transactions and low balances create a difficult economic proposition for a financial institution. They are balanced by a few accounts with relatively high balances and few transactions; these accounts generate the necessary income.

This business model has severe drawbacks, especially when the economy is having difficulties that can result in lower deposit levels, lower spreads on accounts as the interest rate environment falls and greater losses that may occur from defaults and collection costs. In difficult economic times, the dividends paid to credit union members also decrease as there are more losses, more draws on the loan loss reserves, and potentially, a reduction in the capital supporting the institution. It can also result in reductions in withdrawals and a slowing in adding new members who want to open new accounts.

Northside's condition reflects some of these characteristics. It has a relatively low level of assets. This is a hindrance as there are fewer economies of scale and less capacity to help its members and to achieve wider impact. The management is very aware of this situation and has targeted growth as one of its major goals.

The profitability is relatively low and needs to be improved. There is also a need for growth in members and assets to better enable the institution to meet the stresses of addressing the financial services needs of low-income households. New members need to be added who can offer more profitable activities (i.e higher, stable accounts and more loans). In addition, some ways to assist the existing members to increase their own personal wealth would help the profitability of the credit union at the same time. Similarly, the level of capital is relatively low (although meeting regulatory requirements) and this could make it more difficult to meet major emergencies. Management is very clear about these needs as well, and is taking steps to address it.

The Northeast Community Federal Credit Union in San Francisco, offers a different approach. Although there are many banks in the neighborhood where the main branch is located, they cater primarily to more affluent customers with higher account balances, who use sophisticated products and higher cost services. Recent immigrants, many small businesses and lower income people were not being served by the commercial banks. The Credit Union targets these households and businesses, and is very accessible to these members, most of whom face economic stratification and a system of low wage jobs (restaurants, curio shops, tourism, garment work, etc.) and industries. Many are forced to work multiple jobs to survive in an area with a very high cost of living and scarce resources. Without access to affordable financial services and capital, this stratification would be perpetuated.

The Credit Union opened its second branch in the Tenderloin neighborhood of San Francisco, a very different situation from the main branch neighborhood. Its goal is to serve very low and low-income people, including recent immigrants and the homeless and near-homeless. In an area with no regulated financial institutions, the Credit Union now offers basic banking services to these populations. Its goals are expansion of these services to more residents, to offer an alternative to the fringe banking institutions and to help members begin to build wealth. There were roughly 450 Credit Union members in this branch in early 2002.

The Credit Union established this branch in the Tenderloin neighborhood of San Francisco, the highest density neighborhood in the city and one whose residents generally have very limited economic means. Most of the area's 30,000 residents are renters (over 90%). The area's population is still growing rapidly as its relatively low housing costs attract recent immigrants and others looking for a new start. Unlike Chinatown, where the main branch is located, there are no regulated financial institutions in the Tenderloin and the banking needs are great. There are many fringe banking institutions that often charge predatory rates and fees. The Tenderloin branch is designed to increase the availability of affordable financial products and lifeline services to the very low-income and low-income members, including homeless and near-homeless people, in the area.

The Credit Union offers a range of financial services at this branch. The savings accounts require a minimum of $25 to open and the member must maintain that minimum balance in order to keep the account open. Northeast has many members who cannot maintain this level and must close their accounts; as a result, the Credit Union often re-opens accounts for many members. There is no charge for opening an account and the cost is $5 for re-opening an account. Dividends (interest) are paid when the account is greater than $100 with daily compounding. Free withdrawals are limited to 5 per month and cost $.50 for each one thereafter. There is a limit of $50 cash withdrawal per day and there is no fee for withdrawals. For amounts over $50, the Northeast writes a check and charges $.50.

There are no checking accounts at this time, but members may obtain a teller's check to pay bills (e.g., rent, utilities, phone, merchants, etc.). There is no cost for the checks up to 5 per month; the Credit Union charges $.50 for each additional check over 5 in a month. The checks are cashed free of charge at the nearby Golden 1 Credit Union (up to $500) and at the Bank of America's Chinatown branch, at which there is no limit on the check amount (some members probably use check cashing outlets to cash these checks).

Northeast does not cash checks the way a check cashing outlet does. There is a hold of seven business days for non-government checks (payroll or private). Government checks are limited to credit union members only and limited to $50 cash withdrawal per day. Direct deposit is available for both government and payroll checks.

Loans are available—personal, auto, business and home loans. A member must maintain a minimum account balance of $100 in order to apply for a loan. There are three types of personal loans. One is called the "Fresh Start" loan. A loan amount up to $3,000 is secured by a deposit and is used for building a positive credit record. The rate is the higher of 2% over the rate paid on the savings account or 7.5%; it has a term of up to two years with simple interest payments.

The second loan is a payday loan alternative. It is called a "Grace" loan and requires membership for at least one year and direct deposit of either a government or payroll check. The maximum loan amount is the lower of 30% of the direct deposit amount or $300. The term is two weeks. The rate is 18%, or $54 if the loan were repaid after one year. However, the loan is due in two weeks, so the interest earnings are $2.04 over two weeks. There is no fee (a $10 fee was disallowed by the regulators). The Credit Union only allows this type of loan to be made a maximum of three times a year for any member.

The third type of loan is a personal loan. It has a one year term with an 18% rate and no fee. This loan is unsecured and is underwritten by Northeast's staff. The other loans are not underwritten in the same way, although there is a somewhat detailed application form. Most of the Credit Union's Tenderloin members do not qualify for the unsecured personal loan. While applications for some of the loans may be taken at the Tenderloin branch, all personal loan applications go through the main branch for approval through the Credit Committee.

The Credit Union uses "branch accounting," a very important mechanism to understand the actual financial conditions occurring in an institution. Northeast generated investment income of $37,479 in 2001, mostly from below market investments in the Credit Union targeted at supporting the Tenderloin branch. These investments, typically CDs, were made by friendly institutions and individuals at below market rates (presently 0 or 1%); investors included other credit unions (e.g., Patelco Credit Union, Chevron CU), PMI Mortgage Insurance Company (which made a $100,000 deposit at zero interest for five years in 2001), other conventional lenders (e.g., Wells Fargo, Bay View Bank, CalFed Bank, First Republic Bank), special community development lenders, CDFI Fund, etc.

Northeast earned $659 from interest income made on loans to Tenderloin members, $1,803 from fees (a large portion of which came from members who re-opened accounts at a cost of $5), and $572 from IDA investment income. The Credit Union also received a grant of $62, 512 from the City's CDBG program (amounting to half of a $50,000 grant from the previous fiscal year and half of a $75,000 grant from the present fiscal year), which will increase to $75,000 in the coming fiscal year. The total income for the Tenderloin branch in 2001 was $103,026.

The operating costs for the Tenderloin branch in 2001, which are based on a low cost model of operating, totaled $122,907. The primary costs were salary and fringes, rent which has been increasing annually since the first two years of free rent, general office expenses (e.g., utilities), travel and losses (see next section). The Credit Union also paid $2,463 in dividends (interest) to the members who held qualifying accounts at the branch. The Credit Union experienced one "grace loan" writeoff and had a total of $3,564 in losses in 2001, mostly due to few bad checks. In addition, this level of costs does not include the overhead borne by the central office for activities such as supervision, accounting and auditing, membership services, reporting, annual reports, insurance, planning, personnel, technology updates and coordination, etc.

The Credit Union lost $22,343 from the direct costs of operating the Tenderloin branch in 2001. This loss amount does not include the overhead costs—and therefore additional losses—resulting from the inability of the branch to generate adequate income to cover these overhead costs borne by the main office. Additionally, the Tenderloin branch had already generated a negative income for the branch of $6,463 through the first two months of 2002 and this figure included a disproportionately high draw of the CDBG funds which will run out after 10.4 months at the present rate. Therefore, this condition would likely increase the present loss level if all other income and expenses continue at the same rate.

The main office generated almost $500,000 in income in 2001 with total expenses of $181,672 (including salaries, fringes, interest payments and loan loss reserves of $25,000) before dividends. It generated net income of $125,110 for the year, after dividends, so the CU was able to handle the negative cash flow at the Tenderloin branch without great difficulty.

The experience of the Northeast Community Federal Credit Union demonstrates that it is very difficult to provide financial services for very low-income and homeless people in general and even more difficult to make these services pay for themselves. There is inadequate income generated to pay for the costs of providing the services. Homeless people cannot be provided these services without extensive subsidy and providing these services for very low-income people will require a great deal of subsidy as well. They have little income so their account levels are low. They use the accounts for liquidity to pay bills and therefore tend to use the accounts frequently, thereby creating more costs for the financial institution.

The members of the Tenderloin branch are mostly (60% to 70%) living on fixed incomes, particularly Social Security, SSI and VA funds that usually include direct deposit accounts, and General Assistance (a city grant for homeless individuals) that does not have direct deposit. About 10% to 20% of the members are homeless or near homeless. The other 20% without government payments are working, but most do not have high incomes or large reserves that can remain in the CU and generate income and they either do not need loans or they are unable to qualify to repay them. Therefore, the members of the Tenderloin branch produce very little income to cover the costs of operations. An expansion in the number of members will not increase the income if the new members bear the same characteristics; in fact, it could make the financial situation worse with more costs and very little new income.

At the same time, the Credit Union uses a very low cost structure to keep the costs down and keep the negative cash flows at reasonable levels. Much of this low cost structure is visible in relatively low salaries, especially for the San Francisco Bay Area.

This approach has not created an immediate problem because the City provides substantial operating support and the main branch generates adequate net income to cover the remaining negative cash flow, at least for the time being. However, this approach is not an ideal long term solution going into the future. The Credit Union needs to build its overall net worth and its reserves to support additional growth and generate a larger cushion to weather any future problems. In addition, the salary structure is very low and could be increased with the cash flow that is being generated. Finally, Northeast must reduce dividend payments to other members in order to support the Tenderloin branch.

The Credit Union is making remarkable decisions and showing commendable dedication to the neighborhoods and households that it works with. However, it may be useful for Northeast to consider trying to develop a more financially feasible, long term solution.

Other Key Business Model Issues

As true with many other CDCUs, all those in the case studies had a relatively low level of assets. This is a hindrance as there are fewer economies of scale for the operations, less capacity to grow and less capacity to help its members and to achieve wider impact.

Most also had a major dependence on friendly depositors to serve as a base for assets and as a growth vehicle. In one case in particular, one depositor had a disproportionate level of deposits that could devastate the credit union if something were to happen to that organization (which has a long history and is in good financial condition at the present time). Here again, the need for growth and reduced depositor concentration can be highlighted.

The lack of income for institutions serving very low-income people is a very large problem, resulting in a low level of profits or even negative cash flow. Increases in the scale and volume of transactions would not impact this profitability scenario, even with great increases in the volume, if the additional transactions were equivalent to existing ones that result in small, frequently used accounts and low loan volume. To achieve better financial performance, a CDCU would need existing and new members to have fewer transactions, leave funds in their accounts for longer time periods, increase their account levels and take out loans. This type of growth would be very helpful in achieving better financial balance.

The costs of opening new branches can be prohibitive for a lightly capitalized institution. Some form of subsidy often would be necessary. However, multiple branches are often needed rather than one new branch, especially in large metropolitan areas with large populations, even if there is high density. Alternatives may be available through smaller storefronts and partnerships, as is being demonstrated by Bethex.

The interest rate environment also has an impact on these conditions. For example, the existing level of below market interest rate investments is producing lower income than it might in a higher interest rate environment—even compared to the rates that existed one or two years ago. With greater income produced by higher rates, a credit union could cover a larger part of the negative cash flow that it now must pay out of its own operations. This assumes that investors would not ask for an increased return in keeping with the increased economic environment; if the requested returns to investors had to be increased, then a credit union would not be able to benefit much from an increased interest rate environment.

The salaries appear to be very low in all the institutions despite their location in relatively high cost areas. This may make it difficult to attract and retain high quality employees, although the present staffing in all of the CDCUs appears to be doing an excellent job in these areas. It may affect the long term capacity and the ability to grow, as noted above. At the same time, all of the CDCUs used a very low cost structure, in general, to keep the costs down and generate some base level of positive cash flow or to keep the negative cash flows at reasonable levels.

The issue of scale is reflected in the range of products that the credit union offers. While all of the case study examples offered a payday loan alternative, only one of the credit unions had achieved any scale with this product. In addition, they may offer only limited check cashing or not offer check cashing at all; and this is another very important feature in addressing the needs of low-income people using fringe banking institutions.

For example, check cashing is not offered at Northside because of the issues associated with security for the cash that would be needed and the subtle changes that would occur between the Credit Union and its members. In part, this is also an issue of scale. The scale issue is also reflected in the credit union's capacity to withstand losses under any of the higher risk financial services programs. For example, although Northside's loss rate of 3% on its payday loan alternative is excellent in many respects, the Credit Union's capitalization structure and overall size can be strained by this level of losses. A larger, more fully capitalized institution may more easily absorb this level of loss. In order to be a fully effective alternative to fringe bankers, an institution needs to be able to offer the full range of financing products needed by its constituents.

A fuller range of financial products is essential in low-income neighborhoods. For example, cash disbursement is a big issue for many financial institutions serving low-income neighborhoods. Due to security reasons, cost issues and the desire to not separate themselves from the people they are trying to serve (by using bullet proof glass and other methods that offer greater security), many community based groups may not be addressing this need. However, their customers/members are then left with no other option than to use the fringe bankers. More review of this issue needs to occur because these are difficult issues. However, the use of ATMs, cash systems in which employees do not handle disbursements of cash (in some cases, a cash dispensing machine is used and only the armored car personnel have access to it), use of debit cards and some of the new multi-function machines (check cashing, depositing, money wiring, etc.) that are being created may help with these issues. Of course, they may create their own new issues—high costs and fear of technology—but there are some approaches to addressing these new issues as well.

To some degree, some of the alternative institutional approaches have avoided competing with the existing framework of financial services institutions and fringe bankers in situations where the fringe banking institutions are unwilling to try to partner with community based organizations and offer more meaningful and less costly services. However, competition may be worth considering, as it has proven effective in some parts of the country in lowering the costs to consumers of many types of financial services.

Entrepreneurship is an important part of the development of the new approaches. The Bethex partnership, for example, is founded on two entrepreneurs who know their customers and their markets. They are able to enter into a partnership with little in the way of traditional business planning because they know the conditions and their organizations extremely well. They know, internally, what they are going to run into and have a very strong sense of what the results can be and what they are looking for. This entrepreneurship, to the extent that it can be clearly identified, should be strongly supported. The other two credit union examples also demonstrated the need for an entrepreneurial approach for creating new visions and implementing them.

Also key is sound business planning. While one of the new efforts was conceived with little business planning and part of the projections for another one was inaccurate, they all had major aspects of planning to support their efforts. This part of the approach is extremely important, but sometimes difficult to fund and to find an appropriate amount of time. However, the need for reasonably accurate market and feasibility analyses is very critical in this field.

There is little experience in the community development field in the area of financial services, making it more important to produce accurate business plans, market studies and the like (of course, this same lack of experience in the field also makes it more difficult to produce appropriate studies, at the same time). In general, this type of community development effort needs to be better funded up front to provide better protection against problems if the projects do not work according to projections. Otherwise, there may be failures in de novo operations or situations where the sponsor does not have adequate resources or commitment to low-income neighborhoods. If there are a few failures, it will make it even more difficult for community based organizations to move into this field in a substantial way.

The existence of "branch accounting," in which the income and expenses of each branch are tracked separately as well as for the combined institution, is essential to understanding the economic viability of the branches and financial services designed to serve low-income people. The Northeast Community FCU, despite its small size, was one of the few institutions to use this approach and it made internal analysis and understanding of the conditions it addressed far easier . . .

Similarly, it is useful to generate this information so that a clearer picture can be presented to the outside world. In the case of Northeast, this information can be used to demonstrate the issues involved in supporting the banking services for very low-income people and, in their case, hopefully to generate more support and financial assistance for their activities. In all cases, this information can give the institution a clear vision of many of the financial issues it needs to address.

Phasing in the financial products, as Northeast has done, also is very appropriate, especially for a smaller financial institution with a relatively low level of resources. It creates moderate growth that allows the organization to control costs, learn the conditions it is facing and the best approaches and products to meet the target population's needs, and to limit risk and exposure. In addition, Northeast began with a limited range of products, a smart choice in an unknown and potentially difficult environment.

However a slower phasing in also limits impact. Some members of the Northeast undoubtedly use some of the check cashing stores as well the credit union's services. And, with 450 members, Northeast is not reaching the large majority of the residents and employees in the neighborhood. A full range of products is needed to reach more people and have a fuller impact on the financial services available in a given area.

A different marketing approach is usually needed with the new programs and approaches. This has been demonstrated in a number of case studies. The traditional approaches to reach out to people and inform them of the new services do not work very well or they do not work at all. However, the more useful methods, such as neighborhood meetings, require more staff time and cost.

Financial literacy training is a program that is necessary and crucial but, like traditional marketing, it has been less effective for many of the institution in the case studies, especially the general, large workshops. One-on-one training is much more effective—and much more costly. This was a fairly consistent result among the site visits.

There are great variations in regulation of the separate components of these financial services throughout the country. The regulatory differences need to be taken into account in any given local context and any national effort needs to fully understand the differences in the state regulatory conditions. Background research and preparation of materials could be another method of assisting these new efforts.

CREDIT UNIONS

Generic Business Model Issues

While CDCUs are organized explicitly to assist low-income households and neighborhoods, traditional credit unions are founded on a membership base that is connected to one or more employers or industry groups in a region. They typically tend to serve moderate and middle-income households. Their branches are often located near the employers and in commercial areas and/or downtowns. Increasingly, these types of credit unions are seeking new charters, which will allow them to seek members throughout a larger geographic region for anyone living or working in that area.

In general, these credit unions are somewhat similar to banks and the business model that they follow. They probably tend to have higher costs than CDCUs (salaries, office space, amenities, equipment, etc.) although probably not as high as many banks where the office space and amenities may receive more emphasis. Credit unions of all types are more dependent on interest rate spreads from lending and the float from deposits for core parts of their revenues and profits. They have less interest in the more traditional fringe banking products such as check cashing, small loans, bill payment and wiring money. Like banks, one key goal of their involvement in providing financial services to low-income households is to "mainstream" as many as possible not only to assist them but also to generate appropriate levels of revenue and profit.

Moreover, they have less experience in understanding the needs of low-income communities and finding ways to address those needs with appropriate financial products. Some of the credit unions that become involved with low-income initiatives may tend to look at their efforts as "giving back."

Nevertheless, credit unions may be more open to this work than banks due to their mission, although a recent study questioned this track record in one metropolitan area. On the other hand, some credit unions are starting to move in this direction. For example Wright-Patt Credit Union, the largest in Ohio ($717 million in assets), which is offering payday loans for $2 to $3, based on achieving an annual rate of 18%. Ed Gallaghy, president of a Tampa credit union, stated that about 100 credit unions in the country are now offering equivalent payday loans (Bohman).

However, this type of credit union probably has to make more adjustments than a Community Development Credit Union to enter this market on any scale. It needs to change its business model and overall approaches. This necessity was recognized in the initial study performed by Sacramento's American River Health Pro Credit Union. The market study for a new branch to be located in a lower income neighborhood indicated that the branch was very necessary due to the lack of any other institutional lender in the area and the prevalence of check cashing outlets and payday lenders, which charged exorbitant rates and hurt the residents economically. The study also indicated that the Credit Union would have a competitive advantage over other institutional lenders but would be competing against check cashing outlets, at least in the beginning. To enter this competition, the study contended that American River Health Pro Credit Union (ARHPCU) would need to modify its business approach. It would need to add services that were needed in that particular community but not otherwise a major part of its other activities or products throughout the rest of the institution. It would need to charge lower fees than its competitors in the market in order to attract new members. And it would need to undertake various approaches to "mainstreaming" new members, which might require additional effort to assist in becoming more financially astute. These and other business model modifications may be keys to the potential success of similar efforts by credit unions in low-income areas in the future.

These business model and corporate culture changes are essential, but they can be difficult. It is probably very important that any credit union entering into this new arena has a reasonably clear picture of what some of those changes needed to be. It is also very important that a credit union enter into this type of venture with goals that match with the local community's goals—in the case of ARHPCU, growth of the Credit Union combined with a desire to assist the neighborhood and meet the long standing credit union industry goals. Finally, it was also important that ARHPCU entered into the venture with a strong partner that is well accepted in the community.

Another key factor is the overall operations of a credit union trying to serve low-income people. The credit union needs to be efficiently operated and generate profit. ARHPCU, St. Mary's Bank and the Wright-Patt Credit Union all meet this criterion. This efficiency allowed them to enter into these efforts, which were supported out of the credit unions' profits. The scale of the institutions also played a role, with sizable profits that would not be greatly threatened by relatively small outlays for the new, programs.

Examples from the Case Studies

The American River HealthPro Credit Union opened a full service branch in partnership with the Greater Sacramento Urban League in a low-income neighborhood (Del Paso Heights) in north Sacramento. The branch was opened as part of a new facility built by the Urban League offering a range of services and programs to the residents. No other financial institution exists in the neighborhood and only the Credit Union responded to requests made by the Urban

League president to all the local financial institutions to open a branch. The area is heavily populated by check cashing outlets and other similar institutions.

The Credit Union desired to be a source of economic opportunity for a revitalizing community and offer community services. The Credit Union clearly embraced the addition of lower income members to its existing base of middle and upper economic base members. In addition, the Credit Union followed its strategic planning goals of increasing its own size in order to be more fully competitive in the region. The lack of other banking institutions in the neighborhood gave the ARHPCU a competitive advantage. However, the new branch would require a change in the business model perspectives followed by the Credit Union in the past due to the need for different products, a phasing in time line for the products and staffing with different training. This was necessary in order to attract new members to be competitive with the check cashing stores.

The present credit union consists of two merged credit unions, the first of which began in 1955. In 1998, this credit union converted from a federal credit union to a state-regulated credit union and dropped "Federal" from its title. The combined credit union served mostly employees of health care workers and employees in aerospace work. In 1998, these two credit unions merged to form the American River HealthPro Credit Union.

In addition, in 2001, the Credit Union obtained a community charter, which allowed it to attract members in a geographic area in addition to the previously targeted employee groups. The credit union now serves employees of the base companies (GenCorp-Aerojet and subsidiaries, and a number of hospitals and health care employers) in Sacramento County and now with its new community charter, any one who lives, works or worships in Sacramento, El Dorado, Placer or Yolo counties. There are now five branches and an additional 19 ATMs located in supermarkets, corporate sponsors and other locations around the four county area. The total number of members is roughly 20,300.

The Credit Union offers a full range of financial services, including savings and checking accounts, a "holiday" savings account, investments (IRAs, CDs, money market accounts), check cashing, money orders, bill payment, credit cards (12.9% APR with no annual fee) and debit cards, ATMs, first mortgages for home purchase and refinancing, home equity loans and home equity lines of credit, mobile home loans, car loans for purchase and leasing (in addition to a program in which the Credit Union negotiates the prices and terms with the dealers and two types of insurance), and motorcycle, boat and RV loans. The Credit Union also has a "Building Block Certificate" account, to help members begin to save with an initial deposit of $100 and minimum monthly deposits of $50 thereafter.

To open a Premier Checking Account, a member needs to deposit $50. This minimum deposit requirement is waived if the member signs up for direct deposit or payroll deduction. There is a monthly fee of $3, which is waived if the minimum monthly direct deposit is $500 or if the minimum balance is $500. The account can also have overdraft protection (the returned check fee is $15) and it also has no costs for checks or the debit card.

ARHCU has made a special effort to offer check cashing for its members at the new branch. Check cashing for members requires a $5 set up fee and the member is charged 1.5% of the face amount of a government or payroll check. Returned check fee charges were $15. Money orders cost $2. ATM cards cost $2 to issue, but the fee is waived for members with a checking or savings account. There are no charges for making ATM deposits or withdrawals or for point of sale transactions using the debit cards. The checking account charges $3 per month, which is waived under the conditions noted above. If the combined balances on all accounts fall below $100, there is a monthly fee of $5. Automobile loans ranged from 6.74% to 17% in March 2002, depending on type of car loan (new or used car), age of the car and risk of the borrower.

Another traditional credit union uses an entirely different approach in Manchester, New Hampshire. St. Mary's Bank was started in 1908 and is the oldest credit union in the United States. The CU has three branches and is opening a fourth. It provides the full range of financial services for its members, which totaled 61,490 at the end of 2001. Its main lending areas have been real estate mortgages and automobile loans. The total assets were $416,097,439 on December 31, 2001, increasing 39% over the preceding four years.

The Credit Union had wanted to establish ." . . broad, permanent initiatives to serve low-income and minority families" in the community. The Credit Union believes that ." . . credit unions have the responsibility to exemplify the philosophy of community service; we need to be bold enough to live up to our motto with tangible and effective community programs. It is not only our legacy, but may also be a key to our future."

Stemming from these concepts, St. Mary's Bank created a community development program to reach the underserved in their community. They developed an initial set of community outreach programs for which they committed $1 million per year for ten years. The programs were the following:

- **Family Emergency Loans.** The CU makes loans up to $500 available for emergency assistance to low-income families, usually with bad credit or who are unemployed, for utilities/fuel; emergency heating/home repair; medical/dental care; transportation; utility/rent deposits; and community disaster relief. They allocated $10,000 in 1996 (which comprised the pilot program), $30,000 in 1997, $50,000 in 1998 and 1999, and $25,000 in 2000, 2001 and 2002. These funds assisted 25 families in the first year and 65 families in the second year. In the other years, the CU was able to assist between 41 and 65 families, typically using all or most of the allocation. In total, the program has assisted 309 families with $140,814 in loans, with an average loan size of $456 (these loans could be considered to be an alternative to payday loans, in some ways, although this was not the intent of the CU when the program was initiated).

- **Home Ownership Loan Program.** The CU made a $600,000 line of credit loan to the local Neighborhood Housing Services office for short term purchase, rehab and resale to low-income, first time homebuyers. The permanent financing is then provided by bond financing or the secondary market created by the NHS and repays the line of credit interim financing. In addition, the CU was involved in a $3 million pool for second mortgages for first time homebuyers to assist with down payments; the CU committed $1.25 million to the total pool amount. The pool loans are made at market and below market rates. They are secured by second mortgages on the homes.

- **Low-income Rental Housing loans.** The CU makes loans to local non-profit housing developers to be used for the development of low-income rental housing, transitional housing or other housing issues such as lead paint abatement. The CU allocated $150,000 for this purpose in 2002.

- **Economic and Community Development loans.** The CU makes loans to nonprofits to support their lending to small businesses and minority entrepreneurs. The loans are geared to businesses that assist entrepreneurs, create jobs, or provide city renovations and improvements. A total of $65,000 was allocated for this purpose in 2002.

- **Grants.** The CU makes cash grants to nonprofits for the activities that support St. Mary's community outreach programs and/or support the community. 1% of the total annual program allocation (or $10,000) is used for this purpose annually. A total of $53,800 in grants had been made through 2001.

- **Individual Development Accounts.** The CU became the first financial institution in the state to offer IDAs. The program is designed to match up to 50% of savings for a family with a maximum of $500 per family, after completion of a financial training program. As of March 2000, the CU had 29 accounts totaling $9,500. Three of the nonprofit partners are assisting in training for the account holders.

• **Jumpstart Coalition for Personal Financial Literacy.** This is a state program that evaluates the financial literacy of young adults; encourages the development of financial literacy standards for the schools; and promotes the teaching of personal finance.

The results of the program showed a total of $3,729,885 in "funds closed" from 1997 through 2001 out of a total of $6,350,000 committed.

St. Mary's Bank now has a desire to make the program a permanent part of the Credit Union structure. However, it may be possible to go further in these efforts. The Credit Union has somewhat of a "giving back" approach with its programs. In addition to this approach, it may be useful to consider additional concepts—in particular, ways to further incorporate the programs into the St. Mary's regular market activities.

For example, the CU could consider whether it would be possible to make the Family Emergency Loan program, or some part of it, into a regular Credit Union program. It could tighten up the guidelines for some portion of the funds, increase the rate and tie the program to financial management training in an effort to "mainstream" those families who could be identified as having strong prospects for and interest in greater financial participation. Similarly, many lenders have moved in to community lending directly after seeing the success of nonprofits in these fields; the Credit Union may find that there will be some situations where it could become more directly involved in the community development lending process, if needed.

Clearly, an organization with this type of program needs to be profitable. The Credit Union has been able to offer these programs because its own core financial services have been operated in an efficient manner. St. Mary's has control over its costs, while still keeping its fees low and charging reasonable rates on its loans—likely reasons for gaining acceptance from members for the program. This is an excellent combination while still generating strong net income, which allowed the Credit Union to start its large program for the underserved. Some of the efficiency of the CU operations may also be attributable to its scale. At its present size, it is able to generate net income that in turn allows the CU to undertake a program to help low-income people at a fairly large relative scale. The American River HealthPro Credit Union has similar operating characteristics and profit that allow its programs to move forward.

In addition, St. Mary's normal programs have reasonable fees and structures that allow some of the program participants to move into using the Credit Union's financial services and allow other low-income households the opportunity to join the financial mainstream. The checking and savings accounts are relatively low cost and available. The car loans and personal loans are available at excellent rates and offer options for qualifying low-income households. The present lending systems for automobiles, furniture and personal loans need alternatives and models. This Credit Union, as well as most others, offers an excellent model.

Other Key Business Model Issues

The long term financial viability of new approaches instituted by credit unions needs to be carefully ascertained. Different approaches are possible. Credit unions may undertake basically philanthropic approaches or try new efforts aimed at creating large scale new programs for low-income households, but the long term impacts on the institutions need to be carefully considered. In all cases, efforts could be undertaken to mainstream products and customers so that they become essential parts of the financial institutions' long term efforts.

As such, adequate planning needs to be part of the programs. Financial feasibility needs to be studied and methods adopted to assure financial strength over the long term. Programs targeted at low-income people may not make as much profit as programs for middle and upper income people, but they should not represent large losses for the institutions either. If losses are part of the programs, these efforts are likely to be cut in difficult economic times.

Besides appropriate business planning to create sound financial foundations for new efforts, tracking the results of the programs is also important. For example, branch accounting for new branches would be extremely important. Likewise, tracking the costs and revenues of individual programs would be equally important. Lack of these tracking mechanisms prevents a fuller understanding of the economic results of a program or a branch.

An established credit union probably has a very good internal, gut-level sense of what is required, but operations in low-income neighborhoods may be very different from their other programs and branches. Therefore, tracking of branches and programs could be critical to managing these types of programs.

Similarly, financial institutions could track the people who are "mainstreamed" through the programs. This information would be very helpful in understanding when profitability can be reached and which programmatic efforts contribute most to profitability, which would help in selling the program internally if there are any doubts and in discussing the needs externally with funders, if subsidy is needed, and with other institutions to help encourage their participation.

This issue is borne out by the types of transactions that occur in lower income neighborhoods, where the members may keep lower sized accounts, utilize the accounts for more frequent transactions (due to the lack of reserves and household liquidity needs) and lower borrowing capacity. This type of a program requires careful monitoring of the branch's activities in order to achieve break even or profitable operations.

A credit union may encounter some minor conflict with some of its regular policies if it needs to tailor some of its programs more appropriately for low-income people. For example, there may be a need to lower or eliminate some of the fees for minimum balances and/or lower other fees to be more affordable to its target customers. This could create conflicts with its other customers unless there is complete understanding and support from them.

A credit union may find it useful to add other products in order to reach low-income people. For example, a payday loan alternative may be very useful to people in the neighborhood. Money wiring may be another useful product to consider. Credit unions may be an excellent vehicle for the Volunteer Income Tax Assistance program in combination with direct deposit of EITC into credit union accounts. This programmatic approach could be mutually beneficial to both low-income households and creating more economically viable programs for the institution.

St. Mary's Bank made a remarkable commitment. It is using 25% of its profit in 2001 (almost 28% when the program began in 1997) to support their programs. This is a high level of commitment motivated by leadership that wants to help others (not by a desire to achieve a better score with regulators). This commitment not only affects the institution, which passes up an opportunity to strengthen its own capital base; it also affects the members, who, in effect, may forgo higher dividends and/or pay higher fees and rates to make this program possible. However, the program apparently enjoys wide support among members, as well as employees and the community at large. This experience demonstrates that a commitment can be made by all involved and successfully find ways to assist low-income people. It also demonstrates the critical importance of support and vision from the leadership of an institution.

In St. Mary's case, the commitment started with the desire and commitment from the leadership of the organization in its staff and board. The commitment was further strengthened by charging the administration of the program to the Chief Administrative Officer. The program is supported by many elements of the larger community, including its many partners. Moreover, internally, the program involves many staff from all parts of the institution. The program was created in a manner that is based on support from all parts of the affected communities and institutions. This extensive "buy in" from wide sectors of the community and the institution itself is critical to the program's success.

St. Mary's commitment was also long term—ten years, a very long time period for this type of program. However, the length of the term, in addition to the size and the commitment from the organization's leadership, are key elements of the program and its success. If the long term perspective had not been part of the approach, the Family Emergency Loan program could have easily been eliminated when the initial large losses occurred. Instead, the program was revised and continued. Similarly, the programs took awhile to become effective. The volume of activity was relatively low in the first three years and did not begin to approach the committed levels until the fourth year, while greatly surpassing the target level in the fifth year. A lesser level of commitment could have resulted in cutbacks and/or large changes to the program before the programs had the opportunity to start up, undergo modifications, gain acceptance and reach maturity.

As shown by St. Mary's and ARHCU, credit unions are in a potentially excellent position to become more active in low-income neighborhoods and replace some of the more problematic predatory lenders operating there. The normal programs of most credit unions have reasonable fees and structures that could allow many low-income people to move into using these financial services and to join the financial mainstream. Credit unions generally have checking and savings accounts that are relatively low cost and available. The car loans and personal loans are available at excellent rates—especially in comparison to rent-to-own stores, payday lenders, consumer finance companies, automobile companies, etc.—and offer options for qualifying low-income households. The present lending systems for automobiles, furniture and personal loans need alternatives and models. A credit union offers an excellent opportunity to replace the problematic lenders. Moreover, this approach offers institutions greater opportunity to achieve financial viability because lending and deposits offer the best vehicles to profitability and can help balance the low margins from less financially viable programs.

To accomplish this goal, credit unions will have to reach outside of their traditional membership. In the past, credit unions have been available to members with "common bonds," such as employees of a particular company or industry. This has been changing, as the ARHCU's changed membership status attests. The SSA credit union in Baltimore (discussed below) also changed its designation. The federal regulating body for credit unions, National Credit Union Administration, recently proposed rules changes that would allow much more liberal definitions of who members could be. The rules would allow members to be defined as by trades, professions and industries as well as geographically defined communities such as cities and counties (Crenshaw). Credit unions need to take advantage of the existing (and possibly new) regulations to extend their membership to low-income neighborhoods.

To work in this market, it is essential to recognize the importance of initial planning. For example, ARHCU's initial plan set the tone for the institution as a whole and showed the staff some of the issues that would need to be addressed and some of the changes that they would need to make. The plan was probably strongest in considering the issues associated with the build out of the facility and the importance of careful planning and coordination of new products. The weakest part of the plan was the lack of any real financial analysis. The Credit Union management probably had a good internal sense of the costs and revenues, but it would have been useful to make some projections of different possible scenarios.

However, some parts of the plan were not used fully as a guide for the creation of the new programs. For example, the plan proposed a phase in concept with limited financial services in the beginning. Instead, the branch opened as a full service branch, although some additional programs may be placed in service later as experience dictates. In at least one other case study, the initial plan was inaccurate or not followed.

This demonstrates the difficulty of creating a plan that anticipates all of the main issues and approaches that are needed in this type of program while laying out a platform for the organization to follow. It also demonstrates the need for flexibility on the part of the institution, the management and the employees. Changes will almost certainly occur that will be determined by the local needs in the community. The staffing and management will need to be open, flexible and responsive to these requirements from the very beginning of the program concept through the entire planning cycle and throughout the entire time of operations, although the initial implementation period (the first one to three years) may be the most crucial.

This issue of "institutionalization" is also crucial. Where there is a long term commitment and/or where an organization enters into a new program with an open attitude about the future, the program founders eventually will need to address the future of the efforts. In the case of St. Mary's, for example, the program could remain as it is now—basically an important, but less critical part of the overall approach to financial services. Or, it could begin to deepen its functions within the organization. St. Mary's has recognized the need for permanent staffing for the program and is thereby acknowledging their intent to incorporate the program more completely into the organization and to take important steps to make that a reality. This should ultimately make the program stronger and even more permanent and capable of addressing further issues and the creation of additional programs meeting other needs.

These credit unions may also need to find other ways to market to the people in the neighborhoods. Other institutions have uncovered the same situation—that traditional marketing may not effectively reach low-income households—and have focused on different marketing methods that have proven successful.

Location typically plays a key role in the success of check cashing outlets. They are usually in high density areas with a lot of foot traffic. Credit union locations may not be very practical options for serving low-income neighborhoods due to their locations. American River HealthPro Credit Union took a huge step and substantial commitment in recognizing this issue when it opened its new branch. However, it is located in an area with low foot traffic and poor parking opportunities. To address this problem, they are negotiating with the owner of a parcel next to the branch to use the land for parking. This would assist members' ability to conveniently use the branch.

Most credit unions (and banks as well) are closed in the evening and most of the weekends when most check cashing outlets are open. To compete with them, credit unions may need to adjust its hours.

It is important to determine which technologies will be used by low-income members of the credit unions and if there is a need for any additional training in their use. Most observers as well as bankers of all types tend to agree that an important part of this approach could be increased emphasis on training in financial management, budgeting, etc. However, as others have also learned, some credit unions have also realized that financial literacy and management training tends not work as well with large classes, which are often not well attended. To address this issue, for example, St. Mary's tied the training to programs—IDAs and home ownership, as well as to assisting an existing, successful training program in the schools.

Flexibility in conceptualization and implementation of new programs are also essential. St. Mary's was particularly flexible in its program implementation. When an approach did not work, it changed the approach. This was the case with the Family Emergency Loan program, which initially experienced heavy losses. Now, it is operating within acceptable limits and will continue to assist people facing difficult times rather than being eliminated.

In addition, the structure of the guidelines, which are very general, and the charge and makeup of the committee, which has extensive autonomy, contribute to this flexibility and make the program's operations fit the Credit Union's overall approach. This was an area that St. Mary's did not have extensive experience in prior to start up, so the flexibility was an essential element of the program structure. The challenge will be retaining the flexibility as the program grows and becomes institutionalized.

Finally, it is important to review the importance of mission as it concerns banks and credit unions. The issue was discussed in an article describing presentations made to a conference of bankers and some credit unions. "For credit unions, who like to refer to poor people as 'underserved,' the motivation for serving them is to fulfill their mission and to do the right thing, and the revenues that are generated are used to cover the costs and keep other members from subsidizing them. For the banks, which refer to poor people as the 'unbanked,' the motivation is profit, period." (Diekman)

NONPROFIT ORGANIZATIONS

Generic Business Model Issues. For the most part, nonprofit organizations have not been heavily involved in providing financial services to low-income people. While they have been involved in monitoring fringe banking institutions and urging conventional lenders to become more involved, few have been direct participants in providing financial services, other than providing financial literacy training.

However, that may be changing as more nonprofits are becoming aware of the large problems created by fringe banking institutions and as alternative approaches are developed. The Aspen Institute, for example, has been operating a program with support from the Annie E. Casey Foundation that works with local community based organizations to review local conditions and develop some solutions.

To be successful as a nonprofit, especially if homeless and very low-income people are being served, there must be very tight controls on costs. As was shown by the CDCU examples and will be illustrated below, this factor is absolutely essential. Nevertheless, there likely will be a large revenue gap that will need to be covered each year. This grant support is very difficult to obtain. The same problem exists with financial services in general, but the situation is even worse for programs assisting very low-income and homeless people. Funders—both public and private—do not seem to be able to support this issue on any scale at this time.

Even more than financial services for low-income people, financial services for the homeless require subsidy. While other financial services for low-income households may not need much, if any, subsidy, other than initial capitalization, the need to subsidize financial services for the homeless and the near-homeless is essential if some homeless people are to work their way out of this condition.

Therefore, as with financial services for low-income people, there is a need for a low cost structure approach when providing financial services for homeless people.

Financial services for homeless people also need partnerships and assistance from a wide range of parties.

Banks may be able to help create branding for themselves with homeless people as well as the general public interested in working with institutions that are assisting with social problems.

Technology plays a very important role in improving financial service delivery. It can help an organization to become much more efficient and reach greater scale than otherwise possible. Technology can be tailored to fit well with a low cost structure, allowing greater productivity with existing staffing. It can also increase the security for the employees. And it can be structured in a way that is not problematic for the clients. It can offer a good balance in assisting an institution in providing the services without being a problem for the users of the services.

Examples

One of the organizations that are newly interested in financial services is the Operation Reach Out-Southwest, OROSOW, in Baltimore. This community organization saw the problems created for its residents, many of them elderly, by the local fringe banking institutions. They embarked on a process which lead them to review a range of alternatives from buying and operating their own check cashing store to partnering with a local check cashing company that would agree to less onerous financial terms for its products. Neighborhood residents were fully involved in this process.

The SSA National Credit Union recently announced that it would open its first "Neighborhood Contact Office" in the west side neighborhood in addition to its existing 6 branches. The $240 million asset credit union successfully applied to expand its service area to include "underserved areas." The Credit Union will make loans, savings plans and a free checking account without a minimum balance available to new customers. (Baltimore Business Journal; Davis). The CU opened a joint office, called Our Money Place, with A&B Check Cashing in a shopping center. The Credit Union will offer loans, checking and savings accounts and ATM cards while the check casher will offer check cashing, bill payment and money orders. Financial literacy training will be provided by community groups. This will represent a place where all financial services can be obtained in one location.

Also in Maryland, several banks and thrifts pooled $1,000 each to set up a loan fund to offer loans to low-income households for emergency needs. The maximum loan amount is $300 and is available through two community centers. The loans are repaid with monthly payments of $25 and there is no interest rate charged (Sherblom).

Operation Hope in Los Angeles was a partner with Union Bank of California when it purchased Nix Check Cashing in 2000. Operation Hope has three Banking Centers and holds financial literacy classes, offers computer training and houses a Cash & Save branch in one of its locations. Operation Hope recently announced the sale of two of its counseling locations to conventional lenders, which will create full service branches in these locations (Robinson-Jacobs).

Also in Los Angeles, the Skid Row Housing Trust, which works in a very poor area adjacent to the downtown that is home to large numbers of homeless and near homeless people, developed a proposal to assist its employees and residents and then, if successful, other residents and employees in the neighborhood. The proposed program would assess the financial services needs, assess the availability of existing financial services in the neighborhood, and then take steps to address the issues, such as creating financial literacy programs, creating partnerships with institutions like credit unions to bring new resources into the area and create new savings efforts.

Compass Center Bank (which is not a bank despite its name) in Seattle is a nonprofit homeless service provider and shelter, also provides banking services for homeless individuals and other individuals receiving federal payments and who are deemed to require a third party to administer their financial affairs. The Commerce Bank of Washington (the "Bank") supports the Center extensively in this program.

The Center's overall goal is to restore independence to homeless people and break the cycle of homelessness. The Lutheran Church originally founded the Center. The Center is now a separate nonprofit entity loosely affiliated with the Church. In addition to the banking services, the Center provides a wide range of services including an 88-bed shelter for men (currently awaiting repair after the 2001 earthquake), a 40-bed facility for women, transitional housing through 7 homes and a facility for 32 women, free meals (over 110,000 free meals annually), hygiene and laundry facilities, case management and counseling services, information and referral services and mail

Homeless people have even more difficulty finding banking services than low-income people with jobs or government support and housing. They have very low balances that involve frequent transactions and they cannot pay high fees for the services. In addition, many conventional institutions would prefer to keep homeless people out of their lobbies, making it difficult for them to obtain financial services.

The Center wants to offer banking services to help homeless people for many reasons: to help them from being robbed and losing their funds; to help them manage their funds so that they can stretch them as far as possible and utilize them as efficiently as possible; to help those that desire and are able to move out of homelessness with banking services and, at some point, savings as a main part of the support in this process.

The Center states that its original goals (some have already been achieved) for the program include 1) increasing the number of banking accounts up to 600, 2) addressing the federally mandated switch to electronic payments, 3) offering rapid and accurate access to case history, rent and account information, 4) increasing the safety and security issues in handling cash, 5) more adequately providing audit trails and account security, 6) freeing up staff time (up to one FTE) from paper intensive duties required under the old manual system, and 7) delivering improved and more comprehensive services to the homeless.

The Center began offering banking services—acting as a depository—to loggers and fishermen in the early 1900s. The program evolved to assisting homeless people, probably during the early 1980s. The Center offered a low level of banking services for many years. However, all the functions were manual, and all the transactions were done through cash drawers in the office. This limited the efficiency and reach of the program. This method also created issues of security and safety for the staff. In addition, in the late 1990s, the federal government was requiring a movement to Electronic Transfer Accounts (ETA) for all of its support checks. If the Center had not been able to modernize its systems, it would have lost the capacity to offer the existing banking services that it had been offering for so long (ironically, the government later dropped the ETA requirements as banks were not interested in the program due to the lack of fees and other income that would have paid for the costs associated with the program. This is the same problem that the Center is facing).

The Commerce Bank of Washington, through its Managing Director of Administration, became interested in the Center in 1997 when it participated in a "Christmas in April" event. With extensive in-kind and technical assistance from the Bank and funding from several other lenders, the Center developed a computerized system in 1999 that allowed daily internal statements and statements for each account holder, electronic transfers including direct deposits, tracking and corrections, and accounting—all done by machines instead of laboriously by hand. The program required about six months to conceive and begin functioning, including working through various legal and regulatory issues.

The Center has two parts to its banking program. First, it has banking services for homeless people. Most of the Center's clients receive government transfer payments from agencies such as the Veterans' Administration, Social

Security and the Department of Health and Social Services. The Center provides direct deposit capacity for electronic transfers. It also provides check cashing services for government checks that are not wired directly to accounts. It does not cash personal checks. The Center also provides savings accounts through Commerce Bank; withdrawals and deposits are not limited, although there is only one withdrawal allowed per day. And the Center also provides financial planning, budgeting and credit counseling, usually one-on-one.

Second, the Center offers Representative Payee Services for people receiving government support but who are disabled in some way and therefore in need of third party assistance to administer their finances. The Center provides extensive assistance to these individuals—preparation of a monthly budget; paying bills by writing checks on payee accounts; and monitoring mental and physical health, level of sobriety, diet and hygiene. With this assistance, most of the representative payee clients are able to obtain housing.

The Center provides check cashing services at roughly 2% of the face amount of the check with a cap of $15 (compared to 3% or more with no cap in the local check cashing outlets) for government checks (but not personal checks). Direct deposits are free of charge and the counseling is also free of charge. The savings accounts do not pay any interest. There is no charge for deposits or withdrawals and there is no minimum balance requirement. The accounts can stay inactive for up to two years so that people have a safe place to keep their funds while they are transient. The clients under the Representative Payee Services program pay $27 per month, far below the actual costs incurred.

The level of the savings accounts varies depending on the time of the month. In the beginning of the month, when the government checks arrive, the deposit level reaches well over $300,000; during other times of the month, the level of deposits may fall to a little over $200,000. Most of the Center's clients receive monthly checks of $500 or less. However, there are a few accounts with a substantial amount of funds due to workers' compensation settlements, SSI payments or tribal payments.

The Center estimates that it handles about 1,200 transactions per month, including deposits, withdrawals, plus writing up to four or five monthly checks for each Representative Payee account (the post office charges $.90 cents for a money order and the check cashing outlets tend to charge about $2.00).

By shifting to an automated system, the Center increased the number of its accounts from roughly 300 to about 730. Of these, 130 are part of the Representative Payee Services and about 600 are banking accounts. The system has the capacity to handle many more accounts. The main obstacle is lack of income to pay the additional staffing and other costs needed to administer the additional accounts, as the fees and other income do not cover the costs. The available sources of subsidy to pay for these costs are limited.

In addition, the Center does not want to increase the scale of operations for two other reasons. The Center does not want to draw more homeless people into the neighborhood for banking purposes in order to lower the potential for conflict with local businesses in the neighborhood. Second, the Center does not want to compete with the check cashing companies. It is concerned that it does not become "too good" at these services and, therefore, voluntarily restricts the number of clients that it serves.

The Center does not break down its revenues or expenses for the division—called Client Services Office (CSO), which includes the banking program (homeless banking and representative payee services), mail receipt program and information and referral program. Therefore, several of the social services are lumped together when considering the budget for this part of the Center's activities—information and referral, mail receipt and holding, and the counseling—in addition to the representative payee and banking programs. All of these programs are administered at the main office near downtown. However, there are some clear revenues earmarked for just the banking program. The Center earns some small spread on the accounts through a sweep account to a money market account, totaling about $3,100 in 2001. There are some local government contracts/grants totaling a little over $57,000 in 2001 that were mostly targeted to the costs of the representative payee program. The fees charged to the clients under the representative payee program generated about $58,000 in 2001.

The 2001 budget for the entire organization was almost $2.6 million. The budget for the CSO—social services/counseling/representative payee/banking program—was $243,150 in 2001. These expenses are very low. For example, staffing costs/fringes, budgeted at over $218,000 in 2001, are low due to donated services and the low wages—starting salaries are $12 per hour with relatively small annual increases. There are five and one half FTE employees for the CSO activity, social workers, who rotate their work on the bank windows. The banking activities require 4 FTE's of the total in the program; however, the representative payee program includes extensive services that are not really part of the banking program even though the staff is nominally listed as "banking" program staff.

The overall program has about $243,000 in costs with about $114,000 in earned income. The remaining revenue gap of $130,000 must be raised through grants, with some relatively small portion of that amount ($20,000 in 2001) coming from targeted grants from local banks to support the banking operations.

The Center operates its banking programs very tightly—there are very low expenses. Nevertheless, there is a large revenue gap that needs to be covered each year. It is very difficult for the Center to obtain the needed grant support. The same problem exists with financial services in general, but the situation is even worse for programs assisting homeless people. Funders—both public and private—do not seem to understand this issue in any scale yet.

OTHER INSTITUTIONS

Other institutions are competing with banks for their customers. Brokerage firms are now offering free checking and higher interest rates to lure higher income customers away from banks (Coleman and Higgins). Others are also entering the field to compete for lower and middle income customers, in demonstration efforts at present, with the potential for major expansion very shortly. For example, Wal-Mart, with the world's largest net sales of $217.8 billion in 2001, is now offering check cashing, money orders, money transfers and bill payment services in some of its U.S. stores. It has tried to offer its own banking services through an agreement with Toronto-Dominion but was rejected by U.S. regulators. Wal-Mart is now attempting another tactic to offer banking services, applying to buy a small California bank and works with other banks in some of its other stores. The company has been running up against laws regulating the combination of finance and retailing in these efforts. Part of this effort may stem from the desire to recoup fees for debit card transactions now paid to credit card companies (De Paula; Blackwell and Kingson). Another motivation probably stems from the desire to enter into what the company sees as a very lucrative business, enabled by its vast existing network of stores and the wide range of customers.

Other companies are involved as well. Many major grocery chains have entered the field, although several Hy-Vee stores in Des Moines recently announce it is no longer cashing checks, due to the high number of bad checks (Ryberg). Safeway leases space to Wells Fargo in 450 stores and operates its own "private label" bank—Safeway Selects Bank—in 167 stores in six states. The Bank is operated under contract by a subsidiary of the Canadian Imperial Bank of Commerce and its operations are under review at the moment (Pender).

The 7-Eleven chain introduced machines that provide ATM services, cash checks and offer wiring and money orders on a demonstration basis in some of their stores. They are now planning to roll out the services on a national basis (De Paula). The machines, or in-store kiosks called Vcoms manufactured by NCR, will offer telecommunication services through Verizon, e-shopping for

152

movie tickets, flower orders and state fishing licenses, and information services (travel directions, weather reports, lottery results) in addition to check cashing, wring money, obtaining money orders, paying bills and conducting ATM transactions.

After testing the machines in 100 locations, 7-Eleven had planned to place them in 1000 stores approximately by the end of 2002 and place 5,800 of them by the end of 2004. This schedule has been slowed, but the rollout continues. 7-Eleven processed 110 million ATM transactions in 2001 and needs only 10% of its customers to use the machines to break even from the fees and advertising charges. The company already sells about $4.5 billion in money orders annually. The company has 5,800 stores in the U.S. and Canada and has close to $10 billion in sales ($31 billion worldwide—Koenig; PR Newswire). However, glitches (placement in the wrong stores, inadequate marketing, low volumes and resulting high fraud rates, etc.) have contributed to a slower roll-out schedule (Breitkopf). But the company still maintains solid expectations for the use and growth of the machines and its entry into this field.

The Company's goal is to become the main alternative to check cashing companies, the brand of choice for the unbanked. According to Jay Giesen, the VP in charge of the Vcom project, "There is no brand out there that stands for reliable service. That is the positioning we are looking for—a national brand for the 'unbanked'" (Kuykendall). 7-Eleven has been working on the delivery of financial services to walk-in customers for 10 years. They stated with manned service centers; they then moved to automating a narrow mini-bank. The Vcom represents the final step. Mr. Giesen, who came from Western Union and Citibank, has created partnerships with First Data Corporation for money wiring. He is talking with banks about partnerships to accounts, loans and credit cards.

Other institutions are setting up their own banking efforts, although not necessarily connected to providing financial services to low-income households. For example, BMW, Volkswagon, Nordstrom's, Federated Department Stores (owners of Macy's), Drexel University and DePaul University are all opening, or planning to open, banks (Gogoi).

As a side note, it is clear that there are large profits in various parts of this business. The banks have been discussed in this Chapter, along with Wal-Mart, 7-Eleven and the major grocery chains. Also heavily involved are large companies such as First Data Corporation (which owns Western Union), American Express, credit card companies and large manufacturers of new machinery, such as Diebold and NCR. There are further discussion of the impacts of large corporations and connections to the capital markets and stock exchanges in Chapter 4 as well as other sections.

REQUIREMENTS FOR BUSINESS MODELS
IN FINANCIAL SERVICES

There are many obvious issues for creating a successful program to meet the needs of low-income people for financial services while building an economically viable institution that offers better terms than fringe banking institutions. These requirements will vary depending on the type of institution, the particular history of the institution, the target population, geographic location, existence of fringe bankers in the immediate vicinity and the types and costs of the services they offer, etc.

Nevertheless, certain guidelines for these needs are clear.

- Clear definition of the actual model and the guidelines for achieving financial feasibility.
- Clear understanding of the specific target market. It is crucial to have a strong understanding of the local market for financial services. There are many different markets in many neighborhoods—different immigrant groups of many kinds with different interests and goals, individuals, families, seniors, working poor, people with government assistance or social security, etc. Each of these markets tends to relate to financial service needs differently. To successfully address these needs, an institution needs to understand these differences. This is not easily accomplished. Generally, it requires some funding support to obtain this market data—through focus groups, surveys, interviews, market studies, etc.—in order to support the appropriate product design.
- Careful design of new products that both meet the needs of the target populations and fit within the institution's capacities.
- Emphasis on particular, key financial product needs. For example, viable options to payday loans must be developed. There is a major effort throughout the country at present to eliminate or restrict these loans. This effort is very appropriate. However, if payday loans were to end or be rendered ineffective, many borrowers could be forced to find other lenders who could be even worse. Therefore, it is very important to develop viable alternatives.
- Alternative loan products for larger, longer term loans often used for buying automobiles, furniture, computers and other high cost items.
- Reducing the charges for most of the financial services of most fringe banking institutions.
- Achieving scale for new options. Pay day lenders, for example, and other fringe banking institutions and products have spread with remarkable

speed across the country. Therefore, it is equally important to not only develop payday loan alternatives but also to find ways to achieve scale in these efforts. Moreover, it is also important to find ways to make them more accessible to a wider range of people. Credit unions, for example, tend to lend only to their members (and cash checks, usually, only for their members). The check cashing outlets accommodate everyone. Similarly, the check cashing stores have many more branches convenient to their customers and they are open for much longer hours and on the weekends as well. To compete on a larger scale and meet these financial needs, the alternative lending institutions will have to find ways to expand their coverage, locations and hours.

- Access to capital markets. Affordable access is one of the keys to being able to achieve scale.

- Using competition in key markets. Competition, which has proven to effectively reduce the prices of some financial services in some markets, should be one method used to bring changes to the industry. Strategic locations and programs with appropriate pricing may achieve changes in fringe banking institutions through an appropriate level of competition.

- Alternatives need to be developed for people who do not want to join credit unions or other institutions or who do not have access to credit unions or other institutions.

- Offering adequate banking services for the homeless and near homeless. If these services can be provided, they can help stabilize individual conditions and create some incentive to move back into the "mainstream" for some. This also will benefit financial institutions with more stable income for their products.

- Use of new technology. The rapid advancement of technology (discussed later in this report) has opened up the possibilities of reaching many more low-income people in a cost effective manner. However, the use of new technologies faces obstacles in acceptance and methods need to be developed to overcome this resistance.

- Use of advance planning, business plans, financial feasibility projections. Evaluation of each effort is also important once they are operating.

- Allowing adequate time to determine the effectiveness of new programs before making changes or abandoning the efforts. These new strategies can require a long time period to become effective. There is a need to develop a clientele that is committed to the institution that is of sufficient scale to support the program. The growth cannot always be accomplished too quickly, as the experience of UBOC's Cash and Save, which only recently became profitable, demonstrates. All successful approaches will have trade offs that will be part of the structure that need to be addressed. It is also important to give time for new approaches to evolve. It also takes time to help low-income people who may be unused to the banking system to transition into "mainstream" banking. Among other things, it requires an immense time commitment to attend community functions and to provide one-on-one training.

- Support, leadership and vision from the top levels of the organization.
- Creativity, flexibility and openness to develop special approaches. These are essential in working with low-income and immigrant communities. Especially in situations where the residents have mistrust of conventional institutions, where language barriers exist and, in some cases where people are undocumented, the successful startup period may be quite complicated and lengthy. It takes time to build the trust necessary for the banking relationships to gel and reach a financially feasible point for an institution. First Bank of the Americas, for example, found that wiring funds and bill paying may be more important to an immigrant community than free checking accounts.
- Practical implementation skills.
- Dedicated, fully committed people at all levels of the organization and board.
- Management. Strong, tight management is essential to the success of these businesses, as it is in most others. Control over inventories, hiring policies, underwriting policies, selection of the correct products for the specific market, use of technology, cost control, etc. all play a crucial role in the business' profitability.
- Support from the overall community. Working with local businesses, local government and local community organizations is crucial in gaining support for these activities and in helping to market the efforts.
- Use of partnerships. There are many different types of partnerships available to communities for bringing improved financial services to low-income communities. Partnerships are an essential element of this effort and are necessary to their success.
- New approaches to marketing.
- "Branch accounting" and other means of tracking income and expenses.
- Reporting mechanisms for impact of the programs, such as effectiveness in "mainstreaming."

- Literacy training. This element is very important, but improved mechanisms need to be developed in order to become more effective.
- Replication of successful approaches. This concept is essential to finding mechanisms to address the problems and to making widespread changes. Finding the right combination of conditions is possible but may present challenges. The need for vision from the founders, the need for a compatible real estate market and/or other lending conditions, the need for dedicated staff with a unique blend of talents, the availability of capital—these issues are all crucial to successful replication. To achieve replication on the large scale that is necessary will require extensive financial and technical support, as noted below. However, many demonstrations around the country indicate that it is possible to create other, more equitable solutions to the financial services needs of low-income people and generate a profit.

IMPLICATIONS FOR CHANGING FRINGE BANKING IN THE U.S.

The field of financial services for low-income households is very complicated and involved. There are many facets that must be carefully addressed: planning, technology, partnerships, financial feasibility, operations, pricing, selection of financial services, social and community goals, facility buildout, etc. This discussion of business models highlights many of the associated complexities.

The different financial approaches have their own individual requirements and complexities. But there are some key, general issues.

- Generally, it is difficult to provide financial services effectively in low-income neighborhoods.
- Banks and fringe banking institutions are often seen as competitors, but they are really different institutions doing different things. It is possible to combine all, or many, of the needed financial services into one institution, but that is difficult and probably requires modifying existing institutional business model approaches. The result may be an unusual institution.
- Another approach is the combination or partnership of different institutions in some fashion, a very important but sometimes difficult approach.
- Many of these institutions and businesses may prefer that each product stands on its own financially or at least break even. That goal may be very difficult to achieve with this model in low-income neighborhoods.
- Legal limitations can be placed on fringe bankers and some improvements in financial services could result, as discussed in Chapter 2, Pay Day Loans.

- Different products can be combined in some ways to improve other financial needs. For example, savings programs can help increase savings rates, lower costs can be used to reduce the financial pressures on low-income people, programs can be created to help mainstream interested households, etc.
- Although it is not really their business or expertise, conventional institutions can be encouraged to offer fringe banking financial services. However, these services will need to be combined with programs that create profitability.
  - The goal of mainstreaming as many customers as possible to generate earnings to break even or make profit is crucial.
  - Institutions that enter into this arena preferably will be efficiently operated, use a lower cost model, generate appropriate profits and have adequate reserves.
  - Conventional institutions probably will need to modify their business models to successfully address the needs of low-income households through changing the product mix, modifying fee structures and finding methods to improve the ratio of mainstreamed customers.
- With some of these changes, banks can provide many of the needed financial services. They have been involved in a few instances, probably due mostly to Community Reinvestment Act pressures to date. A few are involved because of the potential for new markets but they have not tried to achieve adequate scale that would solve the financial services issues in many neighborhoods. It is important to move beyond demonstrations and "exception" activities.
- Credit unions can play an increased role. One mechanism that is increasingly being used is the expansion of service areas to include low-income neighborhoods and entire cities. As credit unions look for new members in situations where their growth and/or survival depends on finding additional members, this type of expansion can play a key role (Baltimore Business Journal; Virgin; Judice; Lewis).
- Technological changes may offer greater opportunities to reach a higher level of scale, but it is not clear that immigrant and low-income communities are ready to accept these technological solutions without additional motivation and efforts from the institutions.
- Subsidy is necessary for some efforts targeted at very low-income and homeless people and, in some cases, for financial services for low-income households as well. This subsidy can be constructed in different ways.

- Internal or external. An institution may offer a range of financial services by subsidizing the losing products with income from the profitable services.
- An institution may subsidize unprofitable services with revenue from other parts of the bank product line and other locations.
- Public sector/foundations subsidy can be provided.
- Friendly depositors can make below market rate deposits even though there are draw backs—lack of scale, withdrawals, etc.
- Friendly investors may provide patient equity capital, again with the drawbacks that exist.
- A different business model can be employed that uses lower costs.
- Creation of entirely new financial vehicles, institutions and mechanisms.
- These approaches may need extensive capital support, in addition to possible operating subsidies, to work.
- Ironically, improvements in financial services in a low-income area may create the pressures that will result in gentrification. When banks and other financial institutions become more prevalent, an important goal, they may actually be serving higher income people moving into the neighborhood rather than low-income households (Stewart). If that is the case, this movement may be a precursor to helping to push low-income people out of the area. Community development practitioners need to be aware of this possibility and use available tools to address it.

Many different efforts to bring change to financial services for low-income households have been evolving throughout the country. It is likely that many more individual, ad hoc projects will be initiated. However, a much more systemic approach is needed. A more coordinated effort will need to take place and a high level of resources will need to be allocated. The level of assistance needed is extensive. The numbers of people across the country who need help is large. The difficulty in creating financial feasibile business model is substantial. Therefore, future efforts need much more support. A coordinated, systematic method of assisting new programs could include:

- Availability of technical assistance in helping organizations create new efforts;
- Availability of development capacity to create these efforts de novo in areas without any existing capacity to create a new effort; and
- Availability of a financing vehicle to help new financial services programs begin, including startup funds, ongoing subsidies, and investment and

lending support.

- Development of manuals and other materials and approaches (such as franchising) which can detail all the issues organizations need to address;

It would also be critical to include information and guidance on creating partnerships and on the purchase, use and maintenance of various types of technology. Additional effort could be directed at model partnership structures along with research into the legal, regulatory and organizational issues that these partnerships might need to address. Other important areas include assistance and guidelines for marketing and the preparation of market studies and for providing effective financial literacy programs. The technology needed for this effort is increasingly becoming available. In some cases, there may be cost issues associated with the technology. Additional technological advances should be supported to the extent possible and guides to the technology need to be created. There may be a need to initiate additional efforts such as bulk buying in order to keep costs down.

Some of the guiding principles for successful efforts may include

- Widest possible set of services meeting locally defined needs.
- Economic feasibility and self sufficiency if possible.
- Achieving scale in order to appropriately address the magnitude of the problem.
- Use of technologies that enhance the effort.
- Use of partnerships where appropriate—even where the partnerships may at first seem unlikely.

If the community development community in the U.S. want to seriously address these questions, it will need to find ways to address these replication issues—through training and TA, deeper study of workable models, additional capital, creating the capacity to adapt models to local conditions, etc.

Therefore, some method of providing systematic assistance—both financial and technical—on a greater level to support this type of effort is essential to creating a widespread web of financial services institutions capable of having an impact in low-income neighborhoods and changing current financial practices. This would allow some existing as well as new community based efforts to obtain greater assistance in the early stages of developing their programs.

Chapter 4

Obtaining accurate information on the financial feasibility of check cashing and payday lending businesses was extremely difficult. As noted in the Introduction, Chapter 1, these businesses operate out of the mainstream and there are few available sources of information about their inner workings. Those who earn their livelihoods from these businesses typically do not want to discuss this closely held information. Moreover, others involved in these businesses (e.g., accountants) also have generally not been willing to share their knowledge. There no readily available body of existing information on the industry as there might be for other businesses, such as elevators or glass or air conditioners.

Ultimately, however, data was obtained, and offered a generic understanding of the business models. There were several sources for this information, including:

- Focus groups held in Oakland (3) and Los Angeles (2) with different ethnic groups. These indicated that there were different markets and the people had different needs that have to be addressed in different ways.

- An analysis of the impact of typical financial services on a hypothetical low-income family. In the analysis, the costs of these financial services were compared to the costs if the family had had access to more traditional financial services through commercial banks, savings institutions, etc.

- Nine case studies conducted with a range of different financial institutions involved in providing financial services to low-income households in different parts of the country. The case studies were conducted from the viewpoint of developing and understanding a range of existing business models and possible new models, including financial feasibility.

- Professionals in the business who agreed to help me with understanding the financial feasibility of check cashing stores, including payday lending activities, as well as some of the operating business practices of these businesses. The main sources included a software company for check cash-

161

ers—B.E.S.T.—and the company's accountant in Chicago. The information was provided in the forms of interviews, written answers to questions and the development of sample pro formas for typical check cashing businesses.

- Other sources included the review of the financial statements of check cashing businesses that were placed on the market for sale; business plans for new check cashing operations; experience gained from assisting a community based organization in Baltimore considering various options to deal with the financial services needs of the low-income people in its neighborhood and which included information from local check cashing agencies; review of aggregate numbers on the internet for a few public companies listed on the stock exchanges; review of aggregate numbers for all the check cashers in New York State, where they are regulated; attendance at the annual conference of the check cashing industry's trade association; visits to check cashing stores in many locations throughout the country; discussion of these issues with a wide range of people; study of other community development efforts going on around the country; and review of many studies, articles and other information sources.

From this cumulative research and discussion, it was possible to piece together a reasonable understanding of some of the different business models and the financial feasibility of these approaches. There are still gaps in knowledge, and what is presented derives from research rather than from actually operating a business.

INDUSTRY SIZE

The fringe banking industry is quite large by any measure. One recent study (Carr and Schuetz) estimated the sizes of some of the different components in the following way:

	Volume of Transactions	Gross Revenues	Fee Total
Check cashing:	180 million	$60 billion	$1.5 billion
Pay day lending	55 to 69 million	$10-13.8 billion	$1.6 to 2.2 billion
Pawnbrokers	$42 million	$3.3 billion	NA
Rent-to-own	$3 million	$4.7 billion	$2.35 billion
Totals	280 million	$78 billion	$5.45 billion

These numbers are mostly from the late 1990s or 2000; the industry has grown substantially since then.

The New York experience also offers insights into the size of the market. The results from New York which does not allow payday loans (although they are apparently being made anyway through out of state banks, as detailed in Chapter 2) and limits check cashing fees to a maximum of 1.4% of the face amount of certain kinds of checks, demonstrate a very substantial business. In New York, the State Banking Department regulates check cashing companies and requires an annual report. The Department then compiles the information and issues a report with aggregate numbers for the state as a whole. In 1999, according to the report, the industry cashed $14.5 billion in checks. The average check totaled $378.56 and the average check cashing fee was $4.18. Check cashing fees collected totaled $160,183,816 compared to $128,378,056 in 1998. Total fees collected in 1999 were $218,999,857 including electronic benefits transfers and other income from money orders, wiring, lottery fees and miscellaneous transactions.

Fringe banking, in contrast to its name, is a major industry in the United States, although its activities and inner workings remain hidden for the most part.

CHARACTERISTICS OF THE BUSINESSES: VARIABLES IN THE OPERATIONS OF FRINGE BANKING INSTITUTIONS

There are many characteristics that influence the operating costs, revenues and profits of a fringe banking institution. It can be difficult to determine the actual numbers for an "average" store because there are so many factors that enter into any store's operations. These factors can cause wide variation in the operating costs and revenues for the store. Some of the key variables include the following:

- The demographic profile of the surrounding neighborhood will be important. Different characteristics can create different operational results. For example, immigrants will need a certain set of financial services that may be different from households born in this country.
- The income levels and sources of income of the nearby households will also have an affect. People with government benefits payments (social security, SSI, welfare, etc.) as the main source of their income will have one set of needs while lower income working households may have a slightly different set of needs.
- The local conditions will also impact the store to the extent that a community is growing, or at least stable in population.

- In addition, the crime rate will influence the neighborhood and the stores that are located there.
- The competition in the immediate vicinity will also be critical. Almost all of the business typically comes from residents with a 1 to 1.5 mile radius of the store. Some states regulate the proximity of these stores with minimum distance requirements, creating small geographic monopolies, in effect. (New York requires 3/10 of a mile between stores and New Jersey requires 2,500 feet (Sklar).) In other situations, competitors locate next to each other, creating the possibility for greater price and product competition, at least until one or more may be forced from the location and a more dominant company emerges.
- Likewise, the type of competition may also be important—a chain store may be much better capitalized and be better able to withstand a longer term competition for customers. The presence of other financial institutions—banks and credit unions—in some locations may also play a role for some customers. The presence of other stores—convenience stores, grocery stores, etc.—that also cash checks will affect the business as well.
- The type of location can also vary. The density of the surrounding neighborhood can play a role. With higher densities in large cities, the stores should be easily reached by foot or public transportation. A good mix of small and medium businesses in the neighborhood with a greater level of hiring needs is also important. Corner stores are excellent locations and they should be visible and secure. Lower density areas may require cars to be able to reach them. In this case, the availability of parking will also be important. These factors may vary for urban and rural stores.
- The hours that the store is open are also important. Most are open long hours during the week and are open for some period of time on the weekends as well. Some are open 24 hours a day, all week long.

Other business factors play critical roles. For example, the particular mix of financial products is critical. Some products—such as payday loans and check cashing—can be more profitable and serve as the economic engines for a business. However, some states don't allow payday loans; moreover, it may be difficult to mix these products in some locations—depending on the surrounding demographics of the neighborhood—because they can appeal to different groups of people; many people who cash government benefits transfer checks may have no capacity to borrow money because they have no jobs or checking accounts. Moreover, some products are much more profitable than others; payday lending (in addition to consumer finance lending and maybe rent-to-own) can be more profitable than check cashing, which depends even more on larger volumes and smaller margins. Loss leaders may be used by some of the stores, but they are relatively small and each product tends to stand on its own rather than receive much subsidy from the profits generated by other products.

Other financial services products may not generate the same kind of revenue but they can be important for other reasons.

- Some products can generate almost all profit from their revenues once fixed costs are covered by revenues. This condition can occur because these operations have a set of fixed costs—rent, insurance, salaries and benefits, marketing, utilities, etc. Therefore, if a store is open a certain number of set hours and it can add certain products with relatively small costs, most of the revenue from the new services will create mostly profit. This is true for bill paying, money orders, wiring as well as the miscellaneous products such as stamps and envelopes, bus passes, faxing, notary services, etc. There will be some relatively small inventory costs for some products (e.g., money orders, stamps, envelopes, etc.) and relatively small costs for machinery (e.g., fax machine, which would be needed by the business anyway). But most of the revenues from these services would generate profits once the fixed costs are covered with other revenues, presumably from the core financial products such as check cashing. Fringe banking businesses are interested in a high volume of transactions that may be time consuming. They have relatively small fees—at least in absolute terms—that create excellent profits with high volume. This model is in contrast to banks, which desire a smaller number of transactions that lead to large spreads and float income without having to take extensive amounts of time on large numbers of smaller transactions, as discussed in Chapter 3.
- Although some of the products may generate additional amounts of revenue and profit in relatively small increments once the fixed costs are covered, they have additional uses as well. They bring cash into the store that can be used to either lower costs or generate additional income. For example, money wiring and bill payments bring in cash into the store for short periods of time. This cash is then available to be used for check cashing purposes. This use of the cash, in turn, lowers the amount of cash that the store needs to borrow from a bank to cash the checks, thereby lowering the interest costs for the store. Similarly, the cash paid to the store for money orders is available for short term investment until the money orders are cashed. This float adds to the income that the store can generate. However, these possibilities are limited to those check cashing compa-

nies that issue their own money orders.

- The volume becomes a critical matter and it depends on many of the issues discussed above—location, demographics, product mix, competition, etc. After the fixed costs are covered, new revenues that are generated add to the store's profitability. The stores that have the greater volumes can generate more profit. The upper end of the revenue potential is shown in the table below (derived from materials developed by B.E.S.T.) for some sample levels of numbers of checks cashed that average $400 per check with a 2.5% fee (the average store cashes about 100 to 150 checks per day, although some cash up to 500 per day).

Checks per Day	Check Amount	Daily Income
30	$12,000	$ 300
90	36,000	900
120	48,000	1,200
150	60,000	1,500
210	84,000	2,100
270	108,000	2,700
300	120,000	3,000
400	160,000	4,000

If a store is open 6 days a week, or 312 days, and averages 300 checks cashed each day averaging about $600, revenue would be over $1,400,000. Or, with a more typical store, an average of $350 per check and a 2% fee, the annual revenue for 150 checks per day would be $327,600, still an excellent revenue stream. If the store were open 7 days a week, a very reasonable assumption, the annual revenue would be $383,250. These latter assumptions are used in the example that follows.

As discussed in Chapter 3 and as will be further illustrated below in this section, these operations are based on a low cost business model so that much of this revenue becomes profit. Of course, as the volume grows, some other costs will grow—perhaps an added staff position, more accounting, higher interest on borrowed bank funds, etc.—but these costs can be relatively small compared to the added revenues.

It should be noted that a store with this type of revenue would need a very good location—high density, with a large number of working people and people receiving government benefits checks, strong identity in the neighborhood with its patrons and a relatively low level of competition. However, profits such as these could possibly create competition, which could force a lowering of fees and a reduction in volume. Nevertheless, even in these circumstances, the profit potential could still be very substantial. And volume is one of the primary factors in this revenue stream.

This type of revenue stream is then enhanced by revenues from the other products, creating more income that tends to generate mostly profit. Here, too, volume becomes a key, as the stores are open long hours with a high level of fixed costs under any conditions. Finding the best product mix to serve the need of the specific households in any given location then becomes a main issue for the business.

Although this business can be very profitable, it is important to stress the role of management. While profit is potentially available, the businesses must be well managed or they will not succeed. Tight management—whether it is with marketing, employee selection, policies and underwriting of borrowers, collections, control over expenses, etc.—is critical in this business, as it is in others.

FINANCIAL FEASIBILITY

This section will discuss the financial feasibility of a sample store. As noted, it is difficult to define a "sample" store because of wide cost variations and other factors described above. Different cities will have different salary levels, rents, and so on, and these costs will also vary by location within a given city. Also, the population densities will vary along with the level of competition at any site. It is difficult to generalize.

This section includes a breakdown and discussion of stabilized annual revenues by source, a stabilized operating budget and a startup budget for capital costs and working capital needs. Most of the line items will have annotations describing the issues for each of them. There will also be ranges for some of the costs.

This operating statement is stabilized—a budget that reflects income and expenses once the business is has been operating for awhile, any startup losses have ended and profits exist and can be projected into the future. The actual first year budget should reflect losses—the expenses will almost all be necessary while it could take some considerable time to build up the revenues to reach break even and then profitability. It is likely that profits could begin towards the end of the first year, but it could also take more time than that. The timing for reaching profitability is also based, to some degree, on the initial size of the store. Therefore, it is may be useful to consider phasing in the growth of a particular store—by products—to avoid some losses. The losses during the startup period are included in the startup budget, which follows the stabilized budget.

The budgets are intended to show not only the potential for different costs in different locations but also the possible range for a smaller store and a larger store. There is a discussion of cash flows and profits at the end of this section, although they do not include debt service costs for start up; if these costs were included, pre-tax net income would be reduced. These costs are derived from the sources noted in the introduction to this section. Materials from B.E.S.T. provide one primary source, with information from stores in other states, an accountant involved in the check cashing business, business plans, some studies, discussions and other research.

The numbers presented here are representative of a large check cashing operation, presumably in a larger city with higher densities. Many stores operate at far lower volumes, revenues and expenses, and net income.

The numbers are also conservative. The operating expenses and startup costs, for example, are particularly conservative. An experienced owner-operator likely could operate a business with lower costs than those presented here. In addition, these numbers do not include any cost for debt service for startup costs. If these costs were included, the net income would be reduced.

STABILIZED REVENUES

Financial service	# Items Average/Day	Daily Fee–Low Average	Daily Fee— High Average
Check Cashing	125	$625	
Check Cashing	125		$ 875
Money Order sales	150	75	150
Utility Bill processing	50	25	50
Miscellaneous Items	100	25	100
Wire Transfers	10	20	30
Money Order—Float	200	0	0
Daily Income	$ 770	$ 1,205	
Annual Income	$281,050	$439,825	
Pay day loans	10	285	498.75
Daily Income	$1,055	$1,703.75	
Annual Income	$385,075	$621,869	

For purposes of these projections, it was assumed that the store was open seven days per week throughout the year; many are open seven days a week, thereby generating substantially more revenue than stores with shorter hours. However, many are open for fewer hours, as described in Chapter 2. For example, if this sample store were open for six days a week, the annual revenue for the low end projection would fall to $329,160 and the high end to $531,570.

The check cashing revenues are based on assumptions of cashing 125 checks per day. The average check size for the lower end estimate is $250 and the average check size for the higher end estimate is $350. The average check size, at present, is about $350, but this figure can change depending on the economy, location, etc., as described below. The fee charged in this example is 2%; the average tends to be 2.0% to 3% for payroll and government checks and up to 20% for personal checks. In some locations in today's economy, the average fee may have fallen below 2%. Increased competition may also be involved in many locations in lowering the local fee structure.

The assumptions can change the picture dramatically. For example, the number of checks cashed per day per store generally is an average of about 100 to 150. For these projections, an assumption of 125 checks cashed per day was used, which is in the middle of the possible range of the average number of daily checks.

But estimating a higher or lower number can change the outcome substantially. For example, the range of checks cashed per day can start at about 30 and increase to a much higher number; there are some stores that cash 300 to 500 checks each day. In addition, the check size can vary with the income levels of the people near the store's location. The revenues could easily increase or decrease substantially with a larger or smaller number of checks cashed and/or checks cashed with larger or smaller average sizes.

The economic conditions have an impact. In the recent economic downturn, some check cashers tend to be cashing fewer checks and smaller checks. In the smaller towns and rural areas, the check cashing volume is normally lower than in large, high density cities and volume can also be lower in bad economic times. For example, many stores in smaller towns may cash only about 20 to 25 checks per day in this economic setting.

Competition has an impact. More sources have entered the field and that has also created a reduction in fees charged for check cashing. And technology has also played a key role, making it easier for new entrants to join the field. All these factors have lowered the check cashing rates charged in many places around the country recently.

An average check cashing store can sell about 100 to 150 money orders per day, while a few may be able to sell up to 300 per day or more. Most of the business is in the first week of the month because of the need for the customers to pay bills. The fee can be $.25, $.50 or $1.00 per money order. The average amount of the money order is $250 in this example, but this does not affect the fee income (however, the average money order size may impact the need for using cash from a bank for check cashing purposes or the float income for some stores, as shown below). The projections shown here use an average of 150 money order sales per day. Using $.50 per money order and 150 money orders sold per day would result in fee income of $75 per day for the lower end projection compared to $150 per day at $1 per money order for the higher end projection. The difference over one year could be perhaps over $27,000 depending on how many days the store is open. This is an illustration of the ways in which high volume with low margins can impact revenues.

Processing bill payments is another source of fee income. The charge can range from $.50 to $1.00 per bill paid. The average store may process between 20 to 50 bills per day, with some much higher. This example uses an average of 50 bills per day with a fee of $.50 charged for each transaction for the lower end projection. The $.50 fee is based on an assumption that the store charges $1. In the case of bill paying, there is usually a processor, which receives about half of the fee. An alternative approach can be used in which the processor pays the originating store a fee and the store does not include a charge for its efforts in the fee to the customer. The higher end projection assumes either a higher fee charged to the customer or that the store keeps the fee for itself.

Miscellaneous items can vary, but may include postage, faxes, copying, envelopes, bus passes, rolled coins, notary, lottery tickets, prepaid cellular, prepaid ATM cards, prepaid debit cards, prepaid phone cards, foreign exchange, pagers, car title loans, internet connection, etc. The demand for these items changes frequently and depends on location and the surrounding demographic characteristics. The fees can average $.25 to $1.00 per transaction, although some may be much higher, such as the notary service. The range of number of transactions may be 25 per day up to 500 per day. In this example, 100 transactions per day are used.

Money transfer companies pay a commission to check cashing stores that can vary. As an example, the fee for domestic transfers may generate as much as $3 per transaction while international transactions may generate $7 each. This fee level may be attainable presently, but it was probably used more frequently a few years ago when wiring fees were higher. However, the present normal fee may be about $2 per transaction and this number is used for the lower end in the projections in the example (and $3 is used for the higher end). Some companies offer a larger share to the local agent.

Money transfer fees have been falling in recent years due to increased competition, the willingness of many stores to charge very low fees in order to bring in extra business, and having the wiring companies make up the loss in up front fees with higher exchange rate fees at the receiving end of the transaction.

Technological changes are also starting to have a great impact on the economics of wiring money as well.

The example uses ten transactions per day. However, the range of transactions can vary from five per day to 100 or 200, depending on location and the number of immigrant families in the area. The fee in the example ranges from $2 for the lower end projection to $3 per transaction at the higher end.

Money orders can generate float opportunities for those check cashing companies that use their own money orders. This situation occurs only in a few places, such as Chicago and Minneapolis. In those situations, the store may generate interest from depositing the funds into an account. However, most stores use more commonly available money orders, which do not allow the possibility of generating float income.

Payday loans were covered in detail in Chapter 2. In this example, an average of ten loans was assumed per day, an average number. However, some payday loan stores can make over 200 loans per day. The fee used in this example is $15 per $100 of loan amount. The average loan amount for the lower end projection is $200 and the upper end average loan size is $350. A 5% loss rate is built into the numbers. Both of the projected daily fees—the lower and the higher—are based on some combination of fees from new loans and rollover loans. The relative financial importance of the rollovers for profits can again be seen in these proportions. The assumptions for the payday loans are toward the low end of the continuum and could easily have been greater; with assumptions of a larger average loan amount and/or a higher average number of daily loans, the amount of income could be much higher.

Several of these financial products may generate important levels of revenue, mainly because the fixed costs are set and any additional income over these costs from higher volumes of transactions generate higher levels of profit for the store. However, the revenues and profits are only one element of the profitability. These other services are cash transactions. They bring cash into the store. This cash can then be used to cash checks or generate additional income. This lowers the cost for the store because it requires less "buying" or "purchasing" of cash from banks needed to cash checks. "Buying" the cash incurs an interest cost. If the store needs to buy less cash, the interest costs can be reduced and the store can generate more profit.

For example, the money transfers bring in cash for the store if the store is using its own money orders. If the average wire transfer is $200 per day and the store processes 10 of them on average, the amount of cash generated in that day would be $2,000. Similarly, bill payment also creates cash for the store available in the short term for other uses. Processing 50 bills per day generates $2,500 per day if the average bill is $50. Money orders also generate income through interest float until the money orders are cashed as well as fees for stop payments, tracers and re-issued money orders. For example, an average of 150 money order sales per day for an average of $100 per money order generates $15,000 per day in cash.

Using the revenues shown in the Stabilized Revenues table above can illustrate this issue. This cash totals about $19,500 compared to the check cashing needs of perhaps $42.875 (125 checks averaging $350, less fees of 2%). In this example, the store owner would need to borrow almost $20,000 less per day from a bank (or tie up that amount in equity capital) to cover its check cashing needs if the cash from these other sources were not available. Using this revenue stream can result in substantial savings over the course of a year.

However, the averages on any given day do not always mesh with the daily needs for different products. For example, pay checks are most often cashed on Fridays, often in the second and fourth weeks of the month. Government checks of different kinds are usually received once a month at the beginning of a month. Money orders are most needed in the first week of a month, usually to pay bills, and sometimes in the middle of a month. And the bill paying service is most needed at the same time. Money wiring is often done when pay checks are cashed. Sample daily cash needs could be as follows: Monday and Tuesday—$30,000 each; Wednesday—$40,000; Thursday—$80,000; Friday—$175,000; Saturday—$40,000; Sunday—$15,000. These daily cash needs may or may not fall on the days when the cash revenues are most available. Moreover, a check cashing company would need to issue its own money orders to take advantage of the float. If it issues money orders from a money order company instead, the float is not available to the check casher.

STABILIZED OPERATING EXPENSES

Teller #1	37,400	$12 per hour, 60 hours/week
Teller #2	31,200	$10 per hour, 60 hours/week
Teller #3	8,900—20,800	$10 per hour, 40 hours/week
Benefits/payroll taxes	19,200—25,000	28% of wages
Rent	6,000—18,000	$500 to $1,500/month
Phone and data lines	5,000—7,000	
Utilities	2,200—3,500	
Insurance and bonding	6,000	
Armored car service	2,500—6,000	
Security and alarms	1,000	
Computer/data processing	2,000	
Marketing, PR, promotion	12,000	

Outreach/financial literacy counselor	0	
Supplies	12,000	
Legal	2,000—4,000	
Accounting	10,000—15,000	
Collections/court costs	500—1,800	
Bank transaction fees	6,000—20,000	
Losses/Bad Debts	11,000—35,000	3% to 7% of fees
Depreciation	not a cash expense	
Licenses	300—2,000	
Maintenance	500	
Dues	500	
Cell phones	2,500—6,000	
Pagers	500—1,000	
Payroll processing		
Car/travel	6,000—8,500	
Postage	500—1,200	
Internet/DSL fees	included in phone costs	
Equipment	2,500	
Miscellaneous	5,000—15,000	
Debt service, start up loan	0	
Total	**$193,200—$294,900**	

Staffing. Owner/manager (1 FTE); 3 tellers (2 FTE, 1 PT) = 1 FTE); Benefits and Payroll Taxes (25% to 28% of wages): If the typical store is open from 60 to 75 hours, an owner may hire one or one and a half staff. For a 60 hour week, the owner would be there almost all of the time and the full time staff person might be there close to 50 hours as well. If the store is one of two or more owned by the same person or if it is part of a chain, there might be a manager for the store and the owner might shift among stores while spending most of the time at the main office. The part time staff would fill in during high volume times, which could be Fridays, paydays (the first and 15th of each month), etc. The busiest hours for check cashing tend to be 3:00 p.m. to 6:00 p.m. For stores open up to 70 or 75 hours, another FTE may be required. And, although a store may be open for a set number of hours, the owner and employees would need to be on site for additional hours before and after store hours.

Another factor is the number of teller windows in the store. If there are three total windows, the number of staff will increase and the manager may be called upon to serve one window during the busy times. Two windows would be easier to manage, but could create irritation for the customers who wait in line (this is an issue that was raised in various focus groups). Store managers can earn from $12 to $15 per hour. This example assumes a store owner rather than a manager. Tellers earn $10 to $15 per hour. Assume $12 per hour for the FTE, who would be more senior, $10 for the junior FTE, and $9 for $9 for the part time staff at 19 hours per week (so that full time benefits are not paid).

At a larger, more active store, a third full time staff, earning $10 per hour for 40 hours per week was included in the budget. Trustworthy staff are very important to the successful operations of a check casher, as staff are often a major source of losses through various mechanisms; so it may be worthwhile to pay at a higher scale not only for fairness but also to help protect the business. However, some believe that good employees who have been with a company for a long time can become a liability. They gain too much capacity and their salaries must be increased from the starting rate of about $7 an hour. Once the salary is over $15 per hour, it becomes more difficult for the store to afford the employee (Sklar). In general, payroll equals about 28% to 32% of revenues (Sklar).

Office Rent: The rental price for a specific space in an area will depend on local factors. The range is probably $500 to $1,500 per month. Assume $1 per square foot per month for 1,100 square feet, which would include some back office space for the owner and staff plus workspace for bookkeeping, file space etc.

Phone and Data Lines: The phones are needed to verify checks and all the other normal business uses. This can cost $300 to $500 per month. Including the internet costs (assuming high speed DSL or similar connection) could increase this cost by up to $100 per month.

Utilities: This cost will also be set locally (in California, for example, utility costs have become so high that some small business owners depending on reasonable utility costs—restaurants, for example—are having great difficulties). Check cashing stores will have extra costs associated with this business: heating and air conditioning during long work hours; extra electricity for the cameras, computers and other equipment; signage if there are lights as part of the signs; etc.

Insurance and bonding: An employee bond can be relatively expensive, and it may be possible to use it once or twice; the premiums can increase from using this insurance. One factor in this expense is the amount of cash that is kept in the organization's operations. For every $100,000 in cash, the cost is about $4,000 to $5,000 for insurance. And the general liability, workers' comp, unemployment insurance, fire, business interruption, etc. will also add up. These costs could be estimated from $300 up to $500 per month. If an automobile is also being insured (see discussion below in "car/travel"), those costs would need to increase to cover this cost (the ownership structure may also be an issue. For example, if the business is owned by a nonprofit, the parent organization's insurance may increase for general liability and D&O). There may also be a need for errors and omissions insurance.

Armored car courier: This is likely to be around $500 per month if a service is used. However, it could be avoided or reduced depending on the company's banking relationship (i.e. if the bank agrees to cash the checks upon delivery and does not put a hold on them), the company's line of credit (if any) or the company's own available cash, which could be equity, an investment from some source or some type of loan. It will also depend on the volume of business that the store does and when it is done. This volume will most likely be the first day or two of the month and Thursdays and Fridays. The volumes on those days could be well over $100,000 compared to some of the other days of the week at $15,000 to $40,000. On the heavy days, it might be best to have armored car deliveries. The other days may not need it. However, if more cash is needed on any of those days, the staff will probably have to make those "cash" runs in the business' car or a staff person's car, increasing the security risks for staff and the business.

Marketing/publicity/promotion: The first year budget may be especially high because the new store will need to break into the market and develop a clientele. The actual amount spent may depend on the competition and the types of advertising selected (e.g., newspapers, radio, TV, etc.).

Supplies: Including money orders, checks, order forms, computer supplies, office supplies, etc., this item can run from $400 per month to$1,000 per month, depending on the volume of business.

Legal: Perhaps $2,000 to $4,000 per year, after the startup. Some of the legal issues might include preparation of proper forms, collection letters and customer rights, collections themselves in some cases, negotiation of new contracts, dealing with new governmental regulations, occasional disputes with customers/vendors/employees, etc.

Accounting: This cost could be $10,000 to $15,000 per year. Toward the lower end of the range, it could run $200 to $300 per month plus end-of-the-year reports and taxes (regulators may require end of the year statements in some states). A part time bookkeeper (three hours per day) could be required. If an audit were prepared, that would be an additional amount. Alternatively, if Quick-books or a similar system were used, then these costs would be reduced. However, the company would have to hire someone with these skills. The assumptions used in this analysis are toward the higher end of these costs.

Collection services: Usually, the company itself does the collections because it is too costly for a small company to pay for this activity. Also, the companies have better track records for obtaining payment than the collection agencies. If collections are outsourced, the fee is sometimes a percent of the collection amount. This is an expensive service if it is not paid as a percent of the amount recovered, and many owners tend to do this themselves or with the assistance of an employee. This cost could be reduced, therefore. However, there are court costs to take cases through the courts. These are the costs shown in the budget under the assumption that the company does its own collections or hires an agency that works for a percentage of funds recovered.

Bank transaction and account fees: A bank will charge for handling the checks—the costs of processing checks and issuing currency—sent by the check cashing store. In addition, other factors influence this cost. If the types of services offered include services that bring in cash—money orders, wiring money and bill payment—the need for cash will be lower, as this cash can be used for cashing checks and/or making payday loans. This cost may also depend on whether the company has a line of credit to fill cash needs or whether the company has the cash as part of the organization's up front reserves/working capital. Adding interest costs on a line of credit of perhaps $50,000 to $100,000 is assumed in this pro forma. Another factor will be whether the bank cashes all the checks that are sent right away rather than putting a hold on them. If the bank will cash the checks right away and give the check cashing company the opportunity to pay back any bounced checks plus the fees, then the amount of cash needed will be lower. If the bank requires clearance of all checks before giving the company the cash back for the checks, there will be a need for a larger line of credit and/or more working capital up front. Banks probably will not offer to cover all checks, as a rule. The amount (of working capital or borrowed funds, or some combination of both) that will be needed also depends on how long the checks take to clear—a couple of days or up to five working days. The amount of cash needed will vary by the day of the week, with the largest amounts of cash for check cashing required on Thursday and Friday. The amounts on those days could be very high, up to $150,000 or more, depending on the clientele, how many customers there are, when they receive checks and what the sizes of the checks are. For example, if there are recipients of government checks, those tend to be received on the first of the month. If there are a lot of people with these checks using the check cashing service, then the cash needs will have to be adjusted accordingly. Likewise, if the clientele is more weighted toward working people who get paid every other Friday, then the store would have to adjust its cash needs along these lines. Therefore, it might be useful to think about a line of credit of perhaps $100,000 (prime plus two in addition to a 1% annual fee, while still assuming a great deal of startup cash for both reserves as well as meeting cash needs, which is addressed later in the startup capital section) at roughly 7.5%, including the fee.

With an average usage of about two weeks per month, the line would be used mostly on Fridays and the first day of the month, but require some time—until the checks cleared—to pay back. This would cost about $3,750; if the rate were lower—prime plus one, for example, the cost would be about $3,250. For a less conservative approach, usage of one week per month could be assumed. However, rates are at extremely low levels at this time with expectations for an increase within the next year if not earlier; a less conservative approach is therefore more appropriate. It is also important to note that obtaining these bank services has become more difficult recently. Some banks have ended their banking relationships with check cashers, most notably Citibank and Fleet Bank, which believed that check cashers represented a money laundering risk and that they were unprofitable. The industry has been engaged in trying to demonstrate that both assumptions are false (Goldman).

Losses/Bad Debts: There are many possible ways to incur losses—bad checks, fraudulent computer generated payroll checks, other fraud, employees (e.g., not following procedures, cashing checks for friends, etc.). There are also different ways to estimate losses. In one measure, losses from bad checks are supposed to be about 3% to 5% of gross fees, which, based on the above income projections, would be $11, 200 to $$28,000 per year. Some loss percentages can be at 7%, and this number was used for the higher end, $35,000. Some also use a guideline of 1% of profit per month. Another loss measure that could be used is an amount up to 1% of the face amount of the cashed checks. However, by any measure, a new store may be very likely to have a relatively high loss rate. For example, it may be the target for some attempted scams, especially in the beginning. In addition, competitors are likely to refer people to the new store who might be higher risks. And, if personal checks are included in the list of products/services, the losses may be higher because these checks would tend to have higher loss rates. Part or all of any losses from employees could be covered by insurance, but claiming any losses from the insurance may result in higher premiums.

Depreciation: Some of the equipment could be depreciated over three to five years, depending on the specific equipment. This number was left out of the budget because it is not an actual cost expense.

License: This amount varies by state/locality. It can be from $250 to $5,000.

Maintenance: Estimate for repairs to the office.

Dues: Joining the national association of the check cashers (FISCA), etc.

Cell phone: The owner may need a phone and will have to be available on off hours. At least one other staff may need a cell phone.

Pager: The owner and other staff may need a pager too.

Payroll processing: This task is either done by a bookkeeper or an outside processing company; the latter may be preferable, although this budget assumes it is done by the bookkeeper and shows no cost.

Car/travel: The staff may have to make runs to the bank for additional cash or to other locations for supplies. The full range of costs could include lease, repairs and fuel. But employees may be called upon occasionally for various activities that would require using their automobiles; mileage would be charged.

Internet/DSL fees: Included in phone and data transmission, above.

Equipment maintenance: Computers, fax, copier, cameras, etc. may need service contracts to cover the costs of repairs. Parts costs are included in supplies.

Miscellaneous: $5,000 to $15,000

Debt Service: This cost was not included in the pro forma. However, it is possible that the owner of a store obtained a loan as part of the start up capitalization. If that is the case, there will be debt service payments and the pre-tax net income could be substantially higher than the amounts shown in this example.

NET INCOME

The profits possible from a check cashing store range from about $8,000 to $15,000 per month. Some can make much more depending on the mix of products and the volumes. The profits can be 25% of revenue for some of the smaller stores. Profits can begin relatively soon—less than one year after start up, depending on location and the surrounding community needs. Startup costs can be recovered fairly quickly, as well.

Chains sometimes can make less, about $3,000 to $5,000 pre-tax income per month because they may not be managed as tightly as owner-manager stores and because they have additional costs such as higher central overhead.

In this example, the cash flow varied, depending on the assumptions about the size of the checks cashed and the inclusion of payday loans. For the projections without payday loans, the pre-tax cash flow was $87,850 for the lower end revenues with lower expenses ($193,200 in operating expenses). There was no calculation for the lower revenue alternative with higher costs ($294,900 in expenses) because it is unlikely that a store with this level of income would have such high expenses that it would result in an operating loss when stabilized; the business would be forced to close.

When payday loans are included, the profitability increases quite dramatically. The net income for the lower daily average in this case is $191,875 for the lower expense budget. The net income for the higher revenue range is $326,969 to $428.669. The inclusion of payday loans demonstrates the profitability of using a mix of financial services that enhances the revenues of a check cashing store, with all of the attendant caveats (e.g., the loans are permitted in the state, the location is suited to both payday lending and check cashing, expenses don't increase greatly, etc.). The assumptions in this example could have easily been modified with a corresponding change in the net income. For example, increasing the average number of payday loans from 10 to 15, a very reasonable assumption, would increase the higher range of net income to $417,990 to $519,690. Reducing the number of loans to five per day would lower the ranges accordingly.

The effectiveness in generating increased revenues from payday lending is partly due to the cost structure of the business. Once fixed costs are covered, most of the additional income from a new product tends to generate profit, as the overall and variable costs of many of the products are often fairly low. The fixed costs include rent, basic salaries, liability and other insurance costs, utilities, accounting and legal costs. The variable costs are really partly variable in that they may fluctuate on a monthly basis due to changes in sales, advertising and other promotions, differences in seasonal activity, changes in suppliers' charges and other issues. These costs may include phone, supplies and forms, printing, mailing and advertising/promotion (Entrepreneur).

The higher average daily fees yielded higher pre-tax net income. The range was $144,150 to $245,850 without payday loans. Including payday loans, the pre-tax income jumped to $326,969 to $428,669. The payday loan numbers would probably fall somewhat when some additional costs were added. For example, if an extra part time employee were needed, an additional $20,000 might be subtracted from these profits.

As noted above, these figures are geared toward a larger business with a high volume and most likely located in a larger sized city with high density surrounding the store. The financial conditions for a smaller store might be structured as follows:

Revenues	$190,000
Operating expenses	$135,000
Pre-tax income:	$ 55,000

If payday loans averaging $200 were included at a level of 10 per day, the additional income would be over $100,000 per year with some modest increase in operating costs. The pre-tax income could be roughly $155,000.

The summary of these projected, stabilized revenues, costs and pre-tax income figures—including and excluding payday lending—are as follows, although the payday costs are understated and the resulting pre-tax income is overstated:

WITHOUT PAYDAY LOANS

	Small Store	Larger Store— no PD Loans Lower Fee Schedule	Higher Fee Schedule
Revenues	$190,000	$281,050	$439,050
Operations	$135,000	$193,200–$294,900	$193,200–$294,900
Pre-tax Income	$55,000	$ 87,850	$245,850–$144,150

WITH PAYDAY LOANS

	Larger Store— PD Loans Lower Fee Schedule	Higher Fee Schedule
Revenues	$385,075	$621,869
Operations	$193,200–$294,900	$193,200–$294,900
Pre-tax Income	$191,875–$ 90,175	$428,669–$326,969

Please note several important caveats:

- These numbers represent examples only. Actual conditions could vary considerably. Changing the assumptions can increase or decrease the net income substantially.

- Many of the costs presented here are somewhat conservative, geared especially for an owner inexperienced in this field. More experienced operators possibly could be able to both lower costs and increase revenues.

- The numbers represent a range for a fairly high volume store—many operate at much lower volumes while some operate at higher levels;

- They do not include income taxes, which will decrease the net income considerably (for example, the federal income taxes for net income of $191,875 would be $51,466, after deducting state taxes. The state taxes would vary by state; the California tax, for example, would result in an additional $16,962 in taxes, lowering the net income to $123,447).

- They do not include debt service payments for any startup loans or investments, which could considerably decrease the net income before taxes for the first several years of operations. The start-up costs are described in the next section.

This analysis represents a range of possibilities. Revenues and operating expense, for example, could vary widely from those shown in this example. Nevertheless, it is clear that there is considerable income potential from a well-managed fringe banking operation. It indicates that there may be room in the operations of these stores to lower the costs charged to consumers and still make a reasonable profit. Other experiences, reports, information from the industry, and other sources also show that the costs to consumers can be contained while still offering reasonable returns to owners.

Start-up Budget

Startup costs can be separated into several categories: capital, pre-opening operational and other start up costs; losses during the first year or two of operations; working capital needs; and owner salary during the startup. All of these costs are covered in this analysis except for the owner salary during startup.

Startup capital and pre-operating costs can cover a wide range of costs, depending on the type of store that the owner wants, the area and the risks (e.g., high crime area will require greater security costs, during both startup and ongoing operations), the size of the operation (e.g., number of teller windows), etc. These startup costs can range from $25,000/$35,000 up to $150,000 and even higher. The assumptions in this report are based on a store with an open space with some offices already constructed in the back of the space; the remainder of the space needs to be built out. Many of the costs presented here are somewhat conservative, especially for an owner inexperienced in this field. More experienced operators possibly could be able to lower some of these costs.

Some costs will be one time only costs. The initial inventory will have to be purchased. All the equipment and the needed improvements to the space will have to be purchased and completed. Licenses will need to be obtained, significant advertising will need to be completed, staff hired and trained, the store prepared, etc. prior to the opening of the store. As a result, there will be significant costs accrued well before the store serves its first customer. Moreover, once the store opens, it is not likely to reach a break even point for awhile, losing money for potentially several months while it builds its clientele.

Obtaining startup capital is a major issue, although it is not covered in this report. There are many sources, similar to those of other small businesses.

Sources are needed for both debt and equity; potential sources include personal savings, friends and relatives, banks (although start up businesses are sometimes not financed by all banks), the Small Business Administration, finance companies (often using the high rates described earlier in this report), credit cards, and selling equity (private placement with investors or friends through a partnership of some kind; Initial Public Offering for a later stage company) or venture capital firms for equity. This analysis does not include any financing costs or means of financing as part of the start up budget.

Phasing in some of the elements may lower some of the initial capital costs and start up losses. Although some would argue against a phase in, this approach could still be used by phasing in the growth in levels and volume of programs rather than phasing in programs in some sequence. For example, the volume of checks cashed could be phased in based on some projection of growth for a startup, allowing lower costs for staffing, interest, etc. This analysis does not assume any phase in elements.

The following costs are for a three-window storefront. Please also note the following caveats in the startup budget:

- Startup costs can vary in different locations.

- Many of the costs presented here are somewhat conservative, geared especially for an owner inexperienced in this field. More experienced operators possibly could be able to both lower costs and increase revenues.

- There is no salary included for the owner during startup. The owner may draw a salary from any startup capital, savings or net income from other businesses, such as another check cashing store. It is assumed that the owner will draw a salary from the profits of the business once it is operating.

Start Up Budget

Computer system/software	$15,000-20,000
Marketing/outreach	2,000-4,000
Legal set up	2,000-5,000
Startup consulting	12,000-20,000
Property build out	20,000-30,000
Equipment/fixtures	35,000-50,000
ATM	0
Staff training	5,000-6,000
Staff hiring	2,500-5,000
Startup rent and deposit	3,000-4,000
Signage	4,000-15,000
Contingency:	10,000-30,000
Subtotal:	$110,500-$189,000
Projected losses—year 1:	$30,000-$100,000
Projected losses—year 2:	$10,000-$30,000
Working capital for cashing checks:	$50,000-$150,000
Total:	$200,500-$469,000

Computer system/software: With three teller windows installed, each will need a computer along with one or two other computers—for accounting and perhaps, for general business purposes. They will need to be networked. Small cameras are included with each work station. This system could cost from $15,000 to $20,000, or slightly higher up to $25,000.

Marketing/outreach: The initial marketing costs can vary widely. To some degree, it will depend on the location, competition, need for providing information to non-English speaking immigrants, etc.

Legal Set Up: Mostly, startup legal needs cover corporate status and licensing.

Startup Consulting: This item can include a wide range of costs such as business structure (corporate/legal status), location/competition analysis, technology selection, technology implementation (installation of software, hardware set up, equipment installation), branding, general organizational assistance if owner is inexperienced, purchase or development of operations manuals, vendor identification and negotiation, etc. Each organization will require different levels of this assistance, from very little to extensive. The full level of assistance could be quite expensive.

Property Build Out: The build out covers teller windows, security (bullet proof glass and secure doors—some of which can have psychological impacts on both customers and employees that need to be considered), installation of equipment and office space. A three window cage or kiosk can cost about $20,000 to $30,000. Without a kiosk, the buildout costs are much lower. Offices and other construction may also be needed. This total could reach up to $40,000 in some cases.

Equipment/Fixtures: Some basic equipment is needed: one good safe and perhaps a smaller one (there are different kinds, including some that have different cubicles inside with access for different individuals and that can monitor which staff takes out and puts in money and at what times) can cost up to $25,000 ($20,000 is used in this analysis although savings could accrue by using a much less expensive safe as low as $3,000); cameras, alarm systems—$200 to $3,000 ($1,500 is used in this analysis), ID system, cash drawers, calculators, fax, copier, printer(s), bill paying equipment, phone system, time clock, POB or POS terminals depending on products. Other equipment is available but is not absolutely necessary—money counting machines, cash dispensing machines, etc. There will also be a need for furniture—desks, chairs, filing cabinets, tables, etc.

One issue that is probably very controversial is the presence of a gun(s) on the premises. This could increase the risk to employees and if purchased, one or more of the staff would need to know how to use it. One could also argue that the lack of a gun on the premises could also increase the risk to employees. This is a very difficult decision for any organization to face. The total cost for these needs could be $35,000 to 50,000.

ATMs (@ $3,500 to $35,000 each): Many check cashing stores do not include ATMs, although they may increasingly useful. The costs were included here for information; costs for ATMs for check cashers fall into the lower end of this range and banks' ATMs cost more. In addition to ATMs, there are machines that can accept deposits, cash checks, pay bills and wire funds. There are also stored value cards that can be used for debit cards, money wiring and the like. These machines and technologies may not be cost effective yet and there may be some difficulty in gaining acceptance from the target population. However, they are available and their use is increasing. Some form of ATM or other machine will be useful in the future as these transitions occur in the industry.

Staff training: Some companies offer intensive training that costs about $6,000 (it is done on an hourly basis and includes travel costs and expenses from the home office).

Staff hiring: The staff needs to be hired prior to the store's opening. During this time, they are trained and assist with the opening activities, such as marketing.

Startup rent and deposits: The space will need to be rented at least one month prior to opening. The time period will be longer if the build out cannot be carefully scheduled.

Signage: This can be very costly from a few thousand dollars up to $30,000 and even up to $100,000 for very fancy signs. Signage can be important.

Handicap access: This cost can be included in the build out. It is listed here to highlight the need, which could be reflected in the width of doorways and entrances, bathroom layout, stairways, if any, etc.

Contingency: Ideally, it is always wise to include a contingency, if possible. An estimate was included in these projections. It could cover areas such as advertising for the first staff positions, which was not included in the hiring costs, above.

Total start Up Expenses: $110,500 to $189,000. The lower end of the range can be possible in some circumstances, especially for an experienced operator in a lower cost area. Higher cost areas, larger or fancier stores (a few are starting to move "upscale") and/or first-time operators could require the higher cost levels.

Operating Losses: As noted in the introduction to the projections, the budget presented here is a stabilized budget, one that would occur after the income and expenses have settled in to a likely pattern. The first period of time of operations would probably generate losses. For purposes of this report, it is assumed that there are losses for the first year and part of the second year. It is also assumed that the stabilized budget begins at some point in the second year. In fact, the second year could generate losses, be breakeven or generate profits. The profits—as shown in the stabilized budget—might not occur until the third year, or it might require even more time to create the market needed to achieve this scale. The exact amount of the losses can be difficult to predict without doing a monthly cash flow projection and developing a range of possibilities based on different assumptions for a "bad" case, "likely" case and "good" case. This set of projections was not prepared for this report. Therefore, an estimated range of possible losses is used in these projections; the actual figure could be much higher or lower.

Working capital: There are several options for addressing working capital needs, including a line of credit, start up capital from equity, the use of other financial products that generate cash (money orders, wiring money and bill payments) and an agreement with the bank to cash checks immediately instead of placing a hold on them. However, assuming a difficult case scenario, perhaps $100,000 to $150,000, perhaps more depending on the size of the heavy volume days, would be needed in the first year and increasing amounts in the later years as a check cashing business grows. A general rule of thumb is that a store needs

$150,000 in working capital to cash $1 million in checks per month. The highest amounts are needed for the days with the highest check cashing volumes. On other days, much lower draw levels would be needed. These funds, at least at this level, may not be necessary, depending on the availability of some of the other approaches described above (line of credit—difficult to obtain by a startup, cash producing products, rapid cashing of checks by the bank); however, for this analysis, this amount is included. A separate amount of working capital would be needed to fund payday loans if these are included in the line of products.

NEW YORK EXPERIENCE

The Banking Department of the State of New York regulates the check cashing industry, as noted above. The Department publishes aggregate data for the industry. In 1995, the aggregate income, as reported, was $166.9 million. In that year, 31.1 million checks were cashed by licensed operators totaling over $10.4 billion. These checks resulted in fees of almost $103.4 million. Money order fees yielded $12.8 million; utility bill fees generated $5.8 million; and money wiring generated $6.1 million. Miscellaneous products were also very lucrative, creating over $6.3 million in revenues.

The rapid growth is shown by a review of 2001 figures, which actually represented somewhat of a leveling off from 2000. The aggregate income increased to over $246 million in 2001, with 36.9 million checks cashed (down from 40.7 million in 2000) totaling over $14.3 billion (slightly higher than the preceding year). Fees from all sources totaled $246.1 million (an increase from the preceding year).

On the operating expense side, the aggregate total was just over $161.5 million in 1995 and increased to $232.8 million in 2001. New York check cashers lost $6.4 million from robberies, losses from returned checks written off and other sources. Cumulatively, utilities cost $3.7 million; accountants, lawyers and other professional fees cost almost $5.9 million; salaries accounted for $82.25 million; insurance costs were almost $15.9 million; and money delivery service was over $4.07 million.

On the balance sheet, the cumulative net worth for all the check cashers was over $70.1 million in 2001 (an increase from $45.5 million in 1995). The net profit for all regulated New York check cashing agencies was slightly over $13.3 million (compared to $5.4 million in 1995).

The State requires a maximum fee of 1.4% for check cashing and does not allow payday lending. The profits are most likely lower in New York as a result, but nonetheless, fringe banking in the state is still profitable and draws businesses into the industry. In part, the requirement that check cashing stores must maintain a minimum distance from each other helps to offset the other regulatory limitations by creating small market areas where a single store has a distinct advantage.

The check cashing industry in New York has proven itself to be a profitable business approach in the state (Lyke), even with the regulatory framework.

DOVE REPORT

Dove Consulting completed a report for the U.S. Treasury in 2000 (Dove) that surveyed "non-bank financial institutions," mostly check cashing companies with additional services (money wiring, money orders, etc. and in some cases, smaller amounts of payday lending). Dove surveyed these businesses in four cities—Boston, Atlanta, San Antonio and San Diego in December 1999 and January 2000. They were able to obtain responses from 130 out of 371 fringe bankers (Dove included 273 in its initial survey requests) listed in those cities, with at least 30 surveyed in each location. While the results are not indicative of the industry as a whole throughout the country and no conclusions can be drawn from this information, the surveys and the analysis do offer useful information that can be used to compare with other sources and offer insights into the issues that exist.

The operational results do bear some relation to the information obtained from other sources. For example, the gross revenues ranged from roughly $84,000 to $325,000. Check cashing generated the most revenues along with money orders and money wiring. Check cashing was the largest revenue producer, by far, followed by money wiring. In California and Texas, where payday loans were included in the businesses, these loans did not generate a very high percentage of income for these particular stores.

The operating expenses, for the most part, also followed other data. Salaries and rent/utilities were the two highest costs, although "cash and money services" were almost as high location costs. If the percentages shown in the report are extrapolated into costs, the range of operating expenses was about $56,000 to $216,000.

The pre-tax returns on sales (revenues less operating expenses) averaged almost 34% across the four cities. Roughly one third of all revenues became pre-tax profits. The report noted that these profit margins were roughly equal to the 32% average documented in the aggregate report for Massachusetts, compiled by state regulators. The returns ranged from an average of over $32,000 to an average of over $95,000 per store. Sklar also pegged revenues at a similar range; 20% is considered a good return, but the percent could be over 40% in some situations.

The example shown earlier in this section had several differences. The revenues were much higher due to assumptions about volume, which was also much higher in the example. The pre-tax returns were somewhat lower than those of the Dove study, in part due to conservative estimates about operating expenses.

The value of a fringe banking institution is mostly in its cash flow. There are few tangible assets that are of significant value. The location is crucial in generating the cash flow. Therefore, an excellent, long term lease is essential. Without a good lease, the location is not very valuable; lease renewals or re-establishing the business in a new location to obtain a less expensive lease negates the value of the good will of the existing location (Sklar). A check cashing business is valued on its cash flow. However, it is not always clear how much the cash flow actually is, as is the case with many businesses based on cash.

CORPORATE INVOLVEMENT IN PROVIDING FRINGE BANKING SERVICES

There are several large fringe banking companies that now exist. Mostly, they are listed on various stock exchanges. Cash America, for example, provides financial services in the U.S., United Kingdom and Sweden. It is listed on the New York Stock Exchange (PWN). The company makes secured, nonrecourse loans to individuals through 473 locations, commonly known as pawn shops. At the end of 2001, the company had over $76.7 million in outstanding domestic loans. It also has 135 locations (both franchised and company-owned known as "Mr. Payroll") that offer check cashing services. The company also had rent-to-own operations (Rent-A-Tire), which it sold for $3 million in 2002.

Cash America's total revenues for 2001 were $356 million, increasing from $346.4 million the year before. Pre-tax income from operations in 2001 was $12.725 million (52 cents per share), increasing from $701,000 (3 cents per share) the previous year, which included some large, unusual chargeoffs (Business Wire).

ACE CASH Express, the country's largest check cashing chain, was founded in 1968. It is listed on the Nasdaq Stock Exchange (AACE). It now has a total network of 1,178 stores (999 company owned stores and 179 franchises stores) in 35 states and the District of Columbia. A recent press release further describes the company's activities in the following way (PR Newswire):

ACE also maintains automatic self service machines, which provide certain retail financial services without the need for a service associate, at 71 company owned Store locations and 100 automatic self service machines at H&R Block office locations. ACE offers a broad range of financial and check cashing services and is one of the largest providers of Money Gram wire transfer transactions. In addition, ACE offers money orders, bill payment services and prepaid local and long distance telecommunication services. Under ACE's agreement with Goleta National Bank (NB), GNB currently makes small short term consumer loans available to customers at various ACE company-owned stores.

The press release announced that ACE had "achieved record revenue during its second fiscal quarter ended December 31, 2001." Revenues for the second quarter increased to $54.7 million compared to $45.1 million for the previous year's second quarter. The revenues for the fiscal year ending June 30, 2001 were as follows:

Check cashing fees:	$105,479,000
Loan fees and interest:	$54,771,000
Bill payment services:	$10,376,000
Money transfer services:	$10,270,000
Money order fees:	$7,245,000
Other fees:	$6,377,000

The expenses for the stores were just under $38 million for the quarter, including salaries/benefits ($13.97 million), occupancy ($6.755 million), and losses/loan loss provision ($6.8 million). The gross margin for the operations of the stores was $16.7 million for the quarter. Headquarters and regional expenses totaled $8 million, interest was $3.2 million and taxes were $1.364 million. Net income, after depreciation and amortization was $2 million for the quarter.

Check cashing fees increased 12% in the quarter, to $25.7 million from $22.9 million in the corresponding quarter in 2000. Loan fees and interest increased 56%, to $20.2 million. Same store sales increased 21% compared to the previous fiscal year's second quarter.

At the end of 2001, ACE had assets of almost $308 million, consisting mostly of cash and cash equivalents of $153 million, $22.3 million in loans receivable, $39.4 million in equipment net of depreciation and $75 million of good will. The stockholders' equity was $58.5 million.

For the fiscal year ending on June 30, 2001, ACE had the following transactions:
- Face amount of checks cashed: $4,498,000,000.
- Face amount of average check cashed: $358
- Average fee per check: $8.38
- Fee as a percent of the average check: 2.34%
- Number of checks cashed: 12,580,000

- Face amount of returned checks: $26,536,000
- Collections: $17,717
- Net writeoffs: $8,819,000
- Collections as a percent of returned checks: 66.8%
- Net writeoffs as a percent of revenue: 4.5%
- Face amount of money orders sold: $1,709,000,000
- Number of money orders sold: 12,787,000
- New small consumer loans and refinances: $396,783,000
- Average advance: $269
- Average finance charge: $42.30
- Number of transactions—new loans and refinances: 1,477,000
- Gross loans receivable (6/30/01): $27,768,000
- Allowance for loan loss as a percent of gross loans receivable: 48.2%

ACE opened 13 new stores in the quarter, bought 2 company-owned stores and opened 8 franchise locations. The company planned to open 32 newly constructed stores in the remaining six months of the fiscal year while closing 68 stores. The CEO and President of the company highlighted the Goleta National Bank program (payday loans) as "our fastest growing service." The company expected continued growth in the third quarter and projected income from interest and fees of $18 million for the third quarter. (See Chapter 2 for a description of the payday loans and bank relationships with payday lenders).

However, the relationship was prohibited by the OCC, the bank's regulator, in late 2002. The reasons did not include an assessment that payday lending is illegal or inappropriate. The ruling was based on ACE's throwing away 641 client files in a Virginia dumpster and other unsafe and unsound practices by ACE, including excessive exemptions to the Bank's policies and procedures. Both ACE and Bank agreed to pay fines (Beckett; Jackson & Reosti).

In addition to the "self service" machines that have been placed in H&R Block offices, ACE has 71 others in other locations that now exist in 28 states. H&R Block is also a leader in tax refund loans, described earlier in Chapter 2, which is a newer form of a high interest rate loan.

First Data Corporation, a large financial services company, owns Western Union, the money wiring service (Shaver). The company serves nearly 2.5 million merchant locations, 1,400 card issuers and millions of consumers. First Data is a major integrated financial global financial services company that operates in many countries in the world. Its services include a very wide range of financial services products such as electronic payments and transaction services, and logistics, consulting, management and customer service associated with all forms of electronic payments. It offers credit cards, debit cards and stored value cards issuing services and merchant processing services; non-bank money transfer and payment services, bill payment services; transaction services for major credit cards and internet based transaction processing; e-commerce services such as electronic tax processing for banks and government agencies.

First Data Corporation, which is listed on the NYSE (FDC), had net income of $870 million in 2001 with revenues of $6.5 billion. Earnings for 2002 are expected to be $1.26 billion. It is growing rapidly as attested by the increase in processing of merchant transactions, increasing from 6.4 billion two years ago to 8.8 billion transactions in 2001. Western Union is one of the primary engines of growth and profit for FDC. Western Union has over 100,000 agent locations operating in 186 countries (See Chapter 2 for discussion of money wiring services).

First Data Corporation is one of the leaders in credit card transactions. The leader in handling debit card transactions is Concord-EFS, which was later acquired by First Data. The company takes credit card, checking, debit card and other electronic transactions and connects them with the banks. Concord then takes a part of each transaction for its fee. Although its stock price has faced some recent problems, the company is solidly lodged in a major growth sector. Its estimated 2001 earnings are over $400 million on $2.2 billion in revenues. The expected growth is about 25% for next year, although the debit card business is growing at an even faster rate (Savitz).

Rent-A-Center is the largest rent-to-own (RTO) operator in the country. Listed on the Nasdaq stock exchange (RCII), the company now owns and operates over 2,360 stores in 50 states, Washington, D.C. and Puerto Rico. It began in 1986 with 8 stores. A large part of its growth was fueled by mergers. In 1998, Renters' Choice Inc. purchased Rent-A-Center from Thorn Americas, Inc. for $900 million. Other mergers have also occurred recently in the industry. For example, RentWay acquired Ace TV Rentals and Champion Rentals, Inc. in 1998. Aaron's Rental Purchase, the country's oldest rental company, acquired Rentmart's 40 store chain in 1997 from Associates First Capital. In addition, many of these companies are publicly listed and traded; Rainbow Rentals, with 67 stores, went public in 1998 and raised $22.5 million in gross proceeds (Kosta).

Rent-A-Center has experienced extensive growth. Revenues in 1995 were $133,289,000 and increased to $1,808,528,000 by the end of 2001. Similarly, net earnings after taxes increased from $10,712,00 to $97,497,000 during the same period. The operating expenses increased from $113,481,000 to $1,571,942,000 over that time frame. The interest cost also increased from $2,202,000 to $60,874,000. General administrative costs, as a percent of total revenue declined during the period from 4.3% to 3.1%, although the average store expenses as a percent of store revenues increased over the same period (Rent-A-Center).

The presence of large corporations in the industry can change the equation concerning access to capital. Large corporations have access to the capital markets to finance their activities that many other smaller businesses do not have. For example, Cash Systems, Inc, a provider of check cashing services, announced that it had completed two private placements raising common stock proceeds of $777,500 and converted notes totaling $425,000 to company common stock (PR Newswire).

Rent-A-Center announced a conversion of the company's Series A preferred stock into over 7.2 million shares of common stock, allowing the company to reduce its dividends. Rent-A-Center also announced a public offering of 3,120,000 of its common stock. The shares are being offered by affiliates of Apollo Advisors IV, LP and Bear, Stearns & Co. Morgan Stanley is acting as the book-running manager; Lehman Brothers will be a co-lead manager with Bear, Stearns while Wachovia Securities and SunTrust Robinson Humphries will act as co-managing underwriters (Rent-A-Center press releases).

Cash America announced on August 14, 2002, that it had completed two financings that will provide long term liquidity resources for working capital and support other corporate purposes:

- $90 million line of credit from four commercial banks, maturing in 2005.
- $42.5 million of senior unsecured notes issued to a group of institutional holders, maturing in 2009 and carrying a fixed coupon of 7.20%.

The funds are intended to be used for (1) acquisitions, new store openings and the like, and other growth possibilities, and (2) increases in loans to customers "during periods of heavy seasonal demand" (Business Wire, August 14, 2002). Cash America is thus able to access the capital markets at very favorable terms—7.2% for part of the funds and probably a similar rate for the remainder—and then use these low cost funds to make much higher rate loans to individuals so that the company can generate high returns from this transaction.

This scenario apparently occurs frequently: large financial institutions provide financing that supports higher rate financial services in low-income neighborhoods. For example, the *Wall Street Journal* reported in an older article that Resource Equity, Inc., a small Massachusetts lender, which makes very costly rehabilitation loans to people denied loans by large banks, obtained multimillion lines of credit from Shawmut Bank and Bank of Boston (since merged). In one case, a borrower of Resource Equity had been turned down by the larger banks for direct loans and then obtained a 34.09% loan from the smaller lender. When Resource Equity would not refinance the loan at the end of the two year term, the borrower turned to other high rate lenders and eventually faced eviction. The article described similar occurrences in other parts of the country and with other types of consumer finance loans (Wilke).

The article's author states that the mortgage companies ". . . operate on the fringe of the legitimate second mortgage business, which involves some $300 billion of loans. But most of them couldn't survive without backing from banks and access to the secondary mortgage market, where they sell high yielding notes to mainstream banks. And critics say the banks often buy the lucrative paper without applying standards they require of their own loans."

This theme is replayed in other instances. While banks pulled out of low-income areas that did not generate adequate profits, they often finance the fringe banking institutions that replaced them. For example, Fleet Capital and Planters Union, a large bank holding company in the south, have extended secured lines of credit to Title Loans of America, a national leader in making car title loans with over 300 stores. Other companies—such as the check cashing companies, which cash tens of billions of dollars in checks each year and will be described in more detail later in this section, have enormous daily cash needs and these are usually serviced by bank loans (Manning).

Wall Street firms are involved in other ways as well. They bundle loans and sell them on the secondary market to investors. Remittances—funds wired by people working in the United States back to families in their home countries— is now a huge business. These payments are now being *securitized* as *remittance bonds*. These bonds are issued by banks that receive wire transfers from workers and companies abroad. "Before converting the checks or wired funds into local currency to pay recipients, the issuing banks deposit the money into a special offshore account, part of which is used to make bond repayments." For example, one planned offering at the time of the article (1998) was led by Nations-Banc Montgomery Securities LLC and Credit Suisse First Boston for a Turkish bank that receives wire transfers from Germany (Druckerman).

Other corporations are also involved in other ways. Wells Fargo Bank and Capital One Financial Corporation combined with Diebold, Inc. and Cash America to provide $253 million in private financing for InnoVentry, a developer of automated machines that provided check cashing and was preparing machines that would include money wiring, money orders, short term loans and credit cards. The funds were split between a traditional venture capital investment of $115 million and the remainder for working capital and lines of credit. The machines, exclusively manufactured by Diebold, Inc., were placed in kiosks in Albertson's, Circle K, Texaco and Wal-Mart. This financing had been preceded by others, and Wells Fargo, which was part of the original joint venture with

Cash America creating the company in 1998, had been involved in some of those as well. This financing was intended to be the last one before the company planned to have its initial public offering (Kurdek; www.innoventry.com). Despite its apparently strong technology, the company closed down in 2001.

Citibank has also been involved in different ways in providing financial services to low-income households. For example, Citigroup won government contracts to distribute welfare benefits through its ATM cards. By the end of 1998, $640 million of welfare benefits were distributed through Citigroup in this manner in 29 states, including New York. The federal government was seeking a more efficient and less costly means of disbursing welfare and other transfer payments and contracted with institutions that agreed to have the funds deposited in accounts and then have the beneficiaries access the funds through ATM cards. For a variety of reasons, the Citigroup program was not very successful—lack of appropriately located ATMs, added fees for accessing recipients' funds from certain other locations, problems with the cards themselves and the systems, problems with liability for stolen cards, etc. It is important to point out that some of these issues were not due to anything that Citigroup did. However, the venture was not proving to be profitable for Citigroup's competitors or, apparently, for Citigroup itself (Barstow; Sengupta). And, as discussed in Chapter 2, Citigroup is also involved in subprime consumer finance lending.

These corporations represent a sampling of the large corporations involved in fringe banking activities. They also have been discussed in context in different parts of this report. However, when reviewing the wide range of activities from a very wide range of corporations—large grocery and convenience store chains, major banks and other financial services companies, companies manufacturing expensive and sophisticated machines and equipment supporting the industry, investment banks and secondary markets, stock exchanges, credit card companies, consumer lending corporations, etc., in addition to the large corporations that have emerged directly from the industry itself—it is clear that financial services for low-income people is an extensive and profitable business, with excellent profit growth potential in the future for both small and large scale efforts.

These activities are, of course, perfectly legal. However, they contribute to the creation of dual financial markets, helping to segregate lower income households from the mainstream financial institutions and instruments and making it much more difficult for them to move out of poverty. At the same time, these institutions tend not to locate in low-income neighborhoods to offer lower cost financial services. This business approach, while profitable, makes it more difficult for low-income households to change their life situations.

Chapter 5

Low-income people in the United States do not have access to the full range of financial services that most middle and upper income households do. As a result of this inadequate access, these households tend to pay a very high percentage of their available income for interest and fees to obtain these services, compared to most other people in the country. These higher payments significantly affect their ability to move out of poverty and attain higher living standards.

There is a range of institutions that provides a broad offering of financial services to low-income households. It includes check cashing outlets, payday lenders, pawn brokers, rent-to-own stores, consumer lending companies, credit card companies, RAL lenders, mortgage lending companies and automobile lenders. Together, they constitute a financial system that can create great barriers to low-income households in their efforts to improve their standards of living and build better lives for their families.

Many are aware of the check cashers and pawn brokers in low-income neighborhoods. They are aware that low-income people clearly use them. But the extent of the use of the range of these institutions, the number of institutions and the impact on low-income neighborhoods and individual households is often unknown or underestimated.

There is an entire set of financial institutions and practices in low-income neighborhoods that replaces the institutions that the rest of the society uses. It is not just check cashing companies or payday lenders that create the problems. It is an extensive range of institutions that is different from the institutions in the other neighborhoods and that are much more expensive. It is this entire range that low-income households use, not necessarily just an isolated, occasional use of one or two services. It is this entire range of institutions that constitutes a dual financial economy, and it is the problems created by this range of institutions which must be addressed.

The capacity to build assets and escape from poverty can be severely hampered by the costs of the services provided by fringe bankers. The implications of this institutional framework are stark—the rates and fees charged by these institutions help to make it more difficult for low-income people to escape poverty. They represent one more significant challenge for poor people.

This financial system also can counter many of the other community development efforts undertaken in the country. Wealth-building programs, such as IDAs, for example, are likely to be less effective when households are forced to use payday lenders; the high fees that they charge can reduce the impact of the savings programs. Likewise, predatory mortgage lenders take large amounts of equity out of homes that the owners have worked a lifetime to build. The savings provided by affordable housing developments and/or quality child care services can be reduced when the interest and fees on financial services are so extremely high that they may partly or entirely cancel out the housing savings. The new small business started with special financing from a nonprofit CDFI may be endangered at the financial margin due to the higher costs for financial services that it is forced to pay; the additional costs can push the business into failure.

This financial system needs to be altered. It needs to become more affordable for low-income households, although without eliminating profit potential from the industry. It needs to become more efficient, making financial services available on a more widespread basis. And it needs to offer a more complete range of services so that low-income households can more easily move out of poverty.

There are several ways to help create better options for these households.

- Introducing stronger statutory and regulatory efforts.
- Creating political and operational pressures, such as the introduction of viable competition, for existing fringe banking financial institutions to change some of their activities.
- Encouraging presently uninvolved, existing institutions—such as some commercial banks and credit unions—to become more involved in providing affordable financial services to low-income people.
- Encouraging further new approaches by institutions, such as some banks and community development credit unions, which are already involved.
- Creating new alternative institutions, partnerships and financial products.

The last approach, creating alternative institutional approaches, is very important but has been less developed than the others. The Appendix contains a brief executive summary of a business plan that follows these guidelines.

Some of the guiding principles for successful efforts to create these changes include:

196

- Widest possible set of services meeting locally defined needs.
- Economic feasibility and self sufficiency of alternative institutional approaches, if possible, and a reasonable profit level where appropriate.
- Achievement of scale in order to appropriately address the magnitude of the problem.
- Use of technologies that enhance the effort.
- Use of partnerships where appropriate—even where the partnerships may at first seem unlikely.

Although the fringe banking industry often has an unsavory reputation, these businesses provide important services to low-income households that no other institutions are willing to offer in any systematic way. In some situations, the financing fees, rates and products are fairly reasonable, in market terms. In New York, for example, check cashers are limited to charging 1.4% of the face amount and no payday loans are allowed. There are loopholes that exist (payday loans are being made through out-of-state banks) and the regulators created another mechanism that protects stores by preventing more than one store within a set radius. Nevertheless, the industry in New York seems to provide financial services at reasonable prices that allow profits that keep stores in business.

Moreover, other changes have occurred. Just a few years ago, most of this lending was problematic: check cashing mostly required payment of 3% or more; wiring money was much more costly; payday lending was growing rapidly with little legislative or regulatory oversight or restraint; predatory mortgage lending was rampant with little awareness or action taken to prevent abuses; consumer finance companies used abusive practices; etc.

Now, there have been important inroads made in some of these areas. For example, check cashing costs have fallen to 2% or less in some areas where there is competition. Similarly, the costs of money wiring, especially for some destinations, have fallen extensively in some areas due to competition and technological changes. Payday lending is under attack and some restraints have been implemented through regulation and statute. Some consumer finance companies have promised to modify some of their practices such as the use of single premium credit insurance.

While there has been some important progress, it has been completely inadequate in achieving an appropriate level. There is still a very, very long way to go in many areas before a set of fully appropriate financial services for low-income households is available throughout the country.

The fringe banking business is hidden from mainstream awareness. Most people are only vaguely aware of these businesses. Moreover, they are often seen as smaller businesses that face high risks and uncertainty due to the income levels of their customers.

However, it is clear that this business can be quite profitable. Some are relatively more profitable than others. Check cashing, for example, does not seem to generate the same relative profit levels that payday lending or perhaps consumer finance and rent-to-own business may generate. There may be some loss leaders, but mostly, the different financial services tend to support themselves as free-standing products without needing subsidy from other high profit generating products, especially once the core operating costs have been covered by revenues.

While profit is potentially available, the businesses still must be well managed or they will not succeed. Tight management—whether it is with marketing, employee selection, policies and underwriting of borrowers, collections, control over expenses, etc.—is critical in this business as it is in others.

At the same time, it also appears that these businesses do not seem to represent the risk levels that appear from viewing the surface level of the businesses or that pervade the statements of the industry. Certainly there is risk, but it does not seem to justify the high level of prices and profits for the services. There needs to be an appropriate level of profit available to attract and keep businesses in the field. It is important to allow adequate profit incentives to maintain the industry and not regulate or legislate this potential out of existence. It is very difficult to pin down where this profit level actually falls, however.

While the present profit levels can be quite high, the future levels may be greater, as technological changes increase the profit potential further. Moreover, as the scale of these efforts continues to increase, the profit potential may increase and draw more entrants into the field. Also, it is clear that large corporations increasingly are finding methods to provide financial services to low-income households—either directly or indirectly.

At the same time, the increasing entrance by large corporations and the consolidation of the industry through large chains may be creating barriers to entry—e.g., capital requirements, scale, brand creation—for new institutions. There is still time to begin new efforts but the window of opportunity may be lessening.

However, it is clear that there is considerable profit potential from a well-managed fringe banking operation. As a result, there may be room in the operations of these stores to lower the costs charged to consumers and still earn a reasonable profit.

Therefore, these trends can be positive—if methods can be developed to offer a wide array of financial services, including those not easily available to low-income households at present, in a more efficient manner and at reasonable costs. However, if some of the abusive practices are maintained and even intensified, then financial conditions facing low-income households will continue to be harmful.

The appropriate range of financial services needed by low-income households include the following:

- Core Services
  - ✓Check cashing
  - ✓Wiring money
  - ✓Money orders
  - ✓Bill payments
  - ✓ATM
  - ✓Credit cards
- Financial Services—Loans
  - ✓Small, short term loans (up to six or twelve months)
  - ✓Personal loans (furniture, automobile, etc). up to five years
  - ✓Small business loans (relatively small loans—up to $5,000, with relatively short durations up to 3 years)
  - ✓Non predatory home loans—repairs in particular, but also debt consolidation and refinancing
- Financial Services—Other
  - ✓Savings plans—savings accounts, IDAs, EITC, etc.
  - ✓Checking accounts
  - ✓Insurance—health, life, house, liability
  - ✓Investments—CDs, stocks, retirement
  - ✓Tax return preparation, tax anticipation loans and the EITC
- Training Services
  - ✓Financial literacy training
  - ✓Homeownership counseling
  - ✓Credit repair
  - ✓Counseling
  - ✓Savings and investments
  - ✓Technology use

Some of the key issues surrounding these businesses include finding ways of making financial services less costly for those who can least afford them, finding better methods of delivering the services and offering a more complete range of financial services that covers all appropriate geographic areas. Moreover, the structure of the products that are based on the targeting of households with a lack of capacity to use these services needs to be addressed. The methods and technologies are developing that would support this result and still generate adequate profits for participating businesses.

The fringe banking industry is undergoing rapid change. To some degree, it may move in more helpful directions, partly because it is being forced to do so by advocates' pressures, negative publicity, lawsuits and large financial judgements against corporations, and the pressure of market forces. There is consolidation occurring and possible barriers to entry may be emerging as the size to be competitive increases and improved access to capital markets is needed in order to enter the industry. Therefore, these institutions may have a greater interest in presenting a different image and gaining more public acceptance, particularly as they attempt to broaden their market to slightly higher income households.

Many institutions have been involved and many others are considering wider involvement in offering financial services, while still others are thinking about starting to provide financial services. Presently, government officials and regulators have been encouraging banks to find ways to offer more assistance to low-income households (Freeman). There is a major effort to encourage credit unions and CDCUs to become more involved in providing financial services in low-income neighborhoods. Some nonprofits are seriously exploring their role in this arena. Conventional financial institutions are increasingly involved, but they probably will have to change their business models dramatically in order to successfully compete directly on a major scale, assuming that this would be of interest to them.

However, there is no dedicated, concentrated effort—combined with the availability of additional resources—to support this effort. There is no effort to create an initiative that could achieve some type of scale and real impact.

If community development efforts in the U.S. want to seriously address these issues, they will need to find ways to provide extensive assistance in a wide range of areas—training and technical assistance, deeper study of workable models, different types of capital needed to begin and sustain new programs, creating the capacity to adapt models to local conditions, etc. Both public policy and business practice need to address these issues.

Therefore, some method of providing systematic assistance—both financial and technical—on a greater level to support this type of effort is essential to creating a widespread web of financial services institutions capable of having an impact in low-income neighborhoods and changing the financial practices that exist in them.

This assistance needs to come from a wide range of interested institutions and individuals, including public agencies and governments at all levels, foundations, conventional financial institutions and non-traditional financial institutions, religious institutions, the private sector and others.

This type of support would allow some of the existing as well as new community based efforts to obtain greater assistance in the early stages of developing their programs. And one of the goals of any program must be reaching scale. These efforts need to be coupled with some form of increased regulation that will provide a basic, minimal framework for their operations. Without some substantial efforts of this type, market forces will continue to determine the types of services provided and the fees and rates that are charged. Relying solely on the market in this manner will continue to result in great harm to low-income households, at least for the most part in most places.

This study has reviewed many aspects of the industry: the types of businesses and their characteristics; variations in business models and the foundations for successful approaches; the financial feasibility and economic characteristics of these businesses; the profit potential and the roles of large corporations in the industry.

The core of the work in this report has been framed from the perspective of developing and understanding a range of business models, their financial feasibility and possible new, financially feasible models or alternatives. There is an increasing amount of activity and research in this field now. Most of this work, which is of very high quality, focuses on programmatic and policy options. However, there is also a need for work that is aimed at understanding the business models and financial feasibility. These additional steps are absolutely necessary to understand the present situation and develop new approaches to improve conditions.

With further effort in the regulatory, policy, program arenas , and by understanding the economic framework, major changes in the financial services systems supporting low-income neighborhoods can be made that will assist low-income people in moving out of poverty and participating more fully in the economic future of the country.

Chapter References and Notes

I. INTRODUCTION

Caskey, John P. (1994). *Fringe Banking*. New York: Russell Sage Foundation.

Deloitte, Touche, Tohmatsu International (1995). The Future of Retail Banking, A Global Perspective.

II. THE INDUSTRY

Aberdeen American News (November 6, 2002). "What Would Life Be Like on Minimum Wage?"

Allen, Ethan, (2000). The Simple Finance Plan. Ethan Allen Treasury.

Allison, Melissa (February 28, 2002). Household to Alter Practices on Loans. *Chicago Tribune*, p.1.

Associated Press Newswires (September 22, 2002). Pawnshops, Bankruptcy Lawyers, Debt Traders Cash in on Slump.

Association of Progressive Rental Organizations (2004) "Customer Profile," "Average Store Profile," "Transaction Profile," "Facts About RTO." Downloaded from www.apro-rto.com.

Bailey, Jeff (December 11, 1996). HFC Profits Nicely by Charging Top Rates on Some Risky Loans. *Wall Street Journal*.

Bailey, Jeff (April 8, 1998). Conseco Agrees to Acquire Green Tree. *Wall Street Journal*.

Bank of America (2002). Safesend: A New Way to Send Money to Mexico. Downloaded from www.bankofamerica.com/safesend.

Beckett, Paul (December 1, 2000). Citigroup Completes Associates Purchase As It Agrees to Improve Lending Practices. *Wall Street Journal*.

Beckett, Paul (September 6, 2002). Citigroup May Pay $200 Million in FTC "Predatory Lending Case. *Wall Street Journal*, p. A1.

Beckett, Paul & Hallinan, Joseph (October, 11 2002). Household May Pay $500 Million over *Predatory* Loan Practices. *Wall Street Journal*, p. A1.

Beckett, Paul (July 18, 2002). Citigroup's 'Subprime' Reforms Questioned. *Wall Street Journal*, p. C1.

Bergquist, Erick (November 20, 2002). Activists Disagree on Effects of HSBC's Deal for Household. *American Banker*.

Berthelsen, Christian (November 15, 2001). Study Says Fewer Checks are in the Mail. *San Francisco Chronicle*.

Berthelsen, Christian (November 27, 2001). Industry Vet New CEO at S.F. Firm. *San Francisco Chronicle*.

Berthelsen, Christian (January 17, 2002). Providian Sells Best Accounts for $8.2 Billion. *San Francisco Chronicle.*

Berthelsen, Christian (April 17, 2002). Providian Sells Accounts. *San Francisco Chronicle.*

Berthelsen, Christian (May 7, 2002). Surprising Profit for Providian. *San Francisco Chronicle.*

Berthelsen, Christian, (October 12, 2002), "Lender Agrees to Settle," *San Francisco Chronicle*, p. B1.

Berthelsen, Christian (December 12, 2002). BofA Buys 25% of Banco Santander. *San Francisco Chronicle*, p. B1.

Berube, Alan & Forman, Benjamin (November 2001). Rewarding Work: the Impact of the EITC in Greater Chicago. *The Brookings Institution.*

Berube, Alan, Kim, Anne, Forman, Benjamin and Burns, Megan (May 2002). The Price of Paying Taxes: How Tax Preparation and Refund Loan Fees Erode the Benefits of the EITC. *The Brookings Institution.*

B.E.S.T., Inc. (2002). Show Me the Money: A Quick Guide to the Check Cashing Business. Des Plaines, Illinois.

Better Business Bureau (Autumn 2000). Bit or Bounty, Providian to Pay for Provoking its Cardholders.

Bradford, Calvin (May 2002). Risk or Race? Racial Disparities and the Subprime Refinance Market. *Center for Community Change.*

Branch, Shelley (June 8, 1998). Where Cash is King. *Fortune.*

Brazil, Eric (June 24, 2001). Wiring Money Home – Cheaply. *San Francisco Chronicle.*

Breitkopf, David (September 3, 2002). ATMs Gaining in the Money Transfer Biz. *San Francisco Chronicle.*

Breitkopf, David (October 7, 2002). 7-Eleven Slows Down Cash Machine Rollout. *American Banker.*

Bremner, Brain (October 8, 1990). Looking Downscale – Without Looking Down. *Business Week*, p. 62f.

Broome, J. Tol (August 2000). Improving Cash Flow Without Increasing Sales. *Home Furnishings Executive.*

Burger, Albert and Zellmer, Mary (1995). "Strategic Opportunities in Serving Low to Moderate Income Members," Madison, Wisconsin: Filene Research Institute.

Business Wire (January 24, 2002). Cash America press release of financial information. www.cashamerica.com.

Business Wire (April 1, 2002). "Fleet Launches Access Advantage Account."

Business Wire, (June 6, 2002), "Cash America Completes Sale of Rent-to Own Subsidiary."

Business Wire (August 14, 2002). "Cash America Completes $132.5 Million Financing."

Byrnes, Nanette (September 4, 1995). "Nothing Subprime About These Profits," *Business Week*, p. 98.

Cahill, Joseph (March 3, 1999). "Title Loan Firms Offer Car Owners a Solution That Often Backfires," *Wall Street Journal*, p. A1.

Caldor, Lendol (1999), *Financing the American Dream*. Princeton, NJ: Princeton University Press.

California Health and Human Services Data Center, "Electronic Benefit Transfer Project," www.ebtproject.ca.gov.

California Reinvestment Committee, (December 2001), "Stolen Wealth: Inequities in California's Subprime Market."

Canto, Minerva, (November 23, 2002), "Money Wiring Draws Scrutiny," *The Orange County Register*.

Capel, Kerry, (December 23, 1996), "Low Risk Investing in High Risk Loans," *Business Week*.

Caplowitz, David, (1963), *The Poor Pay More*, New York: The Free Press of Glencoe.

Caskey, John P., (1994), *Fringe Banking*. New York: Russell Sage Foundation.

Caskey, John P., *Lower Income Americans, Higher Cost Financial Services, (1997)*. Madison, Wisconsin: Filene Research Institute, Center for Credit Union Research.

Caskey, John P., *The Economics of Payday Lending*, (2002). Madison, Wisconsin: Filene Research Institute, Center for Credit Union Research.

Castaneda, Laura, (April 25, 1998), "Western Union Service Cashes Electronic Federal Benefits," *San Francisco Chronicle*.

Condon, Bernard, (November 2, 1998), " 'I Don't Do Dumb Growth'," *Forbes*.

Consumer Federation of America, (January 2002), "Don't Pay Triple Digit Interest to Borrow Your Own Tax Refund."

Credit Union Journal, (October 7, 2002), "There's Nothing 'Fringe' About the Revenues Being Generated."

Davenport, Todd, (October 18, 2002), "Report: Treasury Undercounting the Unbanked," *American Banker*.

Deloitte, Touche, Tohmatsu International, (1995), "The Future of Retail Banking, A Global Perspective."

Dove Consulting, (April 4, 2002), "Survey of Non-Bank Financial Institutions," prepared for the U.S. Treasury.

Druckerman, Pamela, (March 25, 1998), "Wall Street Repackages Worker Remittances," *Wall Street Journal*.

Eavis, Peter, (August 17, 2002), "Lawsuits and Regulators Shadow Big Lender's Future," *New York Times*.

Economist, November 2, 2002), "A Survey of Migration: the View from Afar," p. 11-12.

Economist, November 23, 2002), "HSBC: Bottom Fishing," p. 66.

Electronic Payments International, (August 16, 2002), "Banks Join Battle for Migrants' Money."

Ellis, Junius, (November 1996), "Countrywide May Soar up to 50%, but Beware of High Flying Aames," *Money*, p. 39.

Entrepreneur Group, (1992), "Check Cashing: Entrepreneur Guide No. 139."

Fair Disclosure Wire, (November 7, 2002), "H&R Block Conference Call Responding to Texas Judge Ruling," Mark Ernst, H&R Block.

Foust, Dean, (April 24, 2000), "Easy Money," *Business Week*, p. 107-114.

Gallagly, Edward and Dernovsek, Darla, (2000), "Fair Deal: Creating Credit Union Alternatives to Fringe Financial Services," *Credit Union National Association, Inc.*

Goldberg, Debby, (Spring 2002), "Single Premium Credit Insurance," *Housing and*

Neighborhoods, Center for Community Change.

Goldman, Gerald, (Fall 2002), "Check Cashers Still Battling Bank Discontinuance," *Checklist*, p. 48ff.

Goldstein, Deborah, (October 1999), "Understanding Predatory Lending," *Joint Center for Housing Studies of Harvard University.*

Gramlich, Governor Edward, (Summer/Fall 2000), "Predatory Lending," *Cascade* (Federal Reserve Bank of Philadelphia), p. 1.

Ha, K. Oanh, (March 20, 2002), "High Interest Rates, Fees Cited," *San Jose Mercury News.*

Hallinan, Joseph, (March 24, 2002), "Conseco Renegotiates the Terms of $1.5 Billion Consortium Debt," *Wall Street Journal.*

Hartnack, Richard C., (Summer 2001), "Union Bank of California – Bringing Convenience Banking to Communities," *Community Developments*, p. 8-10.

Hartnack, Richard C., Vice Chairman, UnionBanCal Corporation, Interviews: March 16, 2000; March 22, 2000; December 21, 2000; April 11, 2001; June 20, 2002. Presentation made to UBOC Advisory Group, February 3, 2001.

Hawke, John D., (Fall 2000), "Focus on Retail Financial Services to Underserved Communities," *Community Developments*, (The OCC's community affairs newsletter).

Heinz, Mark, (June 9, 2002), "Payday/Car Title Loan Business Not Likely to Dry Up in Idaho, Experts Say," Times-News (Twin Falls, Idaho).

Hendricks, Tyche, (March 24, 2002), "Wiring Cash Costly for Immigrants," *San Francisco Chronicle.*

Henriques, Diana, (October 27, 2000), "Extra Costs on Car Loans Draw New Legal Attacks," *New York Times*, p. A1.

Henriques, Diana, (July 4, 2001), "Review of Car Loans Finds that Blacks Pay More," *New York Times.*

Ho, David, (September 20, 2002), "Citigroup to Settle Consumer Class-Action Suit," *San Francisco Chronicle*, p. B3.

Household Bank, "Express Refund Lending." Brochure.

Hudson, Mike, (July/August, 1994), "Robbin' the Hood," *Mother Jones.*

Hudson, Michael, (1996), *Merchants of Misery*, Monroe, Maine: Common Courage Press.

Huffman, Paul J. and Hinton, Marks, (February/March 1997), "Riding the Wave of Acquisition," *Progressive Rentals.*

Immergluck, Daniel and Wiles, Marti, (November 1999), "Two Steps Back: The Dual Mortgage Market, Predatory Lending and the Undoing of Community Development," *Woodstock Institute.*

Johnson, Chip, (May 20, 2000), "Hock Shops Are Pawns to Progress as Oakland Booms," San Francisco Chronicle.

Johnson, Jason, (May 27, 2001), "Pawn Business Booms as Bills Rise," *San Francisco Chronicle.*

Johnston, David Cay, (May 26, 2002), "A Tax Refund Check That Just Keeps Shrinking," *New York Times.*

Johnston, David Cay, (May 21, 2002), "Tax Credit Is Financial Bonanza for 2 Big Tax Preparers," *New York Times.*

Kahn, Joseph, (February 4, 1999), "Banking on the Unbanked," *New York Times.*

Kansas City Business Journal, (January 18, 2002), "H&R Block Uses Texas Company's Machines for Refund Check-Cashing."

Klees, Dee, (March 30, 2002), "Cashing Tax Refunds Can Be Pricey," *Syracuse Post-Standard.*

Kosta, Chris, (September, October, 1998), "From Big to Bigger," *Progressive Rentals.*

Koudsi, Suzanne, (March 4, 2002), "Sleazy Credit," *Fortune,* p. 143ff.

Krebsbach, Karen, (September 6, 2002), "Following the Money," *Bank Technology News.*

Labrinas, James and Kelly, William A., Jr, (1996), "The Effects of Member Income Levels on Credit Union Performance," Madison, Wisconsin: The Filene Research Institute.

Lacko, James M., McKernan, Singe-Mary, and Hastak, Manoj, (April 2000), "Survey of Rent-to-Own Customers," *Federal Trade Commission.*

Leibsohn, Daniel (2005). *Financial Services Programs: Case Studies from a Business Model Perspective.* Manchester: Community Economic Development Press.

Leuty, Ron, (June 22-28, 2002), "Providian Shells Out Another $105 Million," *San Francisco Business Times,* p. 1.

Lewis, Jake, (October 2001), "Renting to Owe," *Multinational Monitor,* p. 1617.

Lipin, Steven and Bailey, Jeff, (February 17, 1998), "Beneficial Corp. Puts Itself on the Market as a Result of Pressure from Wall Street," *Wall Street Journal.*

Lockyer, Sara, (November 23, 2002), "Latinos Wary of U.S. Banks; Immigrants Pay High Fees to Remit Wages," *South Florida Sun-Sentinel.*

Malhotra, Priya, (July 19, 2002), "At the ATM, Another Way to Send Cash," *American Banker.*

Malkin, Elizabeth and Morris, Kathleen, (May 26, 1997), "The Wires are Humming—with Cash," *Business Week.*

Malveaux, Julianne, (May 7, 2000), "Auto Title Borrowing is a Bad Money Move," *San Francisco Chronicle.*

Manning, Robert D., (2000), *Credit Card Nation,* New York: Basic Books.

McCarthy, Brian, (October 2000), "What Financial Factors Best Predict Profitability?," *Western Reporter, Jounal of Home Furnishings.*

McGeehan, Patrick, (June 29, 2001), "Citigroup to End Tactic on Mortgages," *New York Times.*

McNamee, Mike, (October 19, 1992), "Jumping into the Credit Gaps," *Business Week.*

Melcher, Richard and Osterland, Andrew, (February 16, 1998), "High Risk Lenders Land with a Thud," *Business Week,* p. 100.

Mendel, Dick, (Fall/Winter 2001), "Repealing the Hidden Tax," *Annie E. Casey Foundation.*

Millman, Joel, (March 7, 2001), "Big Bank Targets Immigrant Group, Many Illegal," *Wall Street Journal,* p. B1.

Mollenkamp, Carrick, (July 25, 2000), "How Money Store Inspired a Big Change in First Union's Course," *Wall Street Journal,* p. A1.

NeighborWorks Journal, "A Look at the Future of Investment and Financial Services in Revitalizing Communities," Winter 2000, Neighborhood Reinvestment Corporation.

Nendick, Elizabeth, (October 18, 2002), "Ethical Debate Heats Up as Payday Lenders Thrive," *Rockford Register Star* (Illinois).

Nieves, Evelyn, (January 15, 1998), "Poor Credit? Rent-to-Moan is Wooing You," *New York Times.*

Nol, Michael, (August 31, 2001), "Citigroup Ends Alliance with 3,622 Consumer Loan Brokers," *Los Angeles Times.*

Norris, Floyd, (August 6, 1995), "Investors Love to Loans to Deadbeats," *New York Times.*

Northwestern Financial Review, (March 1, 2002), "Bank Offers Tax Help at Laundromat."

Oppel, Jr, Richard, (March 7, 2001), "U.S. Suit Cites Citigroup Unit on Loan Deceit," *New York Times*, p. A1.

Ortiz, Laura, (October 7, 2002), "Partnership Says It Can Save Workers 'Billions'," *Credit Union Journal.*

Osterland, Andrew, (December 1, 1997), "How Green Tree Got Pruned," Business Week.

Peattie, Earl, (1998), "Navigating the Subprime Mortgage," *Consumer Mortgage Education Consortium.*

"Poverty, Inc.," (July 1998), *Consumer Reports.*

PR Newswire, (January 17, 2001), "ACE Cash Express Partners with H&R Block."

PR Newswire, (January 24, 2001), "ACE Cash Express Second Quarter Revenue Increases 21 Percent." www.acecashexpress.com

PR Newswire, (September 27, 2002), "Latino Community Credit Union Teams with US Treasury, USAID and Mexican Credit Unions to Save Latinos Billions."

Pyle, Amy, (February 11, 1999), "Consumer" Groups Attack 'Payday Loans'," *Los Angeles Times.*

Rent-A-Center, Inc., (2002), "ProForma Quarterly Financials, 10Q Format, 1995 – Q2, 2002.

Rent-A-Center Press Releases, (July 29, 2002), "Rent-A-Center, Inc. Reports Second Quarter 2002 Results." See also, www.rentacenter.com.

Reuters, (December 12, 2001), "Net Serves as an Equalizer."

Reuters, (September 7, 2002), "Citigroup to Buy Associates for $31.1 Billion," *Los Angeles Times.*

Reuters, (October 11, 2002), "Household Reaches Settlement with States Over Lending Practices," *New York Times.*

Romney, Lee, (April 6, 1999), "Credit Unions Link Up in Effort to Cut High Cost of Money Transfers," *Los Angeles Times.*

Romney, Lee, (December 15, 2000), "Immigrant Money is Gold Mine," Lee Romney, *Los Angeles Times,* page 1.

Sarkisian, Masis, President, B.E.S.T., Interviews, January 8, 2002; February 28, 2002; March 15, 2002; March 20, 2002.

Saunders, Edmund, (August 26, 2000), "Program to Spur Bank Accounts for Poor Falling Short," *Los Angeles Times*, p.A1.

Saunders, Margot, (July 27, 2001), Testimony on behalf of Low Income Clients before U.S. Senate Committee on Banking, Housing and Urban Affairs.

Scherer, Ron, (December 31, 2001), "Falling Interest Rates Don't Trickle Down," *Christian Science Monitor.*

Scott, Joyce, (October/November 1996), "A Booming New Market," *Progressive Rentals.*

Shaver, Todd, (April 15, 2002), "First Data Corporation," *Bull MarketReport Daily*, section number 8.

Shaver, Todd, (November 11, 2002), "Americredit," *Bull MarketReport In-Depth Report*

Shaver, Todd, (November 11, 2002), "Capital Gains Lead to Capital One Losses," *Bull Market Financial Report.*

Siegel, William, (October 4, 2002), "Check Cashers Play Vital Role in Serving the 'Unbanked'," *American Banker.*

Sinton, Peter, (March 5, 1998), "First Union Buys the Money Store," *San Francisco Chronicle,* p. C1.

Sinton, Peter, (April 2, 1998), "Providian's Gamble Pays Off," *San Francisco Chronicle,* p. D1.

Sklar, Jeffrey, "Business Valuations," (October 6, 2001), FISCA Conference, San Diego, CA. Mr. Sklar is a partner in SHC Consulting in New York.

Smith, Geoffrey, (November 4, 2002), "The Bill Comes Due for Capital One," *Business Week,* p. 47.

Smith, Rebecca, (August 18, 1999), "State Welfare Payments Going the Electronic Route," *San Francisco Chronicle.*

Sorkin, Andrew Ross, (November 15, 2002), "HSBC to Buy a U.S. Lender for $14.2 Billion," *New York Times.*

Sparks, Debra, (August 25, 1997), "Is this Lender Too Hungry for its Own Good?," *Business Week.*

Sparks, Debra, (April 17, 2000), "No Money Grows Here," *Business Week.*

State of New York, Banking Department, (August 30, 2000), "Check Casher Consolidated Statements, 1999."

Stein, Eric, (October 30, 2001), "A Report from the Coalition for Responsible Lending."

Stempel, Jonathon, (November 14, 2002), "Household Bonds Soar on HSBC Merger," *Reuters.*

Tax Smart, "Cash Incentives" and "Frequently Asked Questions." Flyers.

Thompson, Laura, (February 8, 2002), "Tax Filing Service at Minn. Laundromat," *American Banker.*

Timmons, Heather, (May 15, 2000), "First Union Turns Straw Into Gold," *Business Week.*

Timmons, Heather, (July 10, 2000), "How the Money Store Became a Money Pit," *Business Week.*

Timmons, Heather, (March 19, 2001), "Is Citi Bleeding its Weakest Borrowers?," *Business Week,* p. 94.

Timmons, Heather, (July 16, 2001), "Could Citi Make Money by Sending Money?," *Business Week,* p. 83.

Timmons, Heather, (August 13, 2001), "Have Banks Been 'Giving Tequila to a Drunk'?," *Business Week.*

Timmons, Heather, (August 13, 2001), "Good Times for Bad Paper," *Business Week.*

Timmons, Heather, (December 19, 2001), "Do Household's Numbers Add Up?," *Business Week.*

TravelersExpress MoneyGram, (1999), "Open Your Business to a New World of Opportunity."

U.S. Comptroller of the Currency, "Financial Access in the 21st Century," Proceedings of a Forum, February 11, 1997.

U. S. Comptroller of the Currency, (Fall 2000), *Community Developments.*

Vickers, Martha and Timmons, Heather, (October 7, 2002), "The Housing Boom's Dark Side," Business Week. P. 120-4.

Weber, Joseph, (November 5, 2001), "Let the Bidding Begin for Providian," *Business Week,* p. 96.

Western Reporter, (October 2000), "Home Furnishings Industry Averages, *Journal of Home Furnishings.*

Western Union, (2001), "Doing Business in the Fast Lane."

Wilke, John, (October 21, 1991), "Some Banks' Money Flows into Poor Areas - and Causes Anguish," *Wall Street Journal.*

Willis, Rick, (August 14, 1999), "High Cost of Wiring Money from U.S. to Mexico," *New York Times.*

Winn III, Ed, (June/July 1996), "Fringe Banking," *Progressive Rentals.*

Winn III, Ed, (March/April 1998), "Taking a Stab at the Interest Debate," *Progressive Rentals.*

Winn III, Ed, (January/February 2000), "RTO: Yesterday, Today and Tomorrow," *Progressive Rentals.*

Woolley, Suzanne, (April 13, 1993), "Western Union Banks on the 'Unbanked'," *Business Week.*

Wu, Chi Chi, Fox, Jean Ann and Renuart, Elizabeth, (January 31, 2002), "Refund Anticipation Loans," *Consumer Federation of America and the National Consumer Law Center.*

Zellner, Wendy, (November 9, 1998), "How CFS Made Bad Debts Pay So Well," *Business Week,* p. 48.

Zellner, Wendy and Zweig, Phillip, (August 11, 1997), "Bad Debts, Sweet Profits," *Business Week.*

Zuckerman, Sam, (May 5, 2002), "How Providian Misled Cardholders," *San Francisco Chronicle.*

NOTES TO PAYDAY LENDING

Anderson, Mark, (June 9, 2000), "Rival Bills Both Seek to Restrict Payday Advances," *Sacramento Business Jounal.*

Anderson, Mark, (June 8, 2001), "Lawmakers Resume Battle over Payday Advance Loans," *Sacramento Business Jounal.*

Associated Press Newswires, (November 7, 2001), "Bills Compete to Regulate Loan Companies." (Michigan)

Associated Press Newswires, (January 28, 2002), "Short term Loans Still Common Despite Rules." (Oklahoma)

Associated Press Newswires, (March 9, 2002), "Loan Company Will Settle Class-action Lawsuit for $1.4 million."

Associated Press Newswires, (March 26, 2002), "Feds Question Paris Bank's Third Party Loans."

Associated Press Newswires, (April 29, 2002), "Out of State Loan Companies Export High Interest Rates to West Virginia."

Associated Press Newswires, (May 20, 2002), "Briefs from Baltimore."

Beckett, Paul, (October 30, 2002), "Payday Loans are Dealt Blow by Regulators – ACE Cash and California Bank Face Fines as U.S. Controller Seeks to Curb Lending Practice," *Wall Street Journal.*

Berthelsen, Christian, (August 10, 2000), Payday Loan Rules Rejected," *San Francisco Examiner.*

B.E.S.T., Inc. "Show Me the Money: A Quick Guide to the Check Cashing Business," Des Plaines, Illnois.

Blassingame, Kelley, (September 15, 2002), "Payroll Deduction Card Builds up Employees' Credit," *Employee Benefit News.*

Bohman, Jim, (March 31, 2002), "A Responsibility to Help," *Dayton Daily News.*

Bonner, Lynn, (January 15, 2002), "State Sues to Block Pay Day Lender," *The (Raleigh, NC) News & Observer.*

Brooks, Rick, (February 25, 1999), "How Banks Make the Most of Bounced Checks," *Wall Street Journal,* p. B1.

Burns, Judith, (March 19, 2002), "SEC Shuts Down Payday Lender," *Dow Jones New Service.*

Caldor, Lendol, (1999), *Financing the American Dream.* Princeton, NJ: Princeton University Press.

Caplowitz, David, (1963), *The Poor Pay More,* New York: The Free Press of Glencoe.

Carr, James and Schuetz, Jenny, (August 2001), "Financial Services in Distressed Communities: Framing the Issue, Finding Solutions," Washington, D.C.: *Fannie Mae Foundation.*

Caskey, John P., (1994), *Fringe Banking.* New York: Russell Sage Foundation.

Caskey, John P., *Lower Income Americans, Higher Cost Financial Services, (1997).* Madison, Wisconsin: Filene Research Institute, Center for Credit Union Research.

Caskey, John P., *The Economics of Payday Lending,* (2002). Madison, Wisconsin: Filene Research Institute, Center for Credit Union Research.

Coleman, Jennifer, (November 1, 2002), "Feds Order State Bank to Stop Making Payday Loans," *San Francisco Chronicle.*

Community Financial Services Association of America, (2001), "Best Practices for the Payday Advance Industry."

Community Financial Services Association of America, Annual Conference, October 6-7, 2002, San Diego, California.

Consumer Federation of America and state Public Interest Research Groups, (February 2000), "Show Me the Money!."

Consumer Reports, (March 2000), "Cracking Down on Payday Loans."

Cox, Dan, (August 25, 2002), "Instant Money Loan Alert," *New York Post.*

Credit Union Journal, (July 15, 2002), "Why Does Anyone Use a Payday Lender? Study Provides Answers."

Dallas Business Journal, (October 2, 2002). "Judge Dismisses Suit Against ACE Cash Express."

DeMarzo, Wanda, (November 25, 2001), "Aiming to Snap Cycle of Debt, Law Regulates Payday Advances," *Miami Herald.*

Dollar Financial Group, (January 4, 2002), "Dollar Financial Group Announces Agreement with Eagle National Bank," *Business Wire.*

Duran, Nicole, (January 4, 2002), "OCC Orders Bank to Exit Payday Biz," *American Banker.*

Duran, Nicole, (February 8, 2002), "DC Speaks: Stymied for Now, LaFalce Eyes States to Check Payday Lending," *American Banker.*

Duran, Nicole, (November 25, 2002), "Peoples of Texas Loses Second Bid to Dispute OCC's Ruling," *American Banker.*

Eagle National Bank, "Cash Till Payday Loan Application," $100, $200, $300.

Fattah, Geoffrey, (May 23, 2002), "Elderly, Minorities are Prey of Shady Lenders, Panel Told," *Deseret News* (Utah).

Fox, Jean Ann, (November 1998), "A Report on the Payday Loan Industry," *Consumer Federation of America.*

Fox, Jean Ann and Mierzwinski, Edmund, (November 2001), "Rent-A-Bank Payday Lending," *Consumer Federation of America* and *U.S. Public Interest Research Group.*

Frazier, Lynn McKenna, (February 25, 2002), "Northern Indiana Sees Substantial Increase in Bankruptcy Filings in 2001," *New Sentinel* (Fort Wayne, IN).

Gillie, John, (December 7, 2001), "Moneytree Loan Stores Fill Gap Unmet by Banks, President Says," *News Tribune* (Tacoma,WA).

Gordon, Marcy, (November 13, 2001), "Payday Loans Targeted in Report," *Associated Press.*

Gordon, Marcy, (January 4, 2002), "Federal Agency Moves Against Payday Lending," *San Francisco Chronicle,* p. B4.

Gores, Paul, (September 16, 2002), "Credit Union Offers Alternative to Pay day Loans," *Milwaukee Journal Sentinel.*

Greensboro (NC) News & Record, (December 31, 2001), "Close the Loophole for Payday Lenders," editorial.

Grow, Steve, (January 30, 2002), "Payday Advance Loans are the Consumers' Choice," *News & Observer* (Raleigh, NC), guest editorial.

Guart, Al, (April 7, 2002), "Loanshark Bites Big Apple," *New York Post.*

Hackett, John, (November 1, 2001), "Ethically Tainted'", *US Banker.*

Harris, Shane, (December 2000), "A Few Bucks Until Payday," *Governing.* www.governing.com

Hartnack, Richard C., Vice Chairman, UnionBanCal Corporation, Interviews: March 16, 2000; March 22, 2000; December 21, 2000; April 11, 2001; June 20, 2002. Presentation made to UBOC Advisory Group, February 3, 2001.

Hazard, Carol, (February 18, 2002), "Payday Lending: Virginia is Latest Battleground for Small Loan Business," *Richmond Times-Dispatch.*

Hazard, Carol, (June 3, 2002), "Payday Loan Controls Set; New Law Lets State License, Regulate Industry," *Richmond Times-Dispatch.*

Heilman, Wayne, (November 25, 2001), "High Interest Payday Lending Booms in Colorado Springs, Colorado Area," *Knight Ridder Tribune Business News.*

Heinz, Mark, (June 9, 2002), "Payday/Car Title Loan Business Not Likely to Dry Up in Idaho, Experts Say," Times-News (Twin Falls, Idaho).

Hendren, John, (January 12, 1999), "Bending Lending Laws," *San Francisco Examiner.*

Higgins, Michelle, (September 17, 2002), "How to Get Free Money: Use Plastic," *Wall Street*

Journal, p. D1.

Jackson, Ben, (January 7, 2002), "Payday Mayday? Weighing the Impact," *American Banker*.

Jackson, Ben (January 31, 2002), "Oxley to OCC: Payday Deals Aren't Illegal," *American Banker*.

Jackson, Ben (May 8, 2002), "Payday Lender Ace Settles Colorado Suit," *American Banker*.

Jackson, Ben (May 13, 2002), "Ace Settlement Another Blow to Payday Lenders," *American Banker*.

Jackson, Ben, (June 6, 2002), "Federal Courts at Odds Over Payday Lending Pact," *American Banker*.

Jackson, Ben (July 9, 2002), "Can't Rent? Payday Shop Files to Buy a Charter," *American Banker*.

Jackson, Ben (August 5, 2002), "Brickyard of Illinois Pressured Over Payday Lending," *American Banker*.

Jackson, Ben (August 27, 2002), "Pay Day Lenders Aim to Strengthen Community Ties," *American Banker*.

Jackson, Ben (September 18, 2002), "Brickyard is Latest to Quit Pay Day Lending," *American Banker*.

Jackson, Ben and Reosti, John (October 30, 2002), "Goleta Will Quit Payday Loan Biz in OCC Pact," *American Banker*.

Kilborn, Peter, (June 18, 1999), "New Lenders With Huge Fees Thrive on Workers with Debts," *New York Times*, p. 1.

Koerner, Brandon, (May/June 2001), "Preying on Payday." *Mother Jones*, p. 19-20.

Kratz, Gregory, (January 27, 2002), "Easy Cash, Hard Reality," *Deseret News* (Utah).

Larson, Sara, (May 1999), "Subprime Lending Hurts the Poor – What is the Price for Credit?," *Housing Washington*, p. 13-14.

Lipp, Linda, (January 21, 2002), "Payday-lend Bill Might Satisfy All," *Fort Wayne News Sentinel*.

Los Angeles Times, editorial, (May 14, 2001), "Stop Legal Loan Sharks," p. B10.

Lydersen, Kari, (October 2001), "Payday Profiteers," *Multinational Monitor*, p. 9-15.

Lynch, Michael W.,(April 1, 2002), "Legal Loan Sharking or Essential Service," *Reason*, p. 38-9.

Lynch, Michael W.,(April 1, 2002), "Finance on the Fringe," *Reason*, p. 32ff.

Manning, Robert D., (2000), *Credit Card Nation*, New York: Basic Books.

Mathosian, Mark, (March 7, 2002), "Mark Mathosian Column," *Port Charlotte (Florida) Sun*.

Money Mart, "Cash Till Payday Loan Application," July 24, 2002.

Morton, Chris, (March 27, 2000), "Fed Amends Truth In Lending Act Regulations to Include Disclosure of Payday Loan Terms," *National Community Reinvestment Coalition* email.

National Consumer Law Center, (2000), "Payday Loans: A Form of Loansharking: the Problem, Legislative Strategies, A Model Act." www.nclc.org

National Community Reinvestment Coalition, (April 11, 2002), "NCRC Calls for Immediate CRA Exams for Abusive Payday Lenders."

Nendick, Elizabeth, (October 18, 2002), "Ethical Debate Heats Up as Payday Lenders Thrive,"

Rockford Register Star (Illinois).

Office of the Comptroller of the Currency, (March 18, 2002), "OCC Files Notice Against People's National Bank of Paris, Texas."

Pankratz, Howard, (May 7, 2002), "Payday Lender Lawsuit Settled: Ace to Refund $1.3 million in Finance Charges," *Denver Post.*

Paskind, Martin, (July 8, 2002), "If you Lend Money, Know the Rules," *Albuquerque Journal.*

Quick Payday, "New Member Application," (July 24, 2002). www.paydayandpaycheckloans.com.

Pepper, Miriam, (June 2, 2002), "The Sad Story of the Payday Loan Bill," *Kansas City Star.*

PR Newswire, (May 23, 2002), "Community Groups Warn Goleta National Bank Shareholders of Dangers of Ace Cash Express Partnership."

Pyle, Amy, (February 11, 1999), "Consumer Groups Attack Payday Loans," *Los Angeles Times,* p. A1.

Rawle, Richard, (July 11, 2002), "Payday Lenders Offer Useful Service," *Deseret News* (Utah).

Rein, Lisa, (March 5, 2002), "Virginia Passes Limits on Loans Till Payday," *Washington Post*, p. B4.

Reosti, John, (October 22, 2002), "Fighting for Payday Loans," *American Banker.*

Richmond Times Dispatch, (February 18, 2002), Study Profiles Payday Loan Borrower."

Rulison, Larry, (April 3, 2000), "State to Watch Over Payday Loan Trade," *Baltimore Business Journal.*

Said, Carolyn, (June 17, 2001), "Long Way from Pay Day," *San Francisco Chronicle*, p. C1.

San Diego Union-Tribune, (September 22, 2002), "Davis Approves Audits, Study of Payday Lending Industry."

Santa Fe New Mexican, (November 17, 2001), "High Interest Loans Damage the Poor," editorial.

Schafer, Shaun, (January 13, 2002), "Payday Loans Seem to be in Last Days," *Tulsa World.*

Serres, Chris, (December 2, 2001), "Lenders' Paydays Get Bigger," *The (Raleigh, NC) News & Observer.*

Shean, Tom, (February 16, 2002), "Payday Loan Bill Draws Criticism from Military," *The Virginian-Pilot and The Ledger Star* (Norfolk).

Skillern, Peter, (April 18, 2001), "How Pay Day Lenders Make Their Money," *Community Reinvestment Association of North Carolina.* www.cra-nc.org.

Skillern, Peter, (2002), "Small Loans, Big Bucks: an Analysis of the Pay Day Lending Industry in North Carolina," *Community Reinvestment Association of North Carolina.* www.cra-nc.org.

Squires, Michael, (December 23, 2001), "Tough Times: Short Term Loan Firms Prospering," *Las Vegas Review Journal.*

St. Louis Post-Dispatch, (June 4, 2002), "A Bad Bill in the Hand . . . ," editorial.

Storey, Charlene Komar, (Summer 2002), "Branding Sweeps Through the Industry," *Checklist.*

Thompson, Estes, (April 11, 2002), "Groups Protest Payday Lending Interest Rates in North Carolina," *Associated Press Newswire.*

Timmons, Heather, (March 10, 1999), "Fast Growing Payday Loan Business: Convenience or

Legal Loan Sharking," *American Banker Online.*

U. S. *Newswire,* (November 14, 2001), "California Consumers at Risk from Overregulation of Payday Loans, Taxpayer Advocate Tells General Assembly."

Wenske, Paul, (May 20, 2002), "Church Based Group Packs Consumer Clout," *Kansas City Star.*

Williams, Marva and Smolik, Karen, (March 2001), "Affordable Alternatives to Payday Loans," Woodstock Institute, *Reinvestment Alert,* number 16.

NOTES ON METHODOLOGY AND SOURCES TO IMPACT ON A HYPOTHETICAL FAMILY

This example was prepared from information in various books and articles, focus groups with low income people using these services, visits to various businesses, and discussions with many people in the field. It was not based on interviews with families, although the results of five focus groups held by Community Development Finance (held in August and September 2000) were broadly incorporated. Typically, the rates used in this example were not the worst ones as reported in the sources but were somewhat more moderate; the results described here, therefore, could be even more severe.

The numbers for the check cashing and the remittances were obtained from visits to many of these stores in the San Francisco Bay Area and Los Angeles. For example, Money Mart, a chain, lists its charges as 3% for payroll checks with identification (3.5% without identification), 10% for personal checks and money orders, etc. These charges were fairly standard. However, in some places, the rates were far less. In parts of Los Angeles, the rates have fallen to an average of 1.75%, according to newspaper accounts and some interviews, probably due to competition from a couple of banks which have entered the field. In New York, check cashing is regulated and 1.4% is the limit that can be charged. In the above example, 2% was used.

Remittances are available from many of these stores through Western Union, which charges based on the amount that is sent. For example, depending on the country and the final location's accessibility, sending $100 to $200 costs $15, $200 to $300 costs $12 and up, and so on. Sending money within the U.S. is sometimes more expensive (about $22 for $200 or less) probably due to a lower volume than some foreign countries. There are also some sources for international service which are far less expensive and/or do not increase as quickly when the amount sent increases.

The rent-to-own numbers were derived from visits to a store in Oakland. The numbers used in the example were the costs associated with the specific items sold at the store. These costs were obtained from visits to the Rent-A-Center, a large rent-to-own chain, on November 9, 1998 and on August 18, 2000 at 14th and Fruitvale in Oakland, California. The terms were $25.99 per week for 94 weeks, a total of $2,443.06 for a 32 inch RCA TV (which was sold by Circuit City, as advertised in the San Francisco Chronicle on January 8, 1999, for $549.99, usually without interest payments for a year). The couch/love seat combination cost $32.99 per week or $3,430.96 total over 104 months. The 21 cubic foot side-by-side, Whirlpool refrigerator also cost $32.99 per week for 104 months, also a total of $3,430.96. The washer/dryer, both Whirlpool, required $19.99 per week for 104 weeks, a total of $2,078.96. The television set was priced on November 8, 1998 and the remaining items were priced on August 18, 2000.

The personal loan numbers used in the example were obtained from conversations with staff of Household Finance and Beneficial Finance on August 30, 2000 and November 20, 2000, respectively. Research from books and articles as well as discussions indicates that rates can be higher than those used in the example.

It should also be noted that not everyone who uses a check cashing outlet also buys household appliances through a rent-to-own store and obtains a personal loan from a personal finance company. Some people may use one type of financial assistance but not another. Although it is certainly likely that many people use all of the services as outlined in this example, different percentages of people tend to use these services with greater or lesser intensity. At the same time, it is also important to note that not all of the financial services institutions working in low income neighborhoods were used in the example. For example, pawn shops and sub-prime mortgage lenders were not part of this example. If they had been included, the results would have been even worse.

NOTES TO THE MATRIX

Depository institutions, particularly banks, tend to not to make loans for less than $1,000 and/or terms of less than a year.

Check cashers charge a fee for cashing checks. They charge different rates for cashing government, payroll and personal checks. The fee may be anywhere from up to 3% of the face value of a government or payroll check to 12% for a personal check. The check cashing institution may charge a fee for an identification card if the user intends to use the service regularly, and may charge a higher fee if the user does not have what they consider "acceptable" identification.

Payday lenders are often stand-alone institutions, or often part of a check cashing institution. They make loans that are comparable to an advance of a person's paycheck or part of the paycheck amount The lender agrees to defer the deposit of the borrower's check for a certain period of time of up to 30 days, similar to writing a post-dated check, not to be cashed until the date agreed upon. These lenders usually require proof of employment and a checking account. They make short-term loans of between $100-$400 with 300%-900% APR, based on fees charged, if the loans are roll over throughout the year. These lenders are not subject to usury laws in many states and the availability of products and services is often a function of state regulations. These lending institutions allow for easy roll over of the loan with associated fees and higher interest rates. The fees for payday loans are often in the range of 10% to 17% of the loaned amount.

Collateralized lenders are a variety of lending operations that either finance the purchase of goods they sell or lend money in exchange for property or title to property. Examples of collateralized lenders are:
- *Pawn shops* lend money on items that have value, including TV's, stereos, jewelry, tools, musical instruments, computers and accessories, recreational equipment, boats, tractors, motorcycles, cameras, etc. Borrowers bring in items that they want to borrow against. The amount of money the borrower receives depends on the make, model and condition of the item. Pawn shops lend anywhere from 20% to 65% of the resale value of the item. The loan is due to be repaid in thirty days but the loan can be extended every month by paying the interest. Pawn shops vary in the fees and interest they charge

and are regulated in some states. As one example, a Virginia pawn shop charged a $2.00 one-time service charge, a 2% storage charge and 10% per monthly interest rate or finance charge.

- *Title lenders* lend money secured by the borrower's clear automobile title. Title lenders may charge 25% or more interest per month. Typically the loan is for thirty days. A borrower may extend the loan for a subsequent month if he or she pays the monthly interest due for the previous month. It is common that a borrower will rollover a title loan several times. There are sometimes additional fees and often times higher interest rates associated with these rollovers. If the borrower is unable to pay the monthly interest or principal that is due, the title lender takes possession of the automobile. Upon sale of the automobile, some lenders retain the proceeds of the sale even if the value of the automobile exceeds the loan amount. Most title loan companies require proof of employment.
- *Sale-leaseback operations* resemble payday lenders, except the borrower signs a paper "selling" personal property to the lender for the amount borrowed but gets to keep the property for a "rental" payment usually around 1/3 of every $100 borrowed. Effective annual interest rates for these transactions can exceed 700% as they are not subject to usury laws in most states.

Rent to Own companies "rent" merchandise, although the structure of the transaction is more like a loan because of the interest and credit insurance involved. These businesses charge a weekly or monthly rent for a stated period, after which the property is owned by the "renter." Because the store is "renting" instead of selling, the store does not have to report how much it is charging in interest. If a borrower is late with a payment, there is no legal limit to how much interest the store can charge in "finance charges," although the company usually repossesses the rental property.

Finance companies are regulated non-bank lenders that provide unsecured short-term loans to high-risk borrowers charging the maximum allowable interest rates and fees. They are sometimes affiliated with conventional banking and insurance institutions. They often encourage refinancing and loan consolidation at rates that are higher than if a borrower went to a depository institution.

Mortgage companies in the fringe lender category specialize in sub-prime (sometimes referred to as non-prime) home mortgage and home equity loans and, in a few instances, car loans. They target those with impaired credit, employing numerous techniques to inflate the amount a person can borrow and charge high interest rates and various fees. Many of these companies are associated with banking institutions that offer additional financial services. Sub-prime mortgage rates are usually 4 to 6 or more percentage points higher than the prime lending rate.

SERVICES

Credit Insurance is often provided by lending institutions receiving a commission on the sale of the insurance. Lenders collect, on average, 30-40 percent of a borrower's first year's credit insurance premium as a commission. Credit insurance is usually structured as a fee to the borrower and sometimes borrowers have no choice and/or may not even know they are purchasing credit insurance as part of their loan. Many fringe lenders require credit insurance even in situations where the risk of default does not warrant the purchase of the credit insurance. In a pawn situation, if the borrower defaults on the loan, a pawn broker often sells the property pawned *and* collects the insurance. Some credit insurance is non-filing insurance which protects the lender who does not file a UCC, thereby self-insuring against risk of not perfecting a security interest in the property used as collateral. In the mortgage industry, single-premium credit insurance (SPCI), where credit insurance premiums are financed into the loan through a single up-front payment, is the most significant predatory mortgage lending abuse. There are some states that regulate credit insurance or some aspects of credit insurance. Premiums vary from state to state. Some types of credit insurance include:

> property coverage
> credit life
> credit disability
> involuntary unemployment insurance.

Electronic Benefits Transfer (EBT) is a vehicle for delivering government benefits to a financial institution using electronic technologies. Under EBT, the government wires funds into an account. The account holder (beneficiary) has limited access to these funds.

Smart Cards, first developed in the 1970s, are credit-card sized plastic cards with an embedded computer chip. Their applications combine use in telecommunications (mobile phones, DirecTV), financial services (electronic purses, bank cards, online payment systems), retail, transportation, and healthcare (insurance card) industries. The card holder puts a certain amount of funds in an account that is recorded on the card and then draws funds from the card for various uses.

CHAPTER 3: BUSINESS MODELS

Allison, Melissa, (July 7, 2002), "Banco Popular Seeks More Non-Hispanics," *Chicago Tribune.*

Anason, Dean, (August 4, 1997), "Float Won't Pay for Costs of Servicing EBT Accounts, Treasury Says," *American Banker.*

Atlas, Riva, (November 12, 2002), "Banks Make Lots of Money Off 'Free Checking' Accounts," *San Francisco Chronicle*, reprinted from the *New York Times.*

Baltimore Business Journal, "Credit Union to Offer Services to City's Poor," November 18, 2002.

B.E.S.T., Inc. "Show Me the Money: A Quick Guide to the Check Cashing Business," Des Plaines, Illnois.

Blackwell, Rob and Kingson, Jennifer, (May 17, 2002), "Wal-Mart's Designs on Processing," *American Banker.*

Blair, Jason, (August 12, 2002), "In the Big City, Smaller Banks Find a Sizable Niche," *New York Times*, p. 1.

Bohman, Jim, (March 31, 2002), "A Responsibility to Help," *Dayton Daily News.*

Breitkopf, David, (October 7, 2002), "7-Eleven Slows Down Cash Machine Rollout," *American Banker.*

Bremner, Brian, (October 8, 1990), "Looking Downscale – Without Looking Down," *Business Week*, p. 62-4.

Brown, Tony, (September 16, 2002), "CDFIs Bring Capital to Poor Areas," *National Mortgage News.*

Bruce, Laura, (April 4, 2002), "Lower Fees, More Free Accounts in 2002," "Highlights of the Spring 2002 Checking Account Pricing Study," *Bankrate.com.*

Business Wire, (April 1, 2002), "Fleet Launches Access Advantage Account."

Business Wire, (July 15, 2002), "Communidad El Banco Nuestra to Celebrate Grand Opening of Roswell Branch."

Calvey, Mark, (April 26, 2002), "Bank Branches in Bloom," *San Francisco Business Times,* p. 23.

Carr, James and Schuetz, Jenny, (August 2001), "Financial Services in Distressed Communities: Framing the Issue, Finding Solutions," Washington, D.C.: *Fannie Mae Foundation.*

Caskey, John and Humphrey, David, (1999), "Credit Unions and Asset Accumulation by Lower Income Households," *Filene Research Institute.*

Caskey, John and Brayman, Susan, (2001), "Check Cashing and Savings Programs for Low Income Households: An Action Plan for Credit Unions," *Filene Research Institute.*

Coleman, Calmetta and Higgins, Michele, (July 10, 2002), "Do You Really Need a Bank?," *Wall Street Journal,* p. D1.

Community Reinvestment News, (Winter 2001), "Westamerica Enters Payday," San Francisco, CA. Page 1.

Crenshaw, Albert, (December 8, 2002), "Credit Unions Seek Broader Membership Rules," *Washington Post,* p. H4.

Davis, Ryan, (November 30, 2002), "SSA Credit Union in Banking on Check-Cashing Office Union; Hybrid Institution Caters to Underserved Areas," *Baltimore Sun.*

De Paula, Matthew, (July 5, 2002), "Wal-Mart's Getting its Foot in the Door," *Banking Technology News.*

Der Hovanesian, Mara, "For Small Banks, It's a Wonderful Life," *Business Week,* p. 83.

Diekmann, Frank, (November 11, 2002), "Banker Thoughts on the Underserved, Um, Unbanked," *Credit Union Journal.*

Distribution Management Briefing, (November 26, 2002), "Case Study: FleetBoston Financial."

Gallagly, Edward and Dernovsek, Darla, (2000), "Fair Deal: Creating Credit Union Alternatives to Fringe Financial Services," *Credit Union National Association, Inc.*

Gogoi, Pallavi, (June 18, 2002), "What's Next – the Bank of Burger King?," *Business Week,* p. 150.

Foundation, Larry, Tufano, Peter and Walker, Patricia, (July-August 1999), "Collaborating with Congregations: Opportunities for Financial Services in the Inner City, *Harvard Business Review,* p. 57-68.

Harlin, Kevin, (April 28, 2002), "Banks Court Unbanked," *Albany Times Union.*

Hartnack, Richard C., Vice Chairman, UnionBanCal Corporation, Interviews: March 16, 2000; March 22, 2000; December 21, 2000; April 11, 2001; June 20, 2002. Presentation made to UBOC Advisory Group, February 3, 2001.

Hartnack, Richard C., (Summer 2001), "Union Bank of California – Bringing Convenience Banking to Communities," *Community Developments,* p. 8-10.

Heintz, Nadine, (December 2002), "Money in the Bank," *Worth,* p. 23-4.

Holland, Kelley and Melcher, Richard, (July 31, 1995), "Why Banks Keep Bulking Up," *Business Week.*

Irwin, Gloria, (October 20, 2002), "Overdraft Protection: Courtesy or Curse?," *Akron Beacon Jounal.*

Jackson, Ben (July 15, 2002), "Popular Aims to Double in U.S.," *American Banker.*

Jackson, Ben (August 27, 2002), "Pay Day Lenders Aim to Strengthen Community Ties," *American Banker.*

Jackson, Ben (September 23, 2002), "Brushing Up on its Spanish, Harris Opens Up a Store," *American Banker.*

Jacob, Katy, Bush, Malcolm and Immergluck, Dan, (February 2002), "Rhetoric and Reality: An Analysis of Mainstream Credit Unions' Record of Serving Low Income People," *Woodstock Institute.*

Jones, Steven, (October 30, 2002), "Slump Hits Banks' Fee-Based Business," *Wall Street Journal.*

Judice, Mary, (July 7, 2002), "Credit Unions Reach New Markets," *The Times Picayune* (New Orleans).

Kelley, Kate, (October 30, 2002), "Well-Baked: With its Business So Slow, Wall Street Shows Hunger for Any Deal," *Wall Street Journal.*

Koenig, David, (July 9, 2002), "Convenience Store Chain Keeps Changing as It Celebrates 75th Birthday," *AP Newswires.*

Kuykendall, Lavonne, (November 8, 2002), "7-Eleven's Vcom Plan is Back in High Gear," *American Banker.*

Lewis, Gregory, (July 29, 2002), "Credit Unions Explored as Empowerment Tool," *South Florida Sun-Metro.*

Lyke, Rick, (April 2001), "New Yorkers Bank on Check Cashers," *Empire State Report.*

Manning, Stephen, (November 25, 2001), "Customers Put their Faith in Religion-Backed Finance," *Los Angeles Times*, p. A34.

Marlin, Steve, (August 1, 2002), "Back to the Future – With ATM Surcharge Boom Over, Banks are Once Again Turning their Attention to Customer Service," *Bank Systems + Technology.*

Millman, Joel, (March 7, 2001), "Big Bank Targets Immigrant Group, Many Illegal," *Wall Street Journal*, p. B1.

National Credit Union Foundation, (2001), "Plan it, Save 4 It: Credit Union Resource Guide."

National Federation of Community Development Credit Unions, (1999), "Community Development Credit Unions at a Glance."

National Federation of Community Development Credit Unions, (1999), "World View: NFCDCU 25," 25th Anniversary Journal.

Nocera, Joseph, (May 11, 1998), "Banking is Necessary – Banks Are Not," *Fortune.*

Pender, Kathleen, (September 19, 2002), "Safeway Halts Bank Growth," *San Francisco Chronicle*, p. B1.

PR Newswire, (July 9, 2002), "7-11, Inc. to Expand Vcom™ to 1,000 Stores."

PR Newswire, (September 16, 2002), "Harris Bank Introduces 'Express' Store Concept to Provide Financial Service Products and Services to All Chicagoans."

PR Newswire, (November 14, 2002), "7-Eleven Launches National Vcom Rollout in Orlando."

Quinn, Lawrence Richter, (June 2001), "The Horizontal Play," *Mortgage Banking*, p. 70ff.

Riera, Jose, (Fall 2000), "Banco Popular and Popular Cash Express: Providing Financial Services to the Unbanked," *Community Developments*, U. S. Office of the Controller of the Currency.

Robinson-Jacobs, Karen, (August 22, 2002), "Banks Branching out with Purchase of Hope Centers Financial Services," *Los Angeles Times*, p. C1.

Ryberg, William, (November 20, 2001), "Big Losses Push Several Hi-Vees to Quit Cashing Checks," Des Moines Register.

Sapsford, Jathon, (May 17, 2000), "A Small Chain Grows by Borrowing Ideas from Burger Joints," *Wall Street Journal*, p. 1.

Sarkisian, Masis, President, B.E.S.T., Interviews, January 8, 2002; February 28, 2002; March 15, 2002; March 20, 2002.

Sherblom, Becky, (July/August 2002), "Beyond the Fringe," *Shelterforce.*

Silvestrini, Marc, (August 20, 2002), "Banking Deregulation Turns Out to be a Boon for Check Cashing Companies," *Waterbury (CN) Republican-American.*

Sloan, Allan, (November 12, 2002), "'Free' Checking's Big Asterisk Won't Bite Your Wallet if You Don't Let It," *Washington Post.*

Stewart, Janet, (November 10, 2002), "Offering Bank Services to Underserved Chicago Neighborhoods Faces Challenges," *Chicago Tribune.*

Storey, Charlene Komar, (Summer 2002), "Branding Sweeps Through the Industry," *Checklist.*

Sullivan, Aline, (September 16, 2002), "Warring Over the Wealthy," *Barron's*, p. 25.

Tatge, Mark, (August 12, 2002), "A Tilt to Simplicity: A Minnesota Bank Makes Most of its Money the Old-Fashioned Way," *Forbes Magazine.*

Virgin, Bill, (November 22, 2002), "Boeing Credit Union Adapts as Airline Industry Slumps," *Seattle Post Intelligencer.*

Waldman, Adelle, (April 2, 2002), "Fleet Offers Free Account to Compete with Check Cashing Services," *New Haven Register.*

Weissbourd, Robert, with Perpetual Motion, Inc., (June 2002), "Banking on Technology: Expanding Financial Markets and Economic Opportunity," prepared for the *Brookings Institution, Financial Services Roundtable* and the *Ford Foundation.*

Wessel, David, (May 2, 2002), "The Economy – Capital: Banking on Technology for the Poor," *Wall Street Journal.*

Wessel, David, (May 8, 2002), "Capital Journal: Technology Gives New Opportunity to the Unbanked," *Wall Street Journal Europe*, p. A2.

Williams, Jaye Morgan, (May 2, 2002), "Individuals Who Do Not Have Bank Accounts," testimony before the U. S. Senate Banking, Housing and Urban Affairs Committee. (Ms. Williams is SVP, Managing Director of Community Investment, Bank One Corporation).

Williams, Marva E., (May 2, 2002), "Developing Opportunities for Affordable Lifeline Banking for Lower-Income Consumers," *Testimony, Before the U.S. Senate Committee on Banking, Housing and Urban Affairs.*

CHAPTER 4: FINANCIAL FEASIBILITY

Barstow, David, (August 16,1999), "ATM Cards Fail to Live Up to Promises to Poor," *New York Times*, p.A1.

Beckett, Paul, (December 1, 2000), "Citigroup Completes Associates Purchase As It Agrees to Improve Lending Practices," *Wall Street Journal.*

Beckett, Paul, (October 30, 2002), "Payday Loans are Dealt Blow by Regulators – ACE Cash and California Bank Face Fines as U.S. Controller Seeks to Curb Lending Practice," *Wall Street Journal.*

B.E.S.T., Inc. "Show Me the Money: A Quick Guide to the Check Cashing Business," Des Plaines, Illnois.

Branch, Shelley, (June 8, 1998), "Where Cash is King," *Fortune.*

Business Wire, (January 24, 2002), Cash America press release of financial information. www.cashamerica.com.

Business Wire, (June 6, 2002), "Cash America Completes Sale of Rent-to Own Subsidiary."

Business Wire, (August 14, 2002), "Cash America Completes $132.5 Million Financing."

Caskey, John and Brayman, Susan, (2001), "Check Cashing and Savings Programs for Low Income Households: An Action Plan for Credit Unions," *Filene Research Institute.*

Dove Consulting, (April 4, 2002), "Survey of Non-Bank Financial Institutions," prepared for the U.S. Treasury.

Druckerman, Pamela, (March 25, 1998), "Wall Street Repackages Worker Remittances," *Wall Street Journal.*

Entrepreneur Group, (1992), "Check Cashing: Entrepreneur Guide No. 139."

Gallagly, Edward and Dernovsek, Darla, (2000), "Fair Deal: Creating Credit Union Alternatives to Fringe Financial Services," *Credit Union National Association, Inc.*

Goldman, Gerald, (Fall 2002), "Check Cashers Still Battling Bank Discontinuance," *Checklist.*

Ho, David, (September 20, 2002), "Citigroup to Settle Consumer Class-Action Suit," *San Francisco Chronicle*, p. B3.

Kosta, Chris, (September, October, 1998), "From Big to Bigger," *Progressive Rentals.*

Kurdek, Robyn, (February 19, 2001), "InnoVentry Punches Out With $253 Million Series C Transaction," *Private Equity Week.* Also, www.innoventry.com.

Lyke, Rick, (April 2001), "New Yorkers Bank on Check Cashers," *Empire State Report.*

Manning, Robert D., (2000), *Credit Card Nation*, New York: Basic Books.

Oppel, Jr, Richard, (March 7, 2001), "U.S. Suit Cites Citigroup Unit on Loan Deceit," *New York Times*, p. A1.

PR Newswire, (January 24, 2001), "ACE Cash Express Second Quarter Revenue Increases 21 Percent." www.acecashexpress.com

PR Newswire, (February 11, 2002), "EZCORP Annual Shareholder Meeting."

PR Newswire, (April 10, 2002), "Popular, Inc. Reports Earnings for the Quarter Ended March 31, 2002."

PR Newswire, (April 23, 2002), "First Cash Financial Services Reports 31% Increase in First Quarter Net."

PR Newswire, (June 24, 2002), "Cash Systems, Inc. Completes New Financing."

Rent-A-Center, Inc., (2002), "ProForma Quarterly Financials, 10Q Format, 1995 – Q2, 2002."

Rent-A-Center Press Releases, (May 7, 2002), "Rent-A-Center Files Secondary Equity Offering."

Rent-A-Center Press Releases, (July 29, 2002), "Rent-A-Center, Inc. Reports Second Quarter 2002 Results."

Rent-A-Center Press Releases, (August 6, 2002), "Rent-A-Center Announces Conversion of Series A Preferred Stock."

Sarkisian, Masis, President, B.E.S.T., Interviews, January 8, 2002; February 28, 2002; March 15, 2002; March 20, 2002.

Savitz, Eric, (August 19, 2002), "Profits from Debits," *Barron's*.

Sengupta, Somini, (July 14, 2001), "State Rethinks Deal to Provide Extended Welfare via ATM," *New York Times*.

Shaver, Todd, (April 15, 2002), "First Data Corporation," *Bull Market Report Daily*, section number 8.

Sklar, Jeffrey, "Business Valuations," (October 6, 2001), FISCA Conference, San Diego, CA. Mr. Sklar is a partner in SHC Consulting in New York.

State of New York, Banking Department, (August 30, 2000), "Check Casher Consolidated Statements, 1999"; "Check Casher Consolidated Statements, 2001."

Wilke, John, (October 21, 1991), "Some Banks' Money Flows into Poor Areas - and Causes Anguish," *Wall Street Journal*.

CHAPTER 5: CONCLUSION

Freeman, Lisa, (October 7, 2002), "Check Cashing Business Worth Investigating, CUs Told," *Credit Union Journal*.